ALL THE BEST IN MEXICO

BOOKS BY SYDNEY CLARK

ALL THE BEST IN BELGIUM AND LUXEMBOURG

ALL THE BEST IN BERMUDA, THE BAHAMAS, PUERTO RICO, AND THE VIRGIN ISLANDS

ALL THE BEST IN THE CARIBBEAN INCLUDING PUERTO RICO AND THE VIRGIN ISLANDS

ALL THE BEST IN CENTRAL AMERICA

ALL THE BEST IN ENGLAND

ALL THE BEST IN EUROPE

ALL THE BEST IN FRANCE

ALL THE BEST IN GERMANY AND AUSTRIA

ALL THE BEST IN HAWAII

ALL THE BEST IN HOLLAND

ALL THE BEST IN ITALY

ALL THE BEST IN JAPAN AND THE ORIENT

ALL THE BEST IN THE MEDITERRANEAN

ALL THE BEST IN MEXICO

ALL THE BEST IN SCANDINAVIA

ALL THE BEST IN SOUTH AMERICA—EAST COAST

ALL THE BEST IN SOUTH AMERICA—WEST COAST

ALL THE BEST IN THE SOUTH PACIFIC

ALL THE BEST IN SPAIN AND PORTUGAL

ALL THE BEST IN SWITZERLAND

SYDNEY CLARK

ALL THE BEST IN MEXICO

WITH ILLUSTRATIONS AND MAPS

DODD, MEAD & COMPANY

NEW YORK

Copyright © 1944, 1949, 1956, 1958, 1959, 1961, 1966 by Sydney Clark

ALL RIGHTS RESERVED
NO PART OF THIS BOOK MAY BE REPRODUCED IN ANY FORM
WITHOUT PERMISSION IN WRITING FROM THE PUBLISHER

40,377

LIBRARY OF CONGRESS CATALOG CARD NUMBER: 66-20192

PRINTED IN THE UNITED STATES OF AMERICA
BY VAIL-BALLOU PRESS, INC., BINGHAMTON, N.Y.

Acknowledgment is hereby made of the research
and editorial services rendered by Lee Tyler.

CONTENTS

Illustrations follow page 86.

THE FOREGROUND OF THE PICTURE

1. WHAT COLOR, PROFI? — 3

2. ON MAKING AN ENTRANCE — 8
   Through the Air
   Over the Road
   Four "En Route Towns" for the Motorist (Monterrey;
     Saltillo; San Luis Potosí; Chihuahua)
   By Ship and by Train

3. MONEY IN MEXICO — 25
   Preview of Prices
   The Designer's Message (Mexican money)
   Tips without Worry

4. TREMENDOUS TRIVIA — 33
   Advisers in Advance
   Border Barriers Demolished
   Altitude Gremlins
   Guides, Philosophers and Friends

THE BACKGROUND OF THE PICTURE

5. A PAGEANT IN FOUR PARTS — 43
   Aboriginal Marvels of Mexico
   The Impact of Spain
   From Independence to Freedom
   The Colors of Revolution

CONTENTS

YOURSELF IN THE PICTURE

6. MEXICO CITY, CENTER OF EVERYTHING   73
   Candid Notes on Hotels
   Big-City Practicalities (Transportation; Letters, Telegrams, Telephones; English-Language Publications; Health Precautions; Cigarettes; Incidentals)
   Seven Foci for Americans
   Shoppers in Paradise
   The Calendar of Festivals in Mexico

7. TOURISTS ON A WILLING LEASH   99
   The Sightseers' Downtown
   The Americas' Largest Cathedral
   Two Palaces and Two Museums
   The Castle of Grasshopper Hill
   The Luxury Section

8. STROLLS WITHOUT A CHAPERON   111
   Tezontle Palaces of Old
   Churches Straight and Tipsy
   Three Marvels for Discovery
   Wandering on the "Left Bank"
   Bargains in the Mount of Piety
   Markets for the Myriads

9. THE SPECTRUM OF MEXICAN ART   126
   The Classics of San Carlos
   Rivera Gives Lessons in History
   The Rockefeller Reject in the Fine Arts Palace
   The Search for the Painted Walls
   The New Mosaic Murals
   Modernity Gone Mad

10. METROPOLITAN FUN   140
   "See You at Sanborn's"
   Eating Around the Capital
   The Sign of the Tilting Glass
   Evenings in All Keys
   The Clubs of Midnight
   Explorers at Tenampa

CONTENTS

11. ### SPORT AND SPEED 163
    The Sunday Bullring
    The Lightning of Jai-Alai
    Futbol *and* Beisbol
    Hipódromo de las Américas

12. ### WONDERS OF THE CITY'S OUTER BELT 170
    The Shrine of the Indian Madonna
    Floating through Xochimilco
    Pyramids Like Mountains
    Toluca Arts and Crafts

13. ### EXAMINING THE HEART OF MEXICO 179
    Four Superlative Provincial Trips

14. ### WESTWARD TO THE FIRE BELT 182
    The Luxury Spa of San José de Purúa
    Colonial Charm in Old Morelia
    By the Waters of Patzcuaro
    When Uruapan Took the Veil
    The Birth and Death of Paricutín

15. ### GLAMOUR AT GUADALAJARA 193
    Delights of Plaza and Portales
    Temptation at Tlaquepaque
    A Day for Lake Chapala
    Two or Three Days for Puerto Vallarta
    More of the Pacific Coast, Barra de Navidad and Mazatlán

16. ### ALLURING TOWNS OF INDEPENDENCE 204
    Freedom's Cast of Characters
    Querétaro, Birthplace of the Plan
    San Miguel, a Patriot's Hearth
    Guanajuato Silver

17. ### THE SIRENS OF THE SOUTH 217
    The Call of Cuernavaca
    Tangents to Tepoztlán and the Caves of Cacahuamilpa
    Lake Tequesquitengo, Five Syllables of Water Fun

CONTENTS

Taxco the Incomparable
Acapulco in Her Bathing Suit
The Call of Zihuatanejo

18. TO PUEBLA AND THE FORT OF FLOWERS — 236

Cholula and Its Calendar of Churches
The Weathered Wealth of Puebla
Fortín, a Floral Millionaire

19. WONDERS OF OAXACA — 244

Plaza Life at Its Best
Two Double Stars for Strolling
Monte Alban and Mitla

20. YUCATÁN, HEARTLAND OF THE MAYAS — 252

Routes to Mérida
The Island of Carmen on the Way
Mérida, the Modern Hub of Mayaland
Entering Antiquity
Hotel Mayaland, Comfort Amid History
Chichén-Itzá, Pride of the New Empire
Uxmal and Its Thousand-Year Palace
The Island of Cozumel, an Escapist's Dream Come True

INDEX — 273

THE FOREGROUND OF THE PICTURE

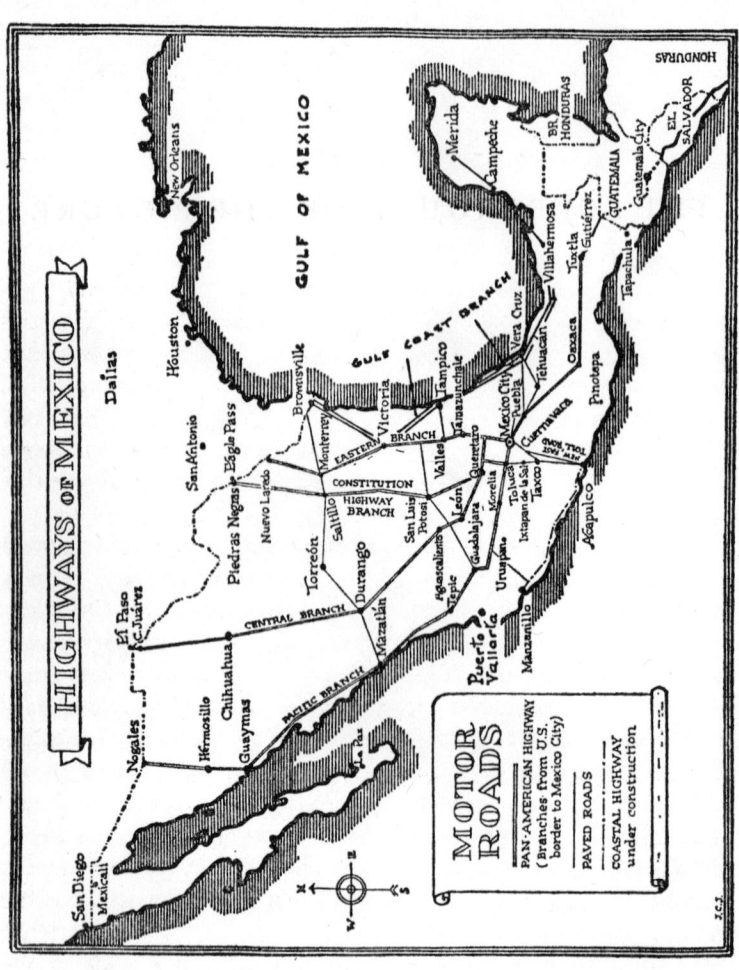

CHAPTER 1

WHAT COLOR, PROFI?

A FRIEND of mine is *Profesora* to the children of a Mexican mine owner near Taxco. They were much excited when she told them that I was writing a book about their country and Alvarito, in particular, was a jumping question mark. He concentrated all of his six years of curiosity into one burning query, "Tell me, Profi—*what color will it be?*" She said she really didn't know, but he was not to be put off. "I mean what *color*, Profi? Will it be black or white—or poorrrple?"

She took the question directly to me but I was as uninformed as she. If one could run through the color chart and say "This is Mexico," one would achieve a major miracle. The color of Mexico attacks the eye with ruthless force and a bewildering variety of unexpected aggressions. The street and market scenes are a perpetual riot of escaped pigments. The roadside and even railroad-side life is a mélange of everything that would be unimaginable north of the Rio Grande. The park and plaza life is by all odds the most appealing to be found in this hemisphere, for every Mexican town, however uninspired, has its lovely central plaza, presumably with a cathedral façade to decorate it. And no town is so poor that it does not have at least one or two beautiful parks and a splendid *alameda*. These areas of siesta are almost invariably clean and attractive to the eye. There is generally a lot of tile work, including sumptuous fountains, decorated benches and a bandstand. Always there are trees, especially Indian laurels of magnificent proportions and assorted tropical palms. These plazas owe their inspiration chiefly to Empress Carlota, who ordered that the existing *Plazas de Armas* all over the country be transformed into gardens of the people.

If you like pretty girls, especially those who do not know they are pretty, you may see tens of thousands of them in Mexico, for the Indian and the mestiza are *naturally* pretty and it is only the unfortunate exception who is not. The faintly Oriental cast of countenance conspires with the clear, light-cocoa skin and the petite figure to build remarkable eye appeal. Almost all of the girls are short, far shorter indeed than the men of the same blood, as every visitor, from the trained ethnologist to the casual tourist, has noted. Five feet is above average for an Indian girl and many are only four feet eight or nine. They are little chocolate dolls (doomed perhaps to be dumpy in middle age) and beside them the tourist girls from the States seem huge, and our six-foot glamazons look like girl giants.

Mexico is so accessible that we can walk into it at a dozen handy points from four states. Important strides are being made to "clean up" the former bad image of the border towns. Tourists entering Juárez from El Paso, for instance, will doubtless have seen the newsy, free magazine, *Amigos*, typical of the new spirit. There's a new museum of Mexican history and art in Juárez, in the center of a 25-acre site that will eventually include hotels, office buildings and a splendid convention hall. In Tijuana, just down the freeway from San Diego, the present city government is sternly dedicated to a drastic cleanup on all fronts, including the sleazy red-light sections, the frumpy tourist traps, the rackets that have long disgraced its community and even, so far as possible, the slum quarters. To inject a bit of civic beauty, it is diverting the Tijuana River to make of its present bed a garden area.

Most of Mexico is as alluringly foreign as if it lay below the equator. Even the capital and the luxury resorts, despite their acquired taste for the benefits of *turismo*, have by no means sold their souls to the transient dollar. They remain stubbornly, appealingly, devotedly, and sometimes irritatingly, Mexican. And the less publicized towns, some two or three dozen of them, which boast the amenities of modern living and yet are scarcely touched by the breath of tourism, are among the most attractive that I, for one, have encountered in many years of traveling.

My enthusiasm, tinctured with an aspersive adjective that crept in among the others, calls for explanation and I shall try to be completely truthful and fair, avoiding the golden glow of the indiscriminate zealot and the shrewishness of the quick-to-complain. What is the power in the magnet that is Mexico? How great and how valid is its pull?

If color is half of it climate is the other half. The climate of the central plateau of Mexico is one of the most docile and predictable of any in the world, possibly surpassing in this respect even the glamorized climate of Hawaii, whose liquid sunshine can sometimes be disobediently wet. But one must distinguish sharply between Mexico's dry winter and her shower-studded summer. And one must distinguish between the high central plateau and the steamy tropical coasts.

The winter weather of the capital and all the high-altitude regions of the heart of the country is so phenomenally fine that it seems an understatement to call it merely perfect. The days are warm and bright and dry—all of them—and the nights are cool and bracing and dry. This delectable period lasts, allowing for some annual variation, from November until April. "And does it never rain in winter?" I once asked a trusted cicerone. "Never," she answered solemnly. "You mean literally that it *cannot* rain?" "It cannot," came the categorical answer. And the next day, which was Christmas Day, it did rain all day long. But that Christmas rain, as I learned for myself, was so rare as to be almost a meteorological phenomenon. In two subsequent winter months I saw only one brief spatter in Mexico City and it was so localized that many sectors of the capital did not get even their fair quota, say one hundred drops. This pleasant constancy does not apply to the north of Mexico, even where the altitude is high. Monterrey and Chihuahua and Saltillo can produce copious rain in December and January as in other months. But, susprisingly, the rule does apply to Acapulco and its region, despite the tropical sea-level temperature of that lovely resort. It never rains in Acapulco's winter; in fact, even "more never" than in the country's capital.

Veracruz and the attractive flower resort of Fortín, which is halfway up the Sierra but still in the Veracruz orbit, demand a special weather note. "Northers" of disagreeable quality and power strike this coast at occasional intervals, sending wild surf and driving rain to the port, and clammy drizzles—with some real rain—to Fortín. These are likely to arrive in winter but they are generally of short duration and if you have the ill luck to strike one while in Fortín, you should ride out the storm, confident that the reward will be enormous when the norther has blown itself out and the sun breaks through upon the trillions of flowers that the rain has nourished. Without occasional soakings, such floral virtuosity as that of Fortín could not exist.

The pull of the Mexico magnet need not submit to conscientious analysis. It is something one feels rather than examines. The very faults of the country can become charms if one is in the mood to be conquered. Tardiness, for instance, becomes a rather delightful insouciance when the Mexican with whom you had an appointment at four P.M. turns up smiling and unperturbed at five, explaining easily, "Of course, you know what P.M. means with us. It's *Puntualidad Mexicana*. But, really, I'm sorry to have kept you waiting." You forgive him instantly, though you know very well that he will be just as late for the next appointment he makes.

You will fuss and fume at times. You will want to commit a slight murder when the bus for which you have a reservation forgets all about you, or when the careful message you have left for a friend at another hotel is never delivered. But if you can induce yourself to *accept these things* as relatively mild visitations of fate, as modest taxes on the vast income of pleasure which the country offers, you will be doing yourself a great favor. The Mexico magnet will get you in the end, in any case, unless you are a miracle of resistance. You may as well succumb at the beginning and call upon your reserves of good nature to meet the "troubles" that are certain to occur. After all, these troubles will make delightful reading in your letters to the home folk and delightful telling as you later exaggerate and build them up to proper dramatic levels for appreciative listeners.

Mexico, when all is said, is a neighbor so endowed with talents and attractions that she is easily forgiven for anything she does or leaves undone. This is especially true in the case of those visitors —and I am told by a friend in a major Mexican travel agency that their number increases each year—who realize that faults are not the monopoly of the other fellow. To many a cultured Mexican many a United States tourist still seems blatant, ill-informed, domineering and contemptuous of anything new to him; and he seems this way because he *is* this way. But his conspicuous race —praise be to Saint Christopher, the patron of travel—appears to be slowly dying out. More speed to this demise. More power to the thoughtful, considerate, informed and patient element in tourism.

CHAPTER 2

ON MAKING AN ENTRANCE

Through the Air

Two MEANS of entering Mexico—to emphasize this point—have won such public favor as to overshadow other means, namely air travel and motor travel. The former is axiomatic in this air-minded age and the latter has been spurred immeasurably by spectacular advances in the Mexican road-building program. Another dramatic and promising development is the new winter service of Canadian Pacific Steamship's *Princess Patricia*, which is opening up all kinds of air-sea possibilities as well as regular cruises. We'll have a quick look, later, at railway and steamer services, but first let's concentrate on the Big Two of Mexican travel. (NOTE: *If you are an armchair traveler, you are cordially invited to skip this rundown. Such listings are deadly dull except to the planner of a do-it-yourself trip, to whom it may be the most intriguing part of the book.*)

American carriers serving Mexico City with jets are: *American Airlines*, with service from New York, Dallas and San Antonio; *Eastern Air Lines*, which has jet flights from New York and from New Orleans, some serving Acapulco; *Pan American Airways* out of Miami, and also Houston; *Braniff International Airways* from Minneapolis–St. Paul, putting down, en route, at Kansas City, Dallas and San Antonio; and *Western Airlines*, from Los Angeles (to which there are direct flight connections from Seattle/Portland, Sacramento, San Francisco, Oakland and Salt Lake City).

Of the foreign carriers, *Mexicana Airlines* is the most convenient, offering jet service to Mexico City from Los Angeles both nonstop and with stops at Mazatlán, Puerto Vallarta and Guadalajara (a magnificent way to be sure of seeing something more of the country than Mexico City!). Mexicana also has direct flights to Mexico City from Chicago, from Dallas (some of these flights make an en route call at Monterrey), and from San Antonio via Monterrey (nonjet). Mexicana also has jet service from Kingston, Jamaica, to Mexico City via Mérida. This airline has applied for three interesting new routes in addition: they would be Chicago to Acapulco; San Antonio, Dallas or Fort Worth to Mexico City; and Corpus Christi to Laredo and Monterrey.

Mexico's second international airline, *Aeronaves de México, S.A.*, has service to Mexico City from both Miami and Detroit (the flights originate in Madrid). Additionally, Aeronaves has applied for rights to serve New York and Miami on the Mexico City–Europe run; Acapulco and Los Angeles; Acapulco and Washington or New York; and Guadalajara and Houston.

The other airlines serving Mexico City are an intriguing international mélange. They include: *Qantas*, Australia's overseas airline, with "Fiesta Service" to Mexico City and Acapulco from London, Bermuda and Nassau (or, coming in from the other direction, from Sydney, Nadi and Papeete); *Varig*, the Brazilian airline, with jet service from Los Angeles (or, coming in the other way, from Rio, Lima and Panama); *Sabena*, the Belgian airline, jetting in from Brussels and Montreal; *Air France*, originating in Paris and stopping in New York en route; *Canadian Pacific Air Lines*, jetting in not only from Montreal and Toronto, but from Rome, Lisbon, Montreal and Toronto; *Iberia Air Lines* of Spain, coming in from Madrid and New York; and *KLM Royal Dutch Airlines*, with jet service from Amsterdam, Montreal and Houston. *Alitalia* and *Japan Air Lines* have also applied for rights to start serving Mexico.

Several Latin American carriers also serve Mexico, should you be thinking of making your entry *that* way. They include our faithful friend, *Pan American*, from Caracas and Panama City; *VIASA*, the Venezuelan airline, from Maracaibo and Panama; *TACA International Airlines*, from just about all the Central American capital cities; and *LACSA*, the national flag carrier of Costa Rica, coming in from Panama and San José, with a way stop at San Salvador.

Air service within Mexico is best provided by three domestic airlines. *Aeronaves* has an "Air Bridge" between Mexico City and Acapulco, with practically continuous DC-6 and jet flights all day long from 7:30 A.M. until 11 P.M. (no advance reservations accepted). The propeller plane makes the hop in an hour, the jet in 45 minutes. *Mexicana* has DC-6 service to Mexico City from Monterrey and from Mazatlán, Puerto Vallarta, Guadalajara and Monterrey. In addition it serves practically all other major Mexican tourist centers, including Veracruz, Minatitlán, Villahermosa, Ciudad del Carmen, Campeche, Mérida, Cozumel, Oaxaca, Tuxtla Gutiérrez, and Tapachula. *Aerolíneas Vega, S.A.*, with head office in Oaxaca, has DC-3 nonstop service between that city and Acapulco, and also serves a variety of small Mexican cities.

Over the Road

Highways in Mexico, as I've already said in a loud shout, have made spectacular advances in the last few years. There are *four* paved truck lines from the U.S. frontier to Mexico City, where they branch out, one continuing south to Oaxaca and clear to the Guatemalan frontier, another going to Veracruz and along the Gulf Coast, across the island of Carmen, on to Mérida and all the way out to the tip of the Yucatán Peninsula.

A magnificent service to automobile tourists is the Mexican Government Tourist Department's *Radio Patrulles de Auxilio Turístico*, better known as the Green Fleet. These are radio-controlled tourist-assistance patrol cars that operate over most of the major Mexican highways and are at your (free) service for minor repairs, tire changes, first aid, etc.

The four main highways from our border to the Mexican capital, all parts of the Pan American Highway System, are: (1) *Highway 85*, the *original* and well-maintained (but curvy) route from Laredo, Texas, to Monterrey, Ciudad Victoria (Highway 101 from Brownsville joins it here) and on to Mexico City (there is Tourist Patrol service as far as Ciudad Mante); (2) *Highway 57*, the *Constitution Highway*, from Eagle Pass, Texas, to Saltillo (close to Monterrey), thence on to San Luis Potosí and Querétaro and Mexico City (Tourist Patrol service ends at Querétaro); (3) the *Central Branch, Highway 45*, from El Paso and Ciudad Juárez through Chihuahua, branching out at Ciudad Jiménez if you want to go to Durango and Mazatlán, otherwise following Routes 49 and 40 more in a straight line down below Zacatecas, rejoining 45 there through León, then picking up a combination of Highways 110 and 57 if you want to see Guanajuato, San Miguel de Allende and Querétaro, otherwise dropping down to Morelia to join Highway 15 to Mexico City via San José Purúa and Toluca. There is Tourist Patrol service most of the way; (4) the fourth main line is the *Pacific Branch, Highway 15* from Nogales (near Tucson, Arizona) to Guaymas, Mazatlán, Tepic, Guadalajara, Morelia and so to Mexico City. There is Tourist Patrol service *all* the way. These last two highways, including the extension from Mexico City to the frontier of Guatemala, are each over 3000 miles long. Also of interest is the *Gulf Coast Highway*, which starts out at Brownsville as 101, then becomes, successively, Highways 80, 120, 130, 140 and 180, clinging close to the coast from Tampico through Jalapa, Veracruz, Villahermosa, across Carmen, Campeche, Mérida, Chichén-Itzá and all the way out to Puerto Juárez.

Connecting lateral roads have developed to such extent that Mexico's claim to have the best and fullest hard-surface network in Latin America is probably quite true. Furthermore, as the AAA road map or those of Mexico's Pemex and Tourism Department will reveal, there are at least five cross-Mexico highways belting the country from ocean to ocean, the longest of them being that from Mazatlán, on the Pacific, to Matamoros (and Brownsville) close to the Gulf.

This development makes many *circuits* practicable in place of the former down-and-back driving. There is, for instance, a *south-central circuit* from Mexico City to Cuernavaca to Taxco to Ixtapán de la Sal (west of Taxco) to Toluca (north) and so back to the capital. The most spectacular highway is the six-lane toll highway from the capital to Acapulco, an easy five-hour drive. Busses race about all over the country and the deluxe and Pullman ones, accepting only as many passengers as can be seated, are generally good, sometimes very good. One of the good services ties in with Greyhound at Laredo for the long run to Mexico City.

A couple of practical pointers may creep in here. First, and by far foremost, the motorist should contact by mail—well in advance—the automobile organization known as *Pemex*, whose head office is at 89 Avenida Juárez, Mexico City. At the same address the Tourism Department maintains an information bureau. Pemex, meaning *Petróleos Mexicanos*, is your informed and intimate friend of highway travel. It has its obvious commercial motive, since it sells you gas and lubricates your car at any of its numerous modern service stations throughout Mexico, but it is also a propaganda organization of unusual energy. It provides essential information about paved highways, all-weather roads and adventure roads throughout the republic and upon request it will map out your whole tour. It offers a wide variety of free booklets and up-to-date maps. Membership in Pemex Travel Club, a nonprofit service organization, is free to foreign motorists, as are all of its informational services. These include, besides the above, impartial advice on hotels and lodging in all parts of Mexico; on facilities for study and research; on shopping, customs formalities, hunting, fishing, sports, special fiestas—in short, on everything that makes up Mexico.

My appreciation of this pervasive organization of Mexican motoring is so enthusiastic that I may be accused of being its paid publicist, but the truth is that I am no more known to Pemex than is any casual American traveler. I stress its services solely by way of presenting a friend in court to the first-time motorist. The second-time motorist already knows all about Pemex, including its conveniently located central information office.

Before writing Pemex, or simultaneously, you might see what luck you have in contacting your nearest office of the Mexican Government Tourism Department. There are many of them now, and you'll find the addresses on page 33, at the head of the chapter called Tremendous Trivia.

Members of the *American Automobile Association* may avail themselves also of the AAA's *very* helpful motoring annual called *Mexico by Motor*, "published for the exclusive use of members." This paperback volume of more than 200 pages may be of even more aid and comfort to the average American motorist than are the Pemex publications, but it is not for sale to nonmembers. Its detailed coverage of the better hotels and motels, together with many illustrated advertisements, is full and easy to follow and its spread of tourist information, including the chief sights and major festivals and how and when to visit them, is impressive. The AAA has also its own first-rate annually revised road map, with city plans of all the border towns, of Monterrey, Guadalajara, Puebla, Cuernavaca, Oaxaca and Acapulco, and two of the capital, but this map, like the guide annual, is for members only.

Since more and more visitors every year are entering Mexico over the road, it might be of help to list here and now some of the leading *hotels and motels* on the four main entering highways, working from north to south in each case.

The best hotels in the tourist heart of Monterrey cluster together in that downtown area that centers around Calle Morelos, Calle Escobedo and Plaza Zaragoza, though three of them, the *Rio*, the *El Paso Autel* and the *Anfa Super Hotel* are a few slingshots farther away. Of those in the immediate area of the seething tourist streets and plaza named, the *Ambassador* is easily the leader. It has a motor-lobby entrance, is air-conditioned throughout, and I can report from personal experience of it that the service is prompt and courteous, especially in the cheerful dining room, where music is, or was at the time of my visit, furnished by a high-spirited band of—canaries. The *Gran Hotel Ancira*, dean of the city's good hotels, has renewed its youth and is very recommendable now. This, too, has a drive-in garage, with entrance direct to the hotel lobby. The *Monterrey*, on Calle Morelos, lacks a drive-in motor lobby but does have a garage with pick-up and delivery service. All three of these places are within a few steps of Plaza Zaragoza, on which is Monterrey's finest restaurant, a luxurious affair, with large separate bar, called the *Luisiana* (spelled in the Spanish fashion) and serving, shall we say, the finest New Orleans-French food. This restaurant, I might interpolate here, is under the same ownership as the *Anfa Super Motel*, which really is superior, situated six miles north of the center on the original Pan American Highway from Laredo. A few dozen more steps along Calle Escobedo brings one to *Sanborn's*, of which I'll tell more presently, and to the city's main drag, named for Morelos, with lots of bright shops and a notably cheerful cafeteria named *Roma*. Every door in this whole area is a wide-open invitation to tourists. "Step in," says one, "we have it." "Whatever you need," says another, "you'll find it here." For the motorist this is the first good chance to "buy Mexican" and almost every woman tourist literally plunges into the exciting pastime of *buying*.

Of the slightly less central hotels the one I know best is the *Rio*, which has an exceptionally interesting background and management, for it was designed and built by two brothers named Agustín and Eugenio Zorilla, who studied engineering at Purdue University. They concentrated their design of the place on providing first-rate, ultramodern bedrooms and baths, all air-conditioned, soundproofed and provided with radio and running ice water, not to mention comfortable beds and the latest in bathroom plumbing. Like the Ambassador and the Ancira, the Rio has a drive-in garage, with direct entrance to the lobby, and it also has a considerable court, backed by a gay ceramic wall, where you may leave your car in the open, handy to hop into, if you wish. As for the *El Paso Autel*, that's an *au*tomobile-ho*tel*, as its name tells us, and instead of being several miles distant, it is only a few blocks north of Plaza Zaragoza, on the broad street named Calle Zaragoza. The *autel* is pleasant, mostly air-conditioned and very moderate in its rates.

Four "En Route Towns" for the Motorist
(Monterrey; Saltillo; San Luis Potosí; Chihuahua)

The heart of Mexico, by which I mean Mexico City and its surrounding towns, is so very far from its "head and shoulders" on the United States border, the distance varying from 600 miles (Brownsville) to 1400 miles (Nogales), that the motorist who is tire-bent to reach the capital often misses some exceedingly interesting towns that he could easily visit en route, and generally he misses them again, or races through them, on the return trip, keyed to home deadlines. Four of these towns, Monterrey, Saltillo, San Luis Potosí and Chihuahua, will be briefly presented here. The first three can be handily knotted together by the motorist entering Mexico from Laredo or Eagle Pass, while the fourth, Chihuahua, is on the highway leading due south from El Paso and Ciudad Juárez. This book's map, called "Highways of Mexico," following the Table of Contents, shows clearly, I think, the main north-south highways and their connecting laterals. It will be noticed how near to each other are Monterrey and Saltillo, though they are on different branches of the Pan American Highway.

Monterrey is a large city, with a skyscraper look, rewarding the visitor for a stay of two or three days. In population it pushes Guadalajara as Mexico's second city, and in wealth and industry it is vastly ahead.

Monterrey is aided in a business way and lessened in picturesqueness by its proximity (146 miles) to Texas, there being in addition to the highway, an excellent air service from San Antonio. Its climate is far less placid and dependable, especially in winter, than is that of the central plateau farther south; but it presents Mexico attractively, with lovely plazas for siesta, with the Chepe Vera hill, appropriately crowned by a ruined ecclesiastical palace (*El Obispado*), and with rugged scenic surroundings. It presents, too, a branch of *Sanborn's*. Few things are more exciting, from the visitor's standpoint, than the institution known as Sanborn's. In the capital, it is one of those places that literally bring to a focus the social and business life of the city. In Monterrey, its pleasant branch focuses local tourist life, both American and Mexican, and lures transients to its cheerful little patio. Sanborn's will be discussed, for it is truly important in the picture of Mexico, in a later chapter on the capital, but it should be underlined here as one of the main attractions of Monterrey. Its Mexican wares—from silver to sarapes—are interesting even to nonshoppers. Its restaurant, around an inner patio, provides an appealing rendezvous. The waitresses, as in the capital establishment, wear Mexican costumes, consisting of a voluminous many-colored skirt, a gay bodice, a yard-wide winged attachment on the shoulders in almost any color that is not harsh, and a broad ribbonlike headdress. The costume is the one formerly worn in a village on Lake Pátzcuaro.

It is not quite decent to mention Monterrey without offering a tribute to its famous Cuauhtémoc Brewery, largest in Mexico, which is a sight of the city. Public tours are made through it at almost hourly intervals and the tourist is rewarded at the end by free beer in the garden. It will be the brand called *Carta Blanca* (White Letter), than which no name in Mexican business or pleasure is better known. Carta Blanca gleams and flashes in neon lights from strategic points in all the towns of the republic, and one becomes so weary of it that one is almost reluctant to concede the truth—that the beer *is* good. Even one who has spent many years in Europe and a few minutes in Milwaukee can make that honest statement.

Monterrey is not *merely* a big city. It is a scenic center, too, with magnificent mountains to the south and west and lesser hills to the north. Motor trips in the environs include visits to a nearby 4200-foot plateau called the *Chipinque Mesa;* to a dramatic ravine called the *Huasteca Canyon,* ten miles distant; and, perhaps the best of all, to a fine waterfall called *Cola de Caballo,* meaning horsetail. The last four miles of this 25-mile trip are on the rough side and the climax involves riding a burro for a little distance, but the goal is superb, and near the cascade is a good restaurant, with a swimming pool. A cableway to the summit (6700 feet) of *Cerro de la Silla,* meaning Saddle Mountain, has been built and is operating intermittently, providing a major thrill for those who enter Mexico by way of Monterrey.

For some four hundred miles due south of Monterrey the highway is merely pleasant and perhaps a bit torrid. It cuts through luscious orange orchards by the score and at all the towns and wayside halts, huge oranges are purchasable for only a few cents apiece. The chief towns and hotels, where halts might be considered to break the long journey, are the following: Ciudad Victoria, with its fair but unpretentious *Hotel Serra Gorda;* Ciudad Mante, with *Hotel Naola;* Antigua Morelos, only a few miles beyond Mante, with its *Tepeyac Courts;* Ciudad Valles, with its large *Hotel Taninul,* a spa with both a hot thermal pool and a cool swimming pool; Tamazunchale, with *Hotel San Antonio;* and, finally, Zimapan, providing two inns of interest, the spectacular-appearing *Hotel Fundición,* in the reconstructed building of a defunct smelting company, and the more conventional *Posada del Rey,* a 50-room affair of some quality, with pool.

At the above-listed town of Tamazunchale, universally called "Thomas and Charlie" by Americans, it suddenly becomes evident that the road has a very stiff climb ahead, mounting from an altitude of 500 feet to 7500 feet. With enormous gusto it tackles the job and the next 200 miles constitute one of the outstanding travel wonders of this hemisphere. Traverse it by sunlight or by full moonlight (as I first did) and you will readily concede that there is no road scenery in Switzerland, or Norway, or Austria's Vorarlberg, or Germany's Bavaria that can surpass it in spectacular artistry. You may prefer more snow, more lakes, and more waterfalls, as seen in Europe, but the changing color effects of this Mexican marvel act to offset that lack. At every turn, and there are hundreds, one color picture dissolves into another. The mountain peaks are in parade formation and the more distant ranks are clad in ever paler colors as they march over the horizon. In moonlight, these pictures are so otherworldly that they reduce the most garrulous gusher of the tourist tribe to inarticulate awe. They are a musician's dream of a moonlight sonata. Through towns and hamlets with strange Indian names, they lead you on and up to the broad central plateau, whose nucleus is the Valley of Mexico, centered by the capital.

If you make this trip by night—with the moon as a silvery lantern—you will enter the vast spreading capital at crisp dawn. Sleepy sentinels at the city limits will look at you, will jot down the registration number of your car for the traffic census, and will wave you on with never a word. You have entered Mexico, D.F.—which is to say *Distrito Federal*.

Saltillo is the first town of interest reached by the motorist entering Mexico from Eagle Pass, traveling on the Constitution Highway Branch. To mention, first off, some hotels along this highway, the best ones in Saltillo are *Hotel Arizpe Sáinz*, an atmospheric place of genuine Mexican charm, and the *Camino Real de Saltillo*, a deluxe air-conditioned motel under Western Hotels management, with pool, patio and a truly elegant restaurant. Matehuala, 160 miles south of Saltillo, has the attractive *Motel Las Palmas*. San Luis Potosí, another 120 miles south, is central Mexico's fast-expanding hub of highway travel and also of agriculture, with several good downtown hotels, all on or near the Zócalo, or central plaza, such as the *Colonial*, the *Gante* and the *San Luis Rey*, and on the western edge of the city a pleasant

FOUR "EN ROUTE TOWNS" FOR THE MOTORIST

motel called the *Tuna Courts*. Other recommendable motels are the *Cactus* and the *Concordia*. Querétaro, 130 miles farther down the middle of the country, has the *Motor Hotel La Mansion*, a bit outside the city on the highway to the capital, the *Hotel del Marques* and the rather old but interesting **Gran Hotel**, this in the very heart of the old city.

Saltillo's scenery is magnificent and the weather will probably be bright and cheerful even if, in Monterrey, only 55 miles distant, it is overcast and misty. Saltillo calls itself the Denver of Mexico, chiefly because it is ambitious and because, like Denver, it lies just a mile above sea level. You will probably arrive in the center of the town on a street surprisingly named Calle Theodore S. Abbott, on or near which are the chief shops.

Saltillo is a city of sunshine and sarapes and the alliteration is not a mere chamber-of-commerce slogan. The sunshine is almost continuous the year around and is doubly delightful in the city's bracing altitude. The sarapes used to be internationally famous but have deteriorated in quality, though not in brilliance of color. These gay and sometimes lurid blankets—the better ones being of wool—are worn as shawls by humble folk, chiefly Indians, throughout Mexico. The sarape is primarily a male garment (its counterpart for women being the less bulky *rebozo*) and is worn in smart or sloppy fashion according to the character of its owner. The sarape market, bordering the main street as you come into town, is a shoppers' rainbow and no woman tourist has ever been known to pass it without entering. You will be accosted, also, by many a sarapemonger on many a street corner. Most of them appear to be named Jesús, and all of them have better sarapes than any of their competitors.

The civic and cathedral complex in the eastern part of the city and the superlative double park (Parque Zaragoza and Parque Porfirio Díaz) in the western part add great distinction. The double park is among the loveliest bosky retreats to be found in Mexico, which makes almost a religion of its parks and plazas.

San Luis Potosí, a mellow city of old Spanish charm with a modern spirit of progress, has been unaccountably neglected by travelers and, so far, by Mexican propaganda as well.

As a bold discoverer, therefore, I present this town, in two brief episodes, the first on foot, the second by taxi.

After a breakfast or lunch, say at Hotel Gante or at the older Hotel Colonial, walk one block to the pleasant Zócalo. Bask in its cool sunshine—the phrase is fair because San Luis lies at 6000-feet altitude—and then enter the cathedral, which fronts upon it. From the Zócalo, walk through the Calle Hidalgo, an attractive *tiled* street for pedestrians only, reminiscent in a small way of old Seville's Serpentería. The best shops and department stores are here. Where the tiles end, turn right at the sign, Mercado Hidalgo, and you are quickly within one of provincial Mexico's gleaming white markets. You will be entranced by its palpitating life and regaled by the smell of millions of flowers. Buy a *mamey* (it looks like a bantam coconut) and upon your return to the hotel, take the fruit to Café La Lonja. Have the soda clerk cut it in two and fill the halves with vanilla ice cream. You have come to the end of a perfect stroll.

Episode Two is a ride to see San Luis' glorious pink-stone churches, *El Carmen, San Agustín, El Santuario;* then along Avenida Carranza to see how prosperous and beautiful a street in colonial-modern Mexico can be.

This city has a considerable past—here González Bocanegra wrote the National Anthem and here the pattern was designed for the Revolution of 1810—and surely it has a bigger future as the business and traffic nucleus of all north-central Mexico, so keep your eye on San Luis Potosí.

The *Central Branch* of the Pan American Highway System (*El Paso–Chihuahua–Durango–Aguascalientes–Querétaro–Mexico, D.F.*) has, of course, some good inns and motor courts along the way. Just across the Rio Grande, called Rio Bravo on Mexican maps, from El Paso is *El Camino Real*, with bungalow-style accommodations surrounding a swimming pool with a sunken bar.

FOUR "EN ROUTE TOWNS" FOR THE MOTORIST

Other hotel conveniences include nightclub, coffee shop, shopping center, and proximity to the race and dog tracks. It is under Western Hotels management, and a stagecoach, the hotel chain's symbol, adds a touch of atmosphere to the scene. Chihuahua's *Palacio Hilton* and *Hotel del Real* are good central places and *El Capitán* and *Santa Rita* are nearby motels. Durango's *Mexican Courts* will be found satisfactory and Aguascalientes can overnight you in the fair *San Marcos Hotel*. Several Querétaro hotels have been mentioned above, in connection with the Constitution Highway, which here joins the Central Branch.

Chihuahua is a silver city in a peculiar sense, for some of its stately old mansions and public edifies are said to have been constructed from the slag and dross of the fabulous Santa Eulalia silver mine near by. Primitive methods of reducing the ore in Spanish-colonial times threw out such rich waste that this material, still known to exist in old structures, actually tempts building wreckers to tear down business buildings and private homes for the silver they contain. More practical attractions for the visitor are found in the group of appealing plazas, in the rich cathedral built from a silver tax and in the Royal Chapel where Mexico's devoted liberator, Father Hidalgo, spent his last hours before being shot and crudely butchered. (The priest-patriot's vivid story is told in Chapters 5 and 16.) A special attraction is found also in the *perro pelón* (bald dog), which will be recognized as the Mexican hairless, though the animal is more properly called the Chihuahueno. And travelers who go for faded celebrities may hunt up the home of Pancho Villa, who was a major headline of this century's 'teens.

The *Pacific Branch* (*Nogales–Hermosillo–Mazatlán–Tepic–Guadalajara–Mexico, D.F.*) has a fair quota of good places for motorists' halts. Hermosillo has several excellent motels. The *Bugambilia* and *El Encanto*, each with swimming pool, are highly recommendable. El Encanto is managed by Western Hotels. Guaymas, the first town on the Pacific Coast, has *La Posada de*

San Carlos, on the beach, with swimming pool and yacht-club privileges, under the same management as the well-known *La Posada* in Santa Fe, New Mexico. Guaymas has also the *Playa de Cortés* inn. Ciudad Obregón has the good *San Jorge Motel*, with pool. Mazatlán has many hotels, among the better ones the *Hotel Playa Mazatlán*, four miles to the north, located on the surf-smitten seafront, the *Hotel de Cima*, the *Freeman*, *Belmar*, and *La Siesta*. Tepic has two recommendable if not pretentious inns, the *Sierra de Alicia* in town and *La Loma* on high ground outside. Guadalajara's hotels and more on Mazatlán will be found in Chapter 15.

By Ship and by Train

Service by ship from American to Mexican ports recently received a much needed shot in the arm by *Canadian Pacific Steamship Co.*, which took its *Princess Patricia* off her regular ferry runs between Seattle and Victoria/Vancouver and her summer cruises up the inside passage to Alaska to try out a winter-cruise service to Mexico. The ship, a 6000-ton beauty, departs Los Angeles on Friday evening, arrives in Puerto Vallarta the following Tuesday, Manzanilla on Wednesday and Acapulco on Thursday, where she remains until Sunday morning. On the homebound leg, she puts into Mazatlán, Monday, for an overnight stay, arriving back in Los Angeles on Friday. One-way rates are available if the whole 14-day cruise is not desired; or you one-way cruise down, lay over for two weeks, and return on the next northbound sailing (at the cruise rate plus 10 per cent). It is also feasible to sail one way and fly the other (cruise fares northbound are considerably less than southbound). The *Princess Patricia*, by current schedule, is to be in Mexico cruise service from December through early April.

The big British ships of *P & O-Orient Lines* call regularly at Acapulco, on sailings both to and from the U.S. West Coast and Europe. You can pick up an Acapulco sailing at Honolulu, Vancouver, San Francisco or Los Angeles—or begin your Mexican

BY SHIP AND BY TRAIN

cruise at London or Southampton, Le Havre, Lisbon, Bermuda, Port Everglades (port for Miami), Nassau, Trinidad, Cartagena or Panama. There's a sailing about once a month.

The *Spanish Line* has two 6000-ton ships in service to Veracruz, which you can pick up at Genoa, Barcelona or other Spanish ports, or at San Juan, Puerto Rico.

Holland-America Line's Maasdam and *Ryndam*, both 15,000-ton liners, come into Acapulco a couple of times a year from Suva, Wellington, Tahiti and Los Angeles, continuing to Panama, Kingston, New York and London. *Shaw-Saville*, a well-known British company, has round-the-world service on its *Northern Star* and *Southern Cross*, ships of 24,000 and 20,000 tons, that come into Acapulco about every three months from Sydney, Wellington, Auckland and Tahiti (sailing on from Mexico to Panama, Curaçao, Trinidad, Barbados, Portugal and England).

Rail travel from the U.S. border to Mexico City has improved enormously, as, indeed, the room for improvement was enormous. First-class coaches and Pullmans now compare rather favorably with their counterparts in the States. The major trains carry dining cars, observation-lounge coaches and club cars, yet the fares are hardly more than a quarter of those for comparable distances and services in the U.S. As an example, the 1225-mile run from El Paso, Texas, to Mexico City is, at present, only $13.01, about one cent a mile, with a Pullman lower berth costing $6.87 more. Top dinner prices in the dining car run to about two dollars, with a martini or daiquiri included. From Chihuahua to Mexico City, a run of a thousand miles, self-propelled Vistacars are operated five days a week, to give maximum visibility on this excitingly scenic route.

A popular innovation is escorted "rail cruises" from New York, in private Pullmans whose route, after reaching the Mexican border, continues to Mexico City, Cuernavaca and Taxco; this is a 16-day cruise now priced at $895. A 23-day cruise, priced at $1095, goes even to distant Acapulco. Still other cruises range in length from 9 to 21 days. All cruises include nights in luxury hotels at several of the chief points and on-board entertainment and guidance throughout the trip.

To tidy up the subject of the main standard lines, the traveler may avail himself of trains of the FNM (*Ferrocarriles Nacionales de México*) from Laredo, via Monterrey and San Luis Potosí, or from Ciudad Juárez, across the Rio Grande from El Paso, via Chihuahua, Torreón and Aguascalientes. And the *Ferrocarril del Pacífico* has a coastal line from Nogales to Guaymas, Mazatlán and Guadalajara, where it ties in with a main FNM line to the capital. Of course, stopovers may be made as desired.

CHAPTER 3

MONEY IN MEXICO

Preview of Prices

THE most absorbing topic in the world of travel is money. It must be so from the frequency with which it is discussed by tourists and it *is* so almost by axiom. What do I get in exchange for my dollar? How much can I buy with what I get? What should I pay for lodging and meals and various incidentals? And what about tips? These are the questions that simmer in the cauldron of travel and come to the seething point in those who, by nature or necessity, are addicted to thrift.

Unfortunately, the mathematics of money, as used in a foreign land, cannot be viewed as a fixed matter, and truthful reports given today may be false tomorrow. This caution is particularly necessary in the case of Mexico, where, despite efforts by the government, inflation-raised prices, then brought devaluation. Returning travelers do Mexico a disservice when they exclaim, orally and in print, that "you can live like a prince down there for the money you'd spend on bare necessities in the States." Even as this book goes to press, I read occasional enthusiastic burblings in the "Letters to the Editor" sections of important United States newspapers about the amazing cheapness of everything in Mexico. These reports simply are not true. They are based on the merest impressionism, perhaps on nothing more substantial than shoeshines and tram fares, which are perhaps one-third to one-fourth what they are in the States. *Some things* are ridiculously cheap. A few are dear. Most things, including basic travel costs, at the present favorable exchange, are considerably less than in the States. The facts may be neatly sorted into three categories and the sorting is substantially fair.

1. Anything that is based primarily on human labor is cheap in Mexico, except where the blind lavishness of tourist spending has vitiated the natural integrity of the people. Servants—and good ones at that—may be had for one-fourth or, in some areas, one-sixth of their "market value" in the United States and, by the same token, railway, bus and trolley fares (as well as haircuts, beauty-parlor treatments, shines and all personal services) are, and will doubtless remain, far under the levels to which we are accustomed, since these costs depend to a large extent on the element of labor.

2. Prices of manufactured goods, except hand-wrought specialties of artists and craftsmen, are frequently high because many of these goods are imported from the United States or can be "moved" from the shelves at prices commensurate with imported goods. If you have to buy a shirt, a hat or a topcoat in Mexico, be prepared to pay as much as you would pay for the same merchandise at home and maybe even more. One wonders how the white-collar worker of Mexico manages to live at all, for he is wickedly squeezed between the millstones of his low salary and the high cost of apparel, to mention only one item.

3. Hotel and restaurant prices have risen a lot but are still reasonable (though not cheap) by our standards. Mounting real estate values and mounting taxes have lifted hotel rates in the capital and in the chief resorts. Food problems, together with general inflation, have lifted restaurant prices. Yet *Hotel El Presidente*, the capital's leader in luxury, lists its rooms, all air-conditioned and with every possible modern comfort, at $15 to $17, single; $17 to $20, double. This is certainly not expensive for such a place, whose tariffs must, in fairness, be compared with the in-season rates of palatial hotels in California or Miami Beach, but it is by no means cheap. It will be seen, incidentally, that couples make out far better in Mexico than single persons, for two usu-

ally pay only 15 to 25 per cent more than one. Restaurant meals in good establishments run from about four to six dollars, including lubrication by a cocktail and a bottle of good Mexican beer. Be prepared, however, to spend considerably more in the *top* restaurants. (Mexican rosy wines such as *Rosa Corina* or *Santo Tomás Rosado,* both dry, or *Vino Rosado Alamo,* sweeter, are inexpensive, but imported wines and liquors, subject to sky-high duties, are sky-high in price—so look out!) In the coffee shops and snack bars, by contrast, which hundreds of Americans patronize right along, life can be rather pleasurably maintained for $1.50 per meal.

In the provinces, excepting a few popular and overcrowded resorts in season, prices of both lodging and meals are far lower than in Mexico City. In fact, the small, unpublicized cities still offer very cheap living, and sometimes great travel rewards as well, to those who enjoy venturing from the beaten track. Six to eight dollars is likely to be enough for a night's lodging *and* a full day's meals in the best hotel—and by no means bad—in these unsung towns of Mexico.

The exchange rate, since the devaluation of 1954, has held, up to this writing, at 12½ pesos to the dollar, the banks and hotels giving the same rate.

The Designer's Message

The Mexican money you receive for your dollars is worth a bit of initial study for two reasons. First, familiarity will enable you to avoid from the outset the mistakes and the confused fumblings that characterize the performance of some tourists for days or even for their entire stay. Second, the money has informative value and romantic interest.

Money *folds,* from one peso, worth eight cents, to a thousand pesos, worth 80 dollars. The big silver clinker, which was the peso until 1942, virtually disappeared for several years, but is now again fairly common, at least in the larger cities. The messages on the more familiar bills, the one, five, ten and twenty, warrant attention, for they present interesting vignettes of the Mexican scene and important sidelights on history.

The *one-peso note* shows, on one side, the Aztec calendar stone, perhaps the most famous work of science left anywhere by primitive America, and on the other, Mexico's tall Independence Monument, at whose base glows the eternal flame to the Unknown Soldier. These are among the chief sights of the country and are seen and admired by all visitors. The calendar stone is the central showpiece of the National Museum, and the Independence Monument topped by a gesturing angel (who fell to earth in the great earthquake of 1957 but was soon restored) rises 150 feet in marble and granite from the fourth glorieta of the capital's famous Paseo de la Reforma, not far from Chapultepec Park and Castle.

The *five-peso note* presents a Mexican beauty with a flower in her hair and a long silver chain looping over her bosom. The silver chain will light fires in the shopper's eye. On the reverse of this note, as on the one, is the Independence Monument.

The *ten-peso note* presents one of the loveliest of Mexico's "types," a girl with head and face framed in a vast white ruff hardly matched by Queen Elizabeth I, or by any of the coifs of Holland. You may chance to see a girl like this in Oaxaca on a day of fiesta, but you are sure to see many of them if you make your arduous way to Tehuantepec at the narrowest point of Mexico's isthmus in the south. The Tehuanas are said to outnumber the Tehuanos almost five to one, the men having been killed off in civil wars. At any rate, the women are a handsome, vigorous and brilliantly colorful breed. As a separate ethnic stock they are threatened with extinction, like the heath hens of Martha's Vineyard. Or will the few remaining pure-blooded males accept the challenge and save the race?

On the opposite side of the ten-peso note is a *Panorámica de Guanajuato;* in other words, a hill's-eye view of one of the most striking and historic small cities in Mexico. Perhaps the picture

THE DESIGNER'S MESSAGE 29

will spur you to make your way to this treasury of romance. In so doing you will be one of few, for Guanajuato has been inexplicably neglected by travelers. If you go there before the surge rolls in that direction, you will enjoy the place almost as a personal discovery.

The *twenty-peso note* pictures the patio of the delightful government palace in Querétaro (cradle of the Independence movement) on one side; on the other, a stern-visaged woman called *La Corregidora*. You will run across this woman frequently in Mexico, for despite her dour appearance, as of a cross between Queen Victoria and a militant temperance reformer, she was a great patriot, and symbolizes the country's unquenchable determination to achieve liberty. *Corregidor* means mayor (or local governor), and *La Corregidora* was the wife of the governor of Quarétaro. It was she who helped hatch the earliest plot for liberty and dramatically warned the patriot leaders when the plot was discovered by the Spanish oppressors. Look for *La Corregidora* in bronze in Mexico City's Plazuela de Santo Domingo, and look for her—much more pointedly—in Querétaro, the city of her devoted activity. If the ten-peso and twenty-peso notes lure you, respectively, to Guanajuato and Querétaro they will have done a job quite as valid as helping to pay for your stay there.

The silver coins of Mexico are simple to handle and to understand. The list of them is brief, starting with the five-peso silver coin and then the gleaming silver-dollar-sized peso (picturing the patriot Morelos), with the words *Independencia y Libertad* stamped around its rim. Below this comes the big copper 50-centavo piece and then the 20-centavo piece, still as large as a British penny, and the 5-centavo piece, in two different sizes. There are also copper coins of ten and five centavos, but I, at least, encounter them so seldom that they seem hardly worth listing. The chief ornaments on the subsidiary coins are the cap of liberty, the Toltec pyramids and the conspicuous symbol of Mexico, an eagle standing on a cactus and devouring a snake. *La Corregidora* is present, too, on the obverse of the copper 5-centavo piece in both sizes.

Gold coins, though not in ordinary use for purchases or commercial transactions, are available at the banks in limited amounts; however, they *may not be legally imported* into the United States. The most costly coin is the 50-peso gold *centenario* with 37.5 grams of pure gold. Since the gold peso is worth, if I'm correctly informed, 10.59 times as much as the paper peso, this means that your centenario will cost you 50 x 8 x 10.59 U.S. cents, which is to say $42.36. There is also a 20-peso gold coin called an *aztec*, a 10-peso coin called a *hidalgo* and a five-peso coin called a *half-hidalgo*. In our day and our country such exotic coinage in pure gold produces a sort of nostalgia for the good old monetary times when we, too, had gold eagles and double eagles.

A curiosity of Mexican money and transactions is that the peons in all parts of the country prefer money which they can ring rather than fold. It does not seem like money to them unless it makes a clatter when dropped. The result is that in many of the provinces hard money is hoarded, despite anything that the government can do, and change is consequently scarce. Often this causes an embarrassing impasse. In small transactions neither purchaser nor seller admits having any change at all. How shall the deal be consummated? More than once in past years, though not recently, I have been forced to submit to the most direct and primitive solution imaginable. I have offered a paper peso for a 50-centavo purchase, and the tradesman or vendor has promptly torn the note in two and given me one half in change.

Tips without Worry

The question of tips is a perplexing one discussed in confidential tones by all tourists. Mexico does not help out by adopting the European custom of adding a fixed 10 per cent service charge on hotel and restaurant bills and letting it go at that. Fifteen per cent is, however, a generous and convenient rule in quality establishments (10 per cent is enough in modest places) and the adoption of it will eliminate worry. In the case of meals taken in an American Plan hotel one may estimate the approximate cost of each meal and leave 15 per cent of the amount on the table. Many Americans are far more lavish than this and sometimes ridiculously so, to the sharp annoyance of Mexicans, who cannot compete with such largess. If the extravagant tippers would curb their natural tendencies by recalling the 15 per cent rule and if devotedly thrifty persons would temper the application of the rule by an occasional bit of "immoral generosity," the net result all around should be fairly satisfactory. And if every traveler would manage to have on hand at all times an ample supply of paper one-peso (eight-cent) notes, the worst worry of all—lack of change—would be demolished at the outset. This plan is not always easy to put into practice, except in the capital, but for that very reason it is important to attempt it. In small communities the recipient of your favors will seldom admit having change and to avoid embarrassment you will give far too much. But whenever you make a *purchase* of anything, including a meal, you are entitled to present a note larger than one that will barely cover the amount. You may then insist upon change.

Porters—but that subject has never been solved by any rule. Tariffs often exist and are often flouted both by givers and demanders of tips, for porters are spoiled by tourists as quickly as fruit by a hot sun. A peso per bag at railway and bus stations should be ample, if not lavish. And if a porter in some provincial or frontier station demands, in his brand of English, "Seventy cents a bag, sir," do not fly into a rage. Assume that he is being moderate and that he means seventy *centavos*. Mexican porters, especially at frontiers, love to befuddle travelers by using the word cents instead of centavos. They hope that in your haste to get along with the business in hand you will be sufficiently rattled to pay a dozen times what the official tariff authorizes. If challenged, they can always point to the tariff and blandly assure you that they asked only 70 centavos, or whatever the figure may be.

But the subject of porter peculations need not intrude further. It can be comfortingly and truthfully said in general that (porters possibly aside) those who serve you in Mexico are honest by nature. The tendency to gyp is merely a tourist incrustation in a few places and has not reached grim proportions. It is by no means second nature, as in some Mediterranean ports.

CHAPTER 4

TREMENDOUS TRIVIA

Advisers in Advance

THE *Mexican Government Tourism Department* has head offices at 45 Paseo de la Reforma, site of the former U.S. Embassy in Mexico City, an information bureau in the Pemex Building at Avenida Juárez 89, and many offices in other cities, including: 2 East 55th Street, *New York City;* 210 North Michigan Avenue, *Chicago;* 1905 Commerce Street, *Dallas;* 809 Walker Avenue, Suite 146, *Houston;* 3106 Wilshire Boulevard, *Los Angeles;* First National Bank Building Arcade, Office 20, *Miami;* 203 St. Charles Street, *New Orleans;* 209 E. Travis Street, *San Antonio;* 1301 Fifth Avenue, *San Diego;* 219 Sutter Street, *San Francisco;* 80 North Stone Avenue, *Tucson;* and 1302 Connecticut Avenue, *Washington 6, D.C.* There are also two Canadian offices, at 1700 Dorchester Boulevard, West (International Aviation Building), *Montreal,* and at 13 Bloor Street, West, *Toronto.*

Supporting and complementing the Mexican Government Tourism Department is a promotional organization, which answers *mail* inquiries only, called the *Mexican National Tourist Council.* It has offices at 2 East 55th Street, New York City, and 9445 Wilshire Boulevard, Beverly Hills, California.

The over-800-page annual called *The South American Handbook,* distributed in the U.S.A. by Rand-McNally, includes Mexico in its coverage, devoting over 60 pages to it and touching many vital topics.

Pemex, with head office at Avenida Juárez 89, is a valuable adviser to the motorist and a tireless publisher of travel booklets. Principal U-Drive outfits inside Mexico, by the way, include *Hertz de México*, Versalles 6, Mexico City; *Auto Rent, S.A.*, Avenida Chapultepec 314, Mexico City; and *Avis Rent-a-Car*, with offices at the Hotel del Prado, Mexico City, and branches in Guadalajara, Mérida and Acapulco.

Several lavish brochures with current travel information are also put out by the big travel agencies, banks and transportation companies, especially by the international air systems.

The *Pan American Union* is a wellspring of travel information. It is, of course, an official bureau of Good Neighborliness and exists primarily to foster friendship and unity in the Western Hemisphere. It has informative literature of every sort and will cheerfully send you, for next to nothing, folders and other helpful material on Mexico, including a full list of hotels. Merely address the Travel Division, Pan American Union, Washington, D.C.

Some forthright comment on guidebooks that stress culture, sights and/or practicalities may be briefly made. *Terry's Guide to Mexico*, newly updated by James Norman, is the Baedeker of the group, packed with comment—historical, artistic, gastronomical and otherwise. Lawrence and Sylvia Martin's *Standard Guide to Mexico* is sprightly and well researched. It is the Mexico portion of their former *Standard Guide to Mexico and the Caribbean*, brought up to date. John Wilhelm's *Guide to Mexico City* and his *Guide to all Mexico* are thorough handbooks written on the spot, or spots, by a resident. Frances Toor's *Guide to Mexico* and *A Treasury of Mexican Folkways* are both excellent (the author is dead, but her books are still being carried on). *Mexico, Three-Storeyed Land*, by A. t'Serstevens, a highly regarded commentary on all phases of Mexican life, is penetrating and without bias. *Mexico*, one of the "Sunset Discovery" series (these books are well-printed, inexpensive paperbacks, brought out by the Lane Publishing Company of Menlo Park, California), has made its good contribution to the guidebook field, and Norman D.

Ford's *Fiesta Lands* is an example of his customary stress on thrift budgetry. AAA members will keep in mind the Association's *Mexico by Motor* as a veritable gold mine of practical up-to-date information.

On other topics than tourist guidance, there is rather a rich literature on Mexico and a good place to browse and buy is the *American Bookstore*, a well-stocked and widely respected shop in Mexico City, at Avenida Madero 25. For standard histories you'll like Lesley Bird Simpson's *Many Mexicos*. For politics and social science you may depend on John A. Crow's *Mexico Today*, or William P. Tucker's *The Mexican Government Today*. In less heavy fields—since you're presumably on holiday—you'll enjoy Patricia Font Ross's *Made in Mexico*, an arts and crafts volume with illustrations by Carlos Mérida; Emmett Reid Blake's exhaustive *Birds of Mexico;* and, finally, Miguel Covarrubias' lavish and beautiful *Mexico South*, an art volume that costs a thumping $12.50—and worth it to those who have that kind of money to spend on a single book. It may also be of interest that more than 20 Mexican schools and colleges have initiated summer courses, in great variety, for foreign (chiefly U.S. and Canadian) students. The most important of them is the *National University of Mexico*, in Mexico City, which great and venerable institution, oldest in the Americas, offers six-week courses, each with two semester hours of credit, from late June through mid-August. The famous *Instituto Allende*, in San Miguel de Allende, offers courses in Spanish "and all fine arts."

Border Barriers Demolished

Scare stories about border formalities used to be a nickel a dozen on both sides of the Mexico–United States line, but nowadays the barriers are as low as any I have ever encountered at any frontier in the world, including the Canada–United States line. This is true, at any rate, for holders of tourist cards, which are valid for six months and which may be promptly secured by U.S. citizens (proof such as birth certificate or passport required) at any Mexican consulate, Mexican Government Tourism Office and at airline and steamship ticket offices. They may also be secured at AAA border offices and even—of all things—upon arrival at the Mexico City airport, though this procedure is not advised.

There are cards for just a single entry and exit of 30 days or six months, and a special one of six months permitting multiple entries and exits, no charge being made for any of the three. For the multiple-entry card only, three photographs must be supplied. Border towns, by the way, such as Tijuana, Nogales and Ciudad Juárez, may be visited by U.S. citizens for periods up to 72 hours without a permit, but personal identification may be required.

Money—which is to say bills and cash—may be taken in or out of Mexico freely in any amounts, without border controls.

Customs inspection is wonderfully innocuous in the case of those who enter Mexico with tourist cards. The country wants you, welcomes you, goes out of its way to make your entrance easy.

Returning to the States is also easy, although in these days the U.S. Customs allowances for returning residents is woefully limited to $100 worth of duty-free souvenirs and gifts, and since 1965 the basis for figuring values has been the retail price rather than the wholesale, as previously. And only one quart of liquor (*adults* only) may be brought in duty-free, instead of the one-*gallon* limit of tradition. Unsolicited gifts, valued under ten dollars, may be mailed to the home folks or Stateside friends, with no restrictions except that no more than one such gift may be mailed to any one person on any one day. Only on a few things, like perfume, are there special rules and you can get information about these from the U.S. Consulate in Mexico City. I have found the Mexican customs guards at the points of departure eager to cooperate in making the exit easy. No doubt they have been instructed by their government to "leave a good impression" on departing travelers, so that they will come again. Over a million tourists, the majority Americans, now visit Mexico annually and leave behind more than $800 million!

Altitude Gremlins

The altitude of Mexico City is officially stated to be 7434 feet. For purposes of comparison one may record that the figure for Mount Washington's summit is 6293 feet and that the Austrian village of Ober-Gurgl, loftiest community in Europe, is just over 6300 feet above sea level. To Mexico City the net result of its lofty situation on the 19th parallel of latitude is a wonderfully exhilarating climate. Says the *South American Handbook*, "The range of temperature is 35°–75° F. with 65° as mean; the nights are always cool." Those words are eloquent. Haiti is on the same latitude as this city. Dakar, across the Atlantic, is only a little south of it. But the sea-level climate of those localities reminds one of a steam *sauna*.

Altitude is a topic of consuming interest in Mexico City. I suppose the net wordage spoken locally on this subject by tourists almost equals that spoken about money and surpasses that spoken about weather. A city 7500 feet above sea level seems to most Americans fantastically high, but to Colombians, Ecuadoreans, Peruvians and Bolivians it seems at a rather low level. I am hardly fitted to worry about it vocally or in print since I became familiar with Andean altitudes before ever seeing Mexico. Tourists concern themselves too much with the subject, I believe, though I should state with emphasis that persons suffering from any heart condition should go easy until they have become adjusted to the higher altitudes. Visitors in the soundest health sometimes expect to collapse if they run a few yards or dance energetically. They expect to be exhausted every evening. They expect to feel their hearts pound and their ears pop if some motor trip takes them from Mexico Valley up over a 10,000-foot pass. A favorite diversion of practical jokers is to tell tourists, when motoring, that the car is at some prodigious altitude and then "watch them suffer," when actually it is rolling along the valley floor; or, more mercifully, to tell them they are still on the valley floor (and watch their expressions of relief), when actually the car is 3000 feet above it. The average person with sound heart is hardly concerned about the altitude of Mexico City after the first day or two, unless he or she is reminded of it. I had, in fact, to be reminded of it by a curious fact of sport. A college classmate of mine was coach of the University of Mexico football team and he expressed his belief that a punt will carry fifteen yards farther in the rarefied air of Mexico, D.F., a mile and a half above sea level, than it will in the air of playing fields in our American seaboard cities. Dropkicks and field goals may be sensibly attempted from points five or ten yards farther from the goal than would be warranted on fields of the United States seaboard.

The Mexico that most transient travelers see is the lofty tableland in the center of the country, the chief exceptions being Acapulco and perhaps the highways from the U.S., or possibly the ports of Veracruz and Mazatlán. Toluca (8700 feet) is the highest city in this central sector and Cuernavaca (4500) is among the lowest. Others may be mentioned as follows: Guadalajara (5200); Morelia (6200); Guanajuato (6500); Puebla (7100); Taxco (5600); Querétaro (5900); Oaxaca (5000). Those who are seriously concerned about altitude will prefer to spend most of their time at places in the brackets below 6000. The road leading to Cuernavaca (and Taxco) touches a mark close to 10,000 feet, and that leading to Puebla is the highest good road in Mexico, with its summit over 10,000 feet, but these high spots are quickly passed. The resort of Fortín de las Flores is one of the few much-visited places in Mexico that lies as low as the 3000-foot level and for this reason, among others, it is favored by those who dread to remain "up aloft."

Guides, Philosophers and Friends

A tourist-agency guide, or one furnished by one of the leading hotels, comes near to being a necessity in Mexico, especially in

GUIDES, PHILOSOPHERS AND FRIENDS

the provinces, a thing that has never been true of the more traveled portions of Europe. It is much less of a necessity if you speak Spanish, but whatever your language equipment it can prove a most comforting buffer. Tourist agencies with central offices in Mexico City are numerous, but I shall mention only a few whose services are personally known to me.

Wagons-Lits-Cook, the world-wide Thomas Cook, has an excellent branch in Mexico City, at 88 Avenida Juárez, the main business thoroughfare. Cook's office is nearly opposite the Regis Hotel, a bit west of the Alameda and is, therefore, conspicuous.

Another great international organization is *Wells Fargo*, linked with *American Express* and located at Calle Niza 22, only two blocks from Hotel El Presidente in the "new downtown" area, on and near Avenida Insurgentes. This ultra-American team of Wells Fargo-American Express, useful for its mail service as well as for travel and exchange, publishes its own brief touring guide, *Mexico? Si, Señor.*

Orbis Turismo de México (*Orbis Travel Service* for you and me) is headed by a dynamic young Mexican named Victor G. Romero. The Orbis office is downtown, on an upper floor of Edificio Juárez, Avenida Juárez 60, in the very midst of the big downtown hotels (del Prado, Prado Alffer, Bamer, Alameda, etc.). Mr. Romero is one of the better-known travel agents of Latin America, a prominent figure in all gatherings of Latin *hoteleros*, and I have found him personally knowledgeable, efficient and courteous.

Among *many* other Mexican travel agencies, some 90 in all, that of *Tony Pérez* is known to me in the person of Tony himself, a most personable and experienced man who has had a major hand in the management of several of the capital's large hotels. His offices are at Calle Volga 1.

Another agency of top importance is *Mexico Travel Advisers*, with head office in Mexico City, at Calle Genova 30. The dynamic head of this agency, perhaps the largest one in Mexico, is James (call me "Jimmie") Dubin. Jimmie is quite a hotel magnate, too, being director of Hoteles Mexicanos Dubin, which owns five hotels in top tourist centers: the Spa Peñafiel in Tehuacán; Monte Cassino in Mexico City; Hotel de la Borda in Taxco; and Rancho Taxco-Victoria (a two-hotel combine), also in Taxco.

Finally I should mention that all the top hotels have travel agencies for the booking of tours, public or personal, in the capital and its surroundings and much farther afield.

My point in emphasizing the service of tourist agencies may warrant repetition. I think Mexico City, and especially its surroundings and the provinces of which it is the natural hub, imperatively call for such service unless you have plenty of time and at least a fair colloquial knowledge of the Spanish language. For 20 years I knocked about Europe practically unaided by any such service, but Mexico is different. Europe has been accustomed to swarms of tourists, British and then Americans, for more than a hundred years. Mexico came more recently into her own. She is progressing at a great clip, but one still needs practical aid, good counsel, good cars, and timely tips both in advance and all along the way.

THE BACKGROUND OF THE PICTURE

CHAPTER 5

A PAGEANT IN FOUR PARTS

Aboriginal Marvels of Mexico

Two mainland countries of Latin America have a past so dramatic and exciting that they make all the others seem a bit pale. These are, of course, Peru and Mexico, the two upon which the scholarship of William H. Prescott seized with such sure grasp in his classics of history, *The Conquest of Peru* and *The Conquest of Mexico*. Both countries boasted wealthy empires and both had elaborate forms of aboriginal civilization. This made the conquest of them thrilling to the adventurous and greedy Spaniards; and the stories of those twin conquests, entirely aside from the style of any historian in recounting them, remain two of the most exciting scenes in the whole drama of history. Peru tapered off in dramatic impact after Pizarro conquered the Incas, but Mexico, after Cortés conquered the Aztecs, has continued to produce one peak of interest after another, even to the present day. Whatever else is said of this country, it can never be accused of being dull.

An informal bibliography of the briefest possible compass, designed for the brusher-up on Mexico, may usefully intrude here. A good and interesting general history, for instance, already mentioned in previous connections, is Henry Bamford Parkes' *A History of Mexico*. The first 20 pages tell, with extreme but intelligent condensation, the entire preconquest story. It is boiled prose, yet it retains its freshness and flavor. These 7000 words can be not only read but studied in one hour. (In the book's remaining 400 pages, the pace of the story is more deliberate.) Various scholarly tomes tell the story of Mexico's *aboriginal* marvels in much detail, but I know of no book covering that pre-Columbian period that combines popular readability with scholarship in the same happy proportions that Philip Ainsworth Means achieved in his books on the Inca civilization of Peru. To me, personally, this seems a real "lacuna" of literature.

For the period of the conquest there is the famous contemporary chronicle written by Cortés' companion, Bernal Díaz del Castillo. It is called *Historia Verdadera de la Conquesta de la Nueva España*, and the priceless original manuscript is in the municipal archives of Guatemala City; but, of course, it has been translated many times and it makes vivid reading in any translation. Probably the best of such translations is that made by A. P. Maudslay from an exact copy of the original MS, edited by Genaro García and published in Spanish in Mexico. An American edition of this scholarly and stirring work, with an introduction by Irving A. Leonard, was brought out by Farrar, Straus & Co., Prescott's *The Conquest of Mexico*, using the chronicle as only one contemporary report, is too well known to need further comment. Despite its length, it is a book that one can hardly lay aside after starting to read or even reread it.

For the Mexico that made its painful way from the first stirrings of independence to the present era of freedom, no adequate review is briefer, fairer or more to the point than Hubert Herring's *Mexico, the Making of a Nation*, published years ago by the Foreign Policy Association as one of its so-called Headline Books and still to be found in libraries. The author condensed the whole story of Mexico's struggle for independence and then for social freedom into less than a hundred pages and yet kept those pages—like their subject matter—unflaggingly interesting.

For today's Mexico, the nation that has taken shape since the Revolution, a simple and electrically interesting quick review (but not recent) is Anita Brenner's *The Wind That Swept Mexico*. Miss Brenner's book deals solely with the years since 1910–1911, when the long-pent-up winds of popular aspiration

ABORIGINAL MARVELS OF MEXICO

grew into a gale and swept away the aging dictator, Porfirio Díaz, and his whole coterie of profiteers. It is wonderfully documented with 184 photographs assembled by George B. Leighton, and there have been few books on Mexico so richly appealing to the eye as is this one. The photographs, excitingly captioned, cover the whole thrilling range of the story, engraving on the mind a composite picture of the country calculated to outlast any words of any text. Tense drama, passion and pathos, snobbishness, misery, hope, struggle, despair, hope again—the pace of the tale never falters. I frankly urge the intending visitor to Mexico to hunt up this book in some library since it probably cannot be purchased, not having been republished for some time.

Parkes points out the fact that Mexico is the principal spot where the ethnological currents of the world, originating in Asia, met and mingled. One current moved eastward, presumably by way of the Bering Strait and the Aleutians, and ultimately inhabited all parts of the hemisphere that makes up the Americas. The other current moved westward until it was stopped by the Atlantic Ocean. The Vikings sent feelers across this barrier but not until 1492 did the barrier become a bridge. And not until 1519–1521, when Hernán Cortés boldly attacked Mexico and conquered it, did the two currents of humanity finally and definitely merge. Intermarriage developed and has continued in Mexico to this day. Asiatics who had become Europeans married Asiatics who had become "Indians," and the human race, long divided, again became one race.

The civilization that Cortés found and that his literary soldier described in the celebrated chronicle was an almost incredible thing and it is no wonder that advance stories of it, seeping through to the approaching conquerors, whetted their natural appetites to the point of sheer greed, which they scarcely bothered to cloak with pious phrases. Says Parkes: "Enriched by the loot of a hundred triumphant campaigns, Tenochtitlán, the Aztec capital—now Mexico City—acquired a splendor which could scarcely be duplicated in Europe." But this splendor was an ephemeral thing, as was the period of Aztec ascendancy. There had been other Indian races whose cultural contributions, even in Mexico, surpassed those of the Aztecs.

It is necessary, in any brief roundup of preconquest Mexico, to reduce the whole complex roster of races to the four that contributed most.

The *Archaic peoples*, not so much a race as a fog of primitive folk lost in antiquity and perhaps roaming the Americas as early as 15,000 B.C., left no great legacy, yet they made a discovery, *probably on the plateau of Mexico*, that had revolutionary consequences. They discovered how to tame a plant called *teosinte* which was native only to Mexico and Central America. This was wild maize or corn and, with its taming, the restless, nomadic tribes of America found it possible to settle down and build cities. Mexican maize anchored civilization in the New World, as wheat and barley anchored it in the Old World.

The *Mayas*, who first appeared some centuries before the birth of Christ, reached two separate peaks of importance—the so-called Old Empire, centering in Guatemala, and the New Empire, centering in Mexico's Yucatán. According to a correlation favored by many students of their calendar and culture (and opposed by other scholars), the Guatemala period lasted from the 4th to the 9th centuries A.D., and the Yucatán renascence lasted from the 12th to the 15th centuries. In the latter centuries of their importance, the Mayas are confusingly intertwined with the Toltecs, and their great hero, whether man or god, was so interchangeable that his "nationality" has never been determined. He was known to the Toltecs as Quetzalcoatl and to the Mayas as Kukulcan, but which race bred him—or invented him—scholarship still does not know.

The Maya civilization, with its three calendars, its scientific advancement and its wonderful architectural and artistic skill, is quite the equal in interest of the Inca civilization in the Andes. It lasted very much longer than did the later Toltec and Aztec ascendancies and it influenced all the strands of culture that have

ABORIGINAL MARVELS OF MEXICO

followed, but it does not belong primarily to the Mexican plateau and hence it does not belong in this review. Though politically a province of Mexico it is often paired for purposes of travel with Guatemala, as it cries to be because of its geography and its historical background.

The *Toltecs* were a tribe of the linguistic family called Nahua, which also produced the Aztecs and all the later migratory peoples. All of these tribes were warlike and all came from the north in successive waves. The Toltecs achieved an advanced and complicated civilization, as every traveler is quickly aware when he visits their wonderful capital, Teotihuacán (near Mexico City), with its elaborate temples and huge pyramids. There is no need to make heavy weather of that name, as many bewildered Americans do. It is merely Tay-o-tee-wah-cáhn. In this truly fabulous place you may first become acquainted with Quetzalcoatl, whose name is also easy to pronounce—merely Ketz-al-quatl. He was many things to many Indian races, especially Toltecs and Mayas, but he is almost always represented as a plumed or feathered serpent. It is quite necessary to know Quetzalcoatl whether or not one ever goes to Yucatán and Guatemala, for the Aztecs "acquired" this god from the Toltecs, and a great part of the success of Cortés was due to a superstition entertained by the Aztecs that the approaching Stranger was a lieutenant of Quetzalcoatl (if not the god himself), coming according to a legendary promise to redeem his people. Instead of throwing him into an Aztec concentration camp, the emperor welcomed the supposed emissary (or god), to his own bitter cost.

The *Aztecs*, a fresh, vigorous, belligerent branch of the Nahua migrants, entered the Valley of Mexico (then called Anáhuac) early in the 14th century and presently acquired some little islands surrounded by swampland. Here they founded the city of Tenochtitlán (easy does it, on pronunciation), which was to become within two centuries the glittering Aztec capital and then the capital of the conquerors' Nueva España. The story of Tenochtitlán, built partly on islands, partly on piles in the marsh or lake and connected by three causeways with the firmer land, is one of the great and tragic stories of history; and it *is* history, not legend. The preconquest happenings are a matter of reliable record, and the city, numbering perhaps a hundred thousand inhabitants that the conquerors found has been described in much detail by excited chroniclers and by more sober historians. It was a true Venice of the New World because it was rich, haughty, imperialistic, and because its streets were canals (destined to be filled in by the demolished Aztec structures when it became the Spanish colonial capital). Many Aztec nobles built sumptuous palaces around open patios, and tribute was exacted from the lesser tribes for hundreds of miles around. The Aztecs delighted in wars because they always won and could then have a handy excuse to levy new imposts and "reparations."

Their tribal god was Mexitl (more commonly and cumbersomely known as Huitzilopochtli) and the people themselves were called Mexica. By an easy transition the conquerors applied the name to the entire country and hence was born the word Mexico. The place where the Mexica-ns settled had special appeal because of the ease with which it could be defended, but also it was pointed out to them by their god who had bidden them settle at the point where they should find an eagle on a cactus plant devouring a snake. They found such an eagle, so engaged, on one of the islands of Lake Texcoco and laid the foundations of their capital there. The eagle attacking the serpent is the familiar symbol of modern Mexico, seen on the national flag, on various coins, on the façades of government buildings and elsewhere.

The character of the early Indians—and it was substantially the same in all the tribes, though the Mayas far surpassed the others in matters of personal cleanliness—is of much more than historic or academic interest to the traveler, for it inheres in the character of Mexicans today. Mexico is an Indian nation, not a Spanish nation with many submerged Indians, as is true of Peru and Ecuador. John Gunther emphasized the fact that "The three greatest men in Mexican history, Cortés excepted, were pure or almost pure Indians—Juárez, Porfirio Díaz (a great man whether you like him or not) and Lázaro Cárdenas." The preconquest Indians were patient to the point of stoicism. Today's Mexicans are infinitely placid about waiting for anything or anybody. Two hours spent in a queue, waiting to buy a railroad ticket or even a single postage stamp for the letter so tightly clutched, seems to them normal and rather pleasant. A similar period of waiting for someone—*anyone*—who is late for an appointment leaves the wait-er totally unruffled, whereas a normal American begins to fume after ten or fifteen minutes.

Courtesy was second nature to the Indians of old. It is second nature to Mexicans of today—to the very great benefit of travelers.

Enjoyment of simple pleasures—of flowers and music, of fireworks and religious celebrations—was the breath of life to the Mexica as it is to the Mexicans.

Life was cheap and it is cheap today. In 1487, when a new temple was dedicated in Tenochtitlán, some 20,000 human victims were sacrificed to the Aztec god, and the gaudily robed priests were splashing in blood from dawn to dusk. Such practices vanished with the conquest, but life has remained pitifully unimportant. It is partly for that reason that rebellions and internecine wars have flourished so luxuriantly.

The obstinate tenacity of the race, the clinging to tradition and to the established way of life, can be considered the outstanding characteristic of Mexicans. Like conservatism in any form, it has its virtues and its defects. The most typically Mexican sound today is the slapping of tortillas by horny-handed women in every town and village. One hears it in many parts of Mexico City (though not on the Paseo de la Reforma!). Exactly the same sounds were heard by Cortés and Bernal Díaz del Castillo. They were heard by Moctezuma II and Moctezuma I, by the hero-god Quetzalcoatl, by the first Maya who appeared on the scene a few centuries before Christ. And the sounds were then probably 35 centuries old. The sound is a symbol. Mexico cannot be modernized overnight, at least in its remoter regions, by outside influences, nor can it by its own government. The mighty force of tradition may be bypassed in some instances, notably in the capital, but it cannot be brushed aside.

The Impact of Spain

The story of the impact of Spain upon Mexico is acted out or danced out in village pageantry in many a Mexican fiesta. Local Indians in full regalia, with multicolored pants, ribboned slippers and enormous chicken-feather headdresses, are the actors (dancers), and they usually devote a half day, or even a whole day, to it for the pleasure of the populace, not to mention their own enjoyment. To fortify their histrionic and terpsichorean talents, they consume vast quantities of mezcal—or of tequila if they can get it, or of pulque if they cannot get mezcal, all being products of their own cactus. A full liter, just over a U.S. quart, of the murderous liquid fire is considered an adequate dram for an average performer, but they carry it amazingly well and are rarely seen drunk—since the show must go on.

I watched the play—or perhaps one should call it a ballet—for some three hours in the village of Zimatlán, near Oaxaca, and was fascinated by the crude color and barbarous energy of it. Mixtec Indians, who are tall, handsome fellows, were selected to play the parts of Moctezuma, his court and his army, while the Spanish invaders were played by Zapotecs (who are a head shorter), and by ill-favored boys who had not attained their growth. Cortés was played by an evil-looking villain suitable for hissing. An unexpected touch was La Malinche (called also Malintzin and Marina), Cortés' celebrated interpreter and mistress. She was played by a girl of seven who was ravishingly beautiful in a long blue gown, blue slippers and a prodigious picture hat, with a vast blue plume. She strutted like a small peacock, and her father, in a natty gray suit and pink shirt, was on the periphery of the show —fairly bursting with pride. I congratulated him and was allowed to shake hands with the charming little concubine. Evidently the village of Zimatlán picked its loveliest little girl for the part and was in no wise troubled by the original Malinche's laxity of morals—unlike the good Prescott, who wrote, in the prose of his period: "Her errors . . . should be charged to the evil influence of him to whom, in the darkness of her spirit, she looked with simple confidence to guide her." (Before looking to Cortés she looked to his friend, Alonso Hernández Puertocarrero, but the girl was so charming that Cortés simply took her.)

A show like this means twice as much to the beholder if he has recently read some full account—and Prescott's remains the best —of the wonderful anabasis made by Cortés and his bold band from Veracruz to Tenochtitlán. It is a story of almost unparalleled courage and resourcefulness, worthy of a better underlying theme than rapacity and glory.

The main facts may be set down here. In 1518, Diego Velásquez de León, governor of Cuba, picked the young man Hernán Cortés—who had once been his private secretary but was then a young-man-about-Cuba—to organize an expedition to explore the unknown land to the west. This mysterious land, rumored to contain large and opulent cities and even an "empire" in the interior, had already been hastily visited—on the coast only—by two previous expeditions. Cortés accepted the assignment and set about his preparations with such astounding energy that Velásquez, in sudden panic lest the young man supersede him in power and importance, sought to call the whole thing off. He was too late. Cortés, hearing of it, set sail immediately from Santiago de Cuba, before the governor could stop him. He cruised about the fringes of Cuba for three months, picking up crews, "marines" and the materials of warfare, and finally set sail in February, 1519, for Yucatán. His force consisted of 11 ships, 500 soldiers, with ten brass guns and four falconets, and, by far the most important of all, *16 horses.*

Luck was with him in a hundred ways, but notably in two. He early acquired interpreters; and the Aztec emperor became convinced that he was, as we have said, the returning god Quetzalcoatl, or at least the god's direct emissary. Cortés cleverly used his 16 horses and his 14 metal tubes that spat out lightning and death-dealing thunder to strengthen immeasurably the rumors of his divine origin or mission.

The interpreters were a team of two: Jerónimo de Aguilar, a Spanish castaway from an earlier expedition who had learned the Mayan tongue and whom Cortés luckily picked up in Yucatán; and the beautiful Malinche whom he picked up in Tabasco. Malinche was an Aztec cacique's daughter whose wicked mother had sold her secretly into slavery. She was sold a second time to Mayas in the Tabasco province and was given by them, with 19 other maidens, as tribute to the white conqueror. Cortés spoke with Aguilar in Spanish; Aguilar could speak with Malinche in Mayan; she could speak with the Aztecs in their own tongue. By this circuitous route, messages could be sent and by the return route the answers could be received. But the clever girl, a born linguist, soon picked up a colloquial knowledge of the Castilian speech, and this shortened the business.

On Good Friday of 1519, Cortés finally landed at the spot which he named Veracruz (True Cross) and was at last in direct touch with the Aztecs. The founding of this town was a political maneuver, since it enabled Cortés to proclaim himself and his band self-governing citizens of New Spain under the direct control of the Spanish crown rather than under the peevish governor of Cuba. Cortés was promptly chosen captain-general, which entitled him to one-fifth of all the loot obtained by the expedition, another fifth going to King Charles I, who was likewise the great Charles V of the Holy Roman Empire. This loot was already starting to roll in nicely. Moctezuma sent to Cortés the turquoise and feather mask of Quetzalcoatl and two enormous disks of solid gold and silver from the chief temple, representing the sun and the moon. Cortés asked outright for a helmetful of gold dust, and this glittering present, too, was promptly sent.

It was at this point that Cortés burned his ships to prevent retreat or defection. And if he only scuttled them, as some claim, it was still an act of boldness that history was to call sheer folly if things went against him, sheer heroism if things went for him—as they did. Cortés, like Pizarro, in Peru, was ruthless, cruel, wily. Like Pizarro, he considered treachery an integral part of warfare. But glory more than personal greed motivated him and he did have certain worthy impulses not connected with either. For one thing, he strove, with a recklessness that often hampered his military strategy, to abolish the religious custom of human sacrifice that he encountered everywhere on his march; and this was only in small part because he foresaw that his own men and he himself might be desirable morsels for the bloody gods. He had no fear of death.

Two points on his march from Veracruz to Tenochtitlán are of outstanding interest to today's traveler. They are Cholula and the volcano Popocatépetl. Cholula, near the present Puebla, was a center of Toltec culture and was famous as the sacred pilgrimage city of Quetzalcoatl. It boasted a huge pyramid (still dominating the landscape and now crowned with a Christian church) and some 400 temples. Here, thanks to the girl Malinche, Cortés learned of a plot against him, instigated by the Aztecs. He decoyed some 3000 Cholulans and Aztec "porters" inside the temple enclosure and massacred every one. Then he erected a Christian cross atop the pyramid and proceeded to destroy and burn the city and its 400 temples (called *teocallis*). He vowed that he would erect a church on the site of each destroyed teocalli and he did indeed make great headway toward it. About 160 of these churches and their successors now dot the landscape of this small *población* and make it one of the most distinctive towns in all Mexico.

The route led from Cholula over a lofty pass between the live volcano Popocatépetl, which still smokes occasionally, and the extinct one, Ixaccíhuatl, "Sleeping Lady," forming together the chief showpiece of Mexican scenery in all ages. The mystery of the former lured one of Cortés' captains, Diego de Ordaz, to make the hard ascent, which is worth mentioning here because

Cortés was destined to make dramatic use of this mountain in his hour of direst need. When his supply of gunpowder was exhausted, he had one of his soldiers lowered into the crater to gather sulphur, so that more powder could be made. Washington at Valley Forge showed no greater tenacity and resourcefulness than Cortés in the Valley of Mexico.

The taking, losing and retaking of Tenochtitlán may be very briefly sketched, though every detail of the tense story is exciting. The Spaniards entered it—between two rows of Aztec nobles in all their splendor—in November, 1519. Moctezuma was brought forward in a jeweled litter and Cortés rode the causeway on his horse. The emperor left his litter and the captain-general dismounted from his horse. Two leaders, representing the two streams of "Asiatic" culture, finally met and eyed each other. Moctezuma perceived that Cortés was a man like himself, but he was more certain than ever that the Spaniard was an authorized representative of Quetzalcoatl. He gave him and his men a palace within the city and the Spaniards settled down there, well aware that their palace could become a trap and that the causeway could be quickly cut.

Cortés' monumental boldness was never more in evidence than now. Although the Spaniards were but 400 against 100,000 possible enemies, he invaded the emperor's quarters, kidnaped him and made him a prisoner. Then he insisted that the worship of Huitzilopochtli, and especially the practice of human sacrifice, must cease. His demand was not instantly granted, so Cortés himself climbed to the top of the sacred pyramid and set about smashing the idols, like a veritable Carry Nation attacking the demon rum. He had an image of the Virgin set up and ordered the singing of hymns and the celebration of Mass. It was a piece of effrontery almost beyond the imagination, as if a small band of Orientals were to invade Washington, seize the President, tear down the Washington Cathedral and set up a statue of Gautama Buddha. But Cortés succeeded. The Aztecs, stunned by his limitless nerve, actually seemed to accept him as their new master.

THE IMPACT OF SPAIN

For six months all was well. Then Pedro de Alvarado, a lieutenant whom Cortés had left in charge of Tenochtitlán while he attended to matters elsewhere, spilled the beans and the maize and the whole rich meal of conquest. In a moment of panic, during a religious celebration of the Aztecs that he imagined was to be climaxed by sacrificing the Spaniards to the outraged pagan god, he ordered an indiscriminate massacre of the celebrants. The people rose in fury and fought the Spaniards to a standstill, despite their terrifying arms and ordnance. The battle raged madly for a week, and finally, on June 30, 1520, those Spaniards who were not slaughtered or drowned made their pitiable escape from the city. This was the famous *noche triste*—sad night—but history should make a courteous nod also to the sad afternoon of the Aztec innocents who were slaughtered in thousands because Alvarado lost his head.

La noche triste should have been the occasion for the utter collapse of Cortés and his dreams of glory, but it served only to stimulate his unquenchable spirit. Although vastly embittered by Alvarado's stupidity, he set about retrieving his fortunes. In a year and a month and 13 days he retook the city, this time without benefit of godhood, for the illusion had been smashed to bits. Also, he was hampered by the fact that the gentle and tractable Moctezuma had been killed and had been succeeded by a nephew, Cuauhtémoc, who was made of far sterner stuff. Cortés, as usual, mixed cruelty with heroism. Because his men were disappointed at the smallness of the loot (much of which had actually been plundered and lost in the lake by the escaping or drowning Spaniards on the "sad night"), he consented to let Cuauhtémoc be tortured, in the hope that he would reveal hidden caches of treasure. The imperial feet were bound, covered with oil and held over a fire, but Cuauhtémoc endured it without the slightest flinching and revealed nothing. Be it said for Cortés that he was presently ashamed of himself and ordered the emperor released, but he could not restore the burned feet.

A little later, Cuauhtémoc was executed on suspicion of hatching a plot—and thus died the last Aztec emperor, and with him the empire. An imposing statue of this magnificent pagan now occupies the most conspicuous *glorieta* on the Paseo de la Reforma of Mexico City. By this tardy tribute the Spanish element of Mexico eases its conscience toward the Aztec race which it dispossessed. The personal story of Cortés ends in anticlimax. He extended his conquest to the whole of Mexico and Central America, but he had increasing trouble with rival aspirants to power and finally he retired to Andalusia with little more than his memories and the empty title of Marqués del Valle de Oaxaca. There, a quarter of a century after his great days, he died in obscurity.

The impact of Spain merged into a steady pressure of imperialistic exploitation. An admirable though futile figure during more than half a century was the idealistic and humanitarian Spanish priest, Bartolomé de las Casas. He fought with unflagging zeal and singleness of purpose to relieve the oppressed. At last, in 1542, he induced Charles, the king-emperor, to issue new and stringent laws for the protection of the Indians, including a law to abolish slavery; but they were so angrily opposed by the privileged classes in Mexico that they were promptly rescinded, whereupon the Spaniards praised God and celebrated with glittering fiestas. Las Casas, then 70, fought on and on, ever noble, ever futile, and died at the age of 90, still fighting for his beloved Indians.

The three centuries subsequent to the arrival of Cortés are not an inspiring portion of Mexico's history, nor even interesting, except from the artistic point of view. The Church was so rich and powerful that it could and did wink at corruption, but at least it was able to advance its own glory by acting as patron of the arts. Literally dozens of great churches were built during the colonial era and, as a whole, they are a delight to the eye; the usual baroque of the period taking on, in later years, an exuberance of ornament hardly matched by rococo architecture anywhere else. This peculiar form of lavish overornamentation, often called "debased baroque," was introduced in the early 1700's by the royal architect, José Churriguera, and has been given his name —churrigueresque. It is a frankly whipped-cream style. The carvings in stone and wood are of remarkable intricacy and effervescence, and interior decorations go in for pink and gold coloring with many fancy scrolls and with innumerable angels and cupids. If you are condemning all this out of hand, I would urge you to withhold judgment until you have seen the two façades of the cathedral *sagrario* in Mexico City and until you have seen the dazzling effects in the churches of Querétaro, Guanajuato, Tepozotlán and Taxco. Secular churrigueresque is astonishingly presented in Puebla in the frosted confection called Casa del Alfeñique, now a provincial museum.

Pre-Churriguera architecture, which still remains in numerous examples, is also fascinating for its sumptuous Spanish baroque. The best of these earlier churches is the opulent Santo Domingo in Oaxaca, but one finds many another in Puebla, Morelia, Guadalajara and San Miguel de Allende. One could, in fact, name almost any town in the heart of Mexico and be sure of finding one or several good churches there. Among the 160 in Cholula is a perfect Mudéjar (Moorish) church, the Capilla Real, with a honeycomb of little domes strikingly like those of the mosque in Córdoba (Spain). There are more than 13,000 churches in the Republic of Mexico and almost all of them date from the colonial period, to the great enhancement of travel pleasure, even though one may actually enter no more than an occasional one.

Of painters who attained local eminence in the colonial period, I will name none (though Manuel Toussaint names 500), and of littérateurs I will name but one, Sor Juana Inés de la Cruz. Born in 1651, and endowed almost from babyhood with precocious abilities, she began as a tiny child to compose verses. She is said to have learned Latin at the age of eight and soon to have spoken it with utmost fluency. She became nationally famous as a prodigy and the viceroy engaged her while still in her early teens as a maid of honor to the vicereine. At the age of seventeen, she became a nun in the convent of San Jerónimo in Mexico City and here she lived the rest of her life. She was a freak of nature, a poetess who could write with tender feeling in an age when feeling had been crushed by Church and state into a pretentious and artificial mold. The delicacy of her *sonetos* and longer poems has excited the wonder of all who have studied her work. Manuel Toussaint called her name "*sin disputa, el más importante de nuestras letras coloniales.*" Others have called her the most sensitive woman poet of the Americas. I know an erudite Mexican lady who long gave regular courses of lectures on Sor Juana Inés de la Cruz, stating as her considered opinion that the Mexican nun possessed poetic gifts so exquisite that they have never been surpassed in delicacy of expression. That is strong talk. I have read in Spanish some of the sonnets, wishing I had a fuller knowledge and appreciation of the language from which no one can adequately translate them. I have studied the nun's pensive face, which seems not at all *troublante*, and have wondered, as one does when gazing at the more vapid portraits of Shakespeare, what is the consistency of genius and whence comes so special a gift. Sor Juana Inés was herself a painter of considerable note and a self-portrait has found its way to the Pennsylvania Museum in Philadelphia, but one knows not how much credence to place in any such revelation. She told with her paintbrush whatever she chose to tell.

From Independence to Freedom

Oppression and Special Privilege have always made a smooth working team to lay the foundations of rebellion, and so it was in Mexico as the 18th century turned into the 19th. The *gachupines* (a nickname given by Mexicans to European-born whites) were at the top of the Special Privilege ladder. They skimmed the cream of colonial wealth for themselves and took all the best jobs. The *creoles*, who were whites born on this side of the Atlantic, came next and did well by themselves in trade. The *mestizos*, of mixed Spanish and Indian blood, were unhappy nondescripts far below the creoles, but by persistent efforts they managed to win

FROM INDEPENDENCE TO FREEDOM

some small degree of economic standing. The *Indians*, of course, were at the base of the ladder, with no hope of getting up even to the first rung. They were abject slaves, accustomed to want as they were accustomed to weather. They knew that not much could be done about either.

But something was done after all—to relieve their want. It required three major upheavals to produce the *very relative* economic freedom that is enjoyed by even the poorest of Mexicans today, and one must be aware of the upheavals to appreciate the cities and towns and even the sublime scenery (so often the enemy of prosperity) encountered in Mexico. I refer to the Mexican War of Independence (1810–21); the War of the Reform (1858–61); THE Revolution (1910–11 and socially to the present day). There were strange interludes, harsh wars and exciting personalities not included in these major events, but it is the three periods listed above that have essentially shaped modern Mexico.

The War of Independence was not planned. It merely happened, in 1810. One is reminded of Paricutín Volcano, which happened in a Michoacán cornfield in 1943. The fuse of independence was lighted almost inadvertently in the town of Querétaro. A group of earnest persons formed a literary and social and art study club that devoted itself less to literature, sociabilities and art than to academic discussions of independence. The corregidor and corregidora of the town were its earliest leaders. Various army officers were attracted, including a bold and restless young man named Ignacio Allende. He in turn drew in a quiet and scholarly cleric about 60 years of age named Miguel Hidalgo y Costilla, the parish priest of the small town of Dolores in the state of Guanajuato. Things moved very fast. The group planned to incite the creoles to expel the gachupines from Mexico, perhaps without a fight. Their plan was discovered and the discovery touched off the fuse. The grim-looking corregidora, dwelling above the Querétaro town jailer, signaled to him by a prearranged system of tapping, that all was known. The jailer instantly warned Allende, who did a Paul Revere by galloping in hot haste to Dolores to warn Hidalgo. The priest, acting purely on impulse, rang the church bell to summon his Indian parishioners. Then, in an impromptu harangue, he told them that the detested gachupines were to be driven from the country. This was the celebrated *Grito* (cry) *de Dolores*.

It was like saying that an investing army was to be expelled by moonbeams, for the rebels had no organization, no money, no weapons. All they had was a burning hatred but it proved to be almost enough to enable them to win immediate victory. Almost but not quite. The fight raged furiously and at first with astonishing success all over the country, but in less than a year the leaders were dead. The grisly heads of Hidalgo, Allende and two of their valiant lieutenants, Aldama and Jiménez, were placed in four swinging iron cages at the four corners of a grain warehouse (Alhóndiga de Granaditas) in Guanajuato town. There they remained for ten years, until the cause for which their owners had been martyred was finally won. Shortly thereafter they were sent to remain in patriotic glory in Mexico City's cathedral, first under the Altar of the Kings and later in the San José Chapel, whence they were taken in more recent years to repose at the base of the Independence Monument.

Another priest named José María Morelos of the town of Valladolid (later to be renamed for him Morelia) joined the rebellion and he picked up the torch that Hidalgo had been forced to drop. With vastly better planning and organization, this able and clear-thinking man—a great man by any yardstick—came even nearer to winning success than had the impetuous Hidalgo, but he, too, was borne down by fate and was executed in 1814. It was left for an able but insincere colonel, Agustín de Iturbide, to win real independence from Spain, only to vitiate the accomplishment by having himself presently proclaimed Emperor Agustín the First. Nevertheless, Mexico was at long last rid of Spanish rule.

It was on September 27, 1821, that Iturbide entered Mexico City in triumph at the head of the curiously named trigarantine army. This referred to the *three guarantees* of the so-called Plan of Iguala, adopted as a plan of independence at the town of Iguala, just south of Taxco. They were as follows: (1) Mexico to be governed by "some European prince"; (2) the Church to retain its traditional privileges; (3) the creoles and gachupines to be equal in every way. Even before his triumph Iturbide let the imperial cat—or kitten—out of the bag by announcing, not too subtly, that the future ruler of Mexico need not necessarily be a prince of a European royal house.

The Church played a curiously jumbled role in the long struggle. There were, in fact, as Hubert Herring has pointed out, "two Churches in 1810—the Church of the bishops and the landholders, and the Church of the village clergy. The Archbishop of Mexico had a salary of 130,000 pesos a year; the village priest often no more than 130 pesos." Each church had its own Virgin, and one of the oddest situations in all religious history developed as the two Virgins engaged in bitter warfare.

The gentle Virgin of Guadalupe was the dearly loved protectress of the oppressed Indians and of the village clergy, including Hidalgo and Morelos. The Virgin of los Remedios was the proud and aristocratic patroness of the Spanish army. She was, in fact, proclaimed by one of the viceroys its commanding general, this "promotion" being accomplished in a glittering ceremony in the cathedral of Mexico City. In many a bloody battle the two Virgins met and each was implored to bring victory to the side of her own espousal. In the end Guadalupe won because she had humanity on her side and humanity will not forever be denied. She still fights for the oppressed and is still devotedly loved, as anyone may see for himself by watching the faces of the faithful as they worship her.

The War of the Reform is important to the traveler if for no other reason than that it explains the word *Reforma*, which one encounters all over Mexico. The capital's leading boulevard and a large hotel are named for the Reform, to the puzzlement of many tourists who never find out the origin of the name. It is not unusual for Americans to worry lest they are being booked for reservations in a temperance hotel when a travel agent in the States tells them he has secured accommodations in the *Reforma*. But if this comment is trivial the Reform itself was anything but trivial. It brought the best leadership and the best spirit that Mexico has had, and the best hope, too, until the coming of the Revolution in the present century.

Specifically, it brought to the scene Benito Juárez, one of the few conspicuous statesmen in history whom one can admire without serious reservation, as one admires Abraham Lincoln and Count Cavour. Juárez was a swarthy Zapotec Indian, a native of Oaxaca, and he came up the hard way. He lived the hard way, too, and even when he became president he never softened his uncompromising devotion to the submerged four-fifths by accepting an easy life for himself at their expense. He had as a foil for his high purpose the short-lived empire of Iturbide, the antics of General Santa Ana, Mexico's most successful opportunist, and the dismal war with the United States, whereby Mexico lost the vast territories of Texas and California. Oppression and Special Privilege were still the drivers of the Mexican chariot and the Church of the bishops and landholders was riding again.

President Juárez was the implacable foe of privilege. He authored the Constitution of 1857, embodying the reforms for which he was to spend the rest of his life fighting. These included free popular education; freedom of speech and of the press; the abolition of class legislation and the sharp curbing of the military and ecclesiastical courts; the separation of Church and state; and the general curtailing of the Church's vast power. The religious orders were suppressed outright and their rich holdings were largely confiscated. Marriage was henceforth to be legal with a mere civil ceremony. Of course, the princes of the Church let out a howl of pain that was heard far beyond the borders of Mexico. It was heard clearly in Europe.

The three-year War of Reform, which put the new laws into effect and established Juárez (in 1861) as constitutional president of the country, was a military triumph; but Mexico was financially ruined and she could not continue interest payments on her foreign debt. Europe stepped in. Britain, Spain and France took joint action and a force was landed at Veracruz to take over the collection of customs. France presently pushed on alone and took over the country, setting up the Austrian prince Maximilian as "emperor" and supporting him with French troops. This was achieved despite a setback at Puebla, the famous Juarista victory of May 5, 1862, for which streets all over the country are still named Cinco de Mayo. Maximilian lasted for five years, but when the United States forced the withdrawal of French troops he was left helpless. Presently he was caught and executed (in Querétaro, June 19, 1867), and Juárez, who had been carrying on the struggle from places of hiding or outright exile, returned to the national leadership. In another five years he in turn died, and without achieving apparent success, though the spirit he injected into Mexico was the sure foundation for success four decades later.

The Maximilian interlude has been embroidered by much romantic writing and by sentimental thought. He was a well-intentioned man utterly unable to head up so ruthless a regime as is basic to foreign domination of any country. He has been glamorized because he looked noble in his tawny beard, because he had back luck, because his wife, Carlota, in attempting to help him broke down and went mad, and above all, because he died with true heroism, refusing to escape unless his comrades in arms could be rescued with him. Carlota, never regaining her sanity, died in a château near Brussels in 1927.

The Díaz dictatorship may serve here chiefly as a backdrop for the Revolution—THE Revolution one may emphasize again—that overthrew and supplanted it. Díaz was an exceedingly able man and though a mestizo by birth and, like Juárez, a native of Oaxaca, he had an abiding predilection for the privileged classes. He was the very personification of successful tyranny. Setting aside the constitutional law against a president succeeding himself, he ruled with iron hand for 35 years. Elections were held at routine intervals but his henchmen counted the votes and had but to announce the victory each time. It mattered not a bit how many actual votes he received. Perhaps he would even have been ashamed to be popular with the masses.

Díaz built railroads and opened up the mineral and petroleum wealth of Mexico, allowing foreign financial interests to exploit the country's wealth on a great scale without fear of serious restraint. Order prevailed and Mexico was, so to speak, well rated by Dun and Bradstreet. The smart or lucky upper crust waxed fat and life was very pleasant. The Virgin of los Remedios was presumably happy but the Virgin of Guadalupe was sad. Her worshipers were in greater misery than ever and their rescue seemed more remote than even in colonial times. The land rumbled with a suppressed but furious discontent. The dictator, however, could not hear the noise and he went his way contentedly. Approximately on his 80th birthday came the centennial (September 16, 1910) of the Grito de Dolores and, without the slightest embarrassment at perpetrating so gross a burlesque, he made it the occasion of an international fiesta in Mexico City. The party cost 20 million pesos and historians record that 20 carloads of champagne were consumed at a single all-night ball in the National Palace, a thing that anyone can believe who has attended a dictator's party anywhere in Latin America. Such goings on were not calculated to allay the growing bitterness of the poor and Mexico grew so ripe and overripe for revolution that before the end of that same year the country literally exploded.

The Colors of Revolution

The slightest spark was enough to touch off the revolution and that spark was Francisco I. Madero, as mild a Milquetoast as could have been found in all Mexico. The unarguable rightness of his cause won him such instant support that he found himself almost against his will a national leader. He was scarcely over five feet in height and unlike another little man—from Corsica—his appearance was wholly insignificant. His voice was so high-pitched that in speeches before large gatherings it could and did squeak distressingly; he had a facial tic that was devastating to dignity. Madero had almost nothing but an honest cause, but that was enough.

He was a liberal, stemming from a very wealthy family of creoles in the northern state of Coahuila, a family numbering in its immediate circle and in collateral branches nearly 200 male members of greater or lesser business vigor. The family, wedded to traditional ideas of privilege, regarded young Francisco as the "tiresome one" of the group, forever thinking and talking of queer humanitarian ideas and even putting them into practice. On his own cotton plantation he devoted every peso of profits to improving the housing, education and medical conditions of his peons. It was easy for his uncles and brothers and cousins to demonstrate the mathematical absurdity of such a performance, leading straight to insolvency. But the very incompetence of Madero—if the term is not too severe—was enough to prove the validity of his case. He launched the revolution with such ineptitude that the dictator and his circle, secure in their great power, must have roared with laughter. Madero asserted that there must be a free election in 1910 in accordance with the constitution. He wrote a mild book, *La Sucesión Presidencial*, organized antireelection clubs and started a newspaper to support them. He even secured an interview with Díaz and explained to the aged tyrant in timid fashion that he was trying to make the Mexican electorate more conscious of citizenship and its privileges.

"An excellent idea," said Díaz, with a straight face. He himself was anxious only to follow the will of the people, as he had always done.

Shortly afterward, as Madero's popularity increased alarmingly, Díaz took the usual precaution of throwing him into jail on a charge of sedition. Then he forgot him and went about the business of having himself reelected for a new six-year term. This was, of course, achieved by the usual foolproof method of having his own henchmen count the votes. It was presently announced that Madero had mustered only 196. "Too bad," said Díaz in effect; and again the old man bowed to the will of the electorate and remained president, surrounded by a little group of almost equally old men who were called *Científicos*. They never interfered with the engine of dictatorship but merely oiled it and helped to keep it humming.

But popular hatred was volcanic. It blazed of itself, and kept blazing. Madero, released on bail, fled to Texas but soon re-entered Mexico and carried on the fight in a curiously mild way. His continual willingness to compromise with his foe made his leadership of doubtful value but the momentum of the Revolution was terrific. Within nine months Díaz was sailing for refuge in Europe on the German ship *Ypiranga*, spending the remaining four years of his life in Paris while the mighty wind of change swept Mexico. Within six months of Díaz' departure, Madero became the first Mexican president ever chosen by the people in completely free elections. The Revolution was launched, but it was not a thing with a beginning, middle and ending. It was, and is today, a state of mind, a continuing force, an unsuppressible demand of a downtrodden populace that knows its power. It is doubtful if any Mexican strong man, however powerful his foreign connections, can ever again ignore it. In fact, it is virtually certain that he cannot. All politicos, from the most patriotic to the most grasping, recognize this force as axiomatic and make haste to proclaim themselves a part of it. No one can deviate too far for too long from giving it actual support as against lip service. For us Miss Brenner has stated the case with clarity. "It is a living story underneath what happens in Mexico now, and tomorrow. *La Revolución*—is the past, and it is a set of beliefs. The phrase runs like a live current through everything public and personal, too; politics and art and business and thought and industry." And of its peculiar importance in Western Hemisphere diplomacy she said: "Because of Mexico's immediate revolutionary past, the country is something like a school for liberal policymakers in many other Latin-American republics; its moral leadership is far beyond its size."

The drama of the living revolution is fascinating, especially as it relates to the Church, to the controversy over the subsoil wealth of the country (particularly oil) and to the drastic land distributions. And the part that Mexican artists have played, and still play, in the unfolding plot is equally enthralling. The artists will be discussed in Chapter 9, but the other topics need brief comment here.

The Church, after long and harsh persecution brought on by its own recurring tendency to amass wealth and to side with Special Privilege, seems now to be coming back. The great majority of Mexicans, of whatever social standing, can be counted as loyal Catholics, but the oppressed four-fifths have hated the hierarchy, and the government has cracked down on the Church in order to keep its own good and regular standing as a revolutionary government. Former President Avila Camacho's dramatic confession of faith ("I am a believer") did much, in its time, to restore ecclesiastical prestige.

The oil controversy had "much to be said on both sides." But basically the foreign interests invited a showdown with the Revolution and took a beating from it. Foreigners, especially the absentee owners of vast properties, simply did not know the strength of the thing with which they grappled.

The distribution of land was a very drastic new-dealish performance (50,000,000 acres expropriated by Cárdenas alone; 882,000 families provided with land to work in *ejido* or communal villages) but it did go a long way to allay the terrible bitterness of the peons.

The chief figures of the Revolution, both the fighting part and the continuing political part, are the most colorful features of the pageant. Among the fighters the two most conspicuous figures of the early days, aside from those already mentioned, were Pancho Villa, the "generous bandit," and Emiliano Zapata, the fierce peasant leader whose theatrical appearance belied his ability. He fought for *land*, which was the central core of the Revolution. You may see him in many a mural, notably in those of the Palacio de Cortés in Cuernavaca, which Diego Rivera painted and for which Dwight Morrow paid.

The many political figures of the struggle have been vastly confusing to the average American and need not be recalled in detail. One can judge something of their individual revolutionary odor by noting whether or not they have had streets and squares and towns named for them. One does not see such honors bestowed upon Huerta or Calles, but one does find the names Carranza and Obregón. Of all the Revolution's presidents, Lázaro Cárdenas left by far the biggest name. He really put the Revolution into effect. And when foreign capital yelled like a banshee, he let it yell and went steadily about his business. His successor, General Manuel Avila Camacho, edged back to the middle of the road and made cooperation with the United States a major feature of his administration. His foreign minister, Ezequiel Padilla, an outstanding figure of internationalism, placed Mexico, despite her real and long-standing grievances, among our Best Neighbors. Miguel Alemán, coming to power in 1946, continued good relations, from a position perhaps a little right of center, and his successors have continued on a friendly course. One of modern Mexico's ablest and most respected presidents was Adolfo López Mateos, who was overwhelmingly elected in July, 1958, and served a six-year term, during which he managed the coup of securing the 1968 Olympic Games for Mexico. The president as of this writing is Licenciado Gustavo Díaz Ordaz, who was inaugurated on December 1, 1964.

Among political parties it is necessary to know the names and significance of only four: the PRI, for *Partido Revolucionario Institucional* (Institutional Revolutionary Party), which is the government, no matter who is president; the PAN, for *Partido de Acción Nacional*—rightist; the PP, for *Partido Popular*—leftist; and the PARM, for *Partida Auténtico de la Revolución Mexicana*—middle of the road).

The social laboratory that is Mexico is a place of undying interest to all visitors who do not shut their eyes to it. Forbearance is often necessary but it has been equally necessary equally often on the other side. The will to understand is one of the rarest of human powers. It is an evidence of strength. Even the most transient of tourists will contribute his worthy bit to inter-American solidarity by striving to develop whatever of this power is in him.

YOURSELF IN THE PICTURE

CHAPTER 6

MEXICO CITY, CENTER OF EVERYTHING

Candid Notes on Hotels

MEXICO, D.F., is enormous. Far larger than Madrid, Barcelona and, with the single exception of Buenos Aires, all other cities that speak Spanish, it is a metropolis of over five million inhabitants. Its hotels, too, are metropolitan, and because of their overpowering importance in everyone's Mexico travels, the selection of hotel headquarters calls for more than casual thought. These candid notes will try to be the opposite of casual.

The growth of the capital's hotels in recent years seems to me little short of phenomenal. In part it reflects the steady growth of Mexican tourism and in part it results from the coming of the jet age, enabling sun-hungry travelers from such centers as New York and Chicago to reach Mexico City in three or four hours. As in Hawaii, Jamaica and other sun-drenched areas of holiday, hotel promotion in Mexico, not only in the capital but in various lesser towns and resorts, jumped the gun and erected new hotels of every type and price bracket to meet the oncoming rush.

This alertness was typified by *Nacional Hotelera*, a corporation headed by a self-made master-*hôtelier* named Cesar Balsa, who was born in Barcelona, the son of a barber, and climbed the rungs of success—bellboy, waiter, maître d, food supervisor (this in Madrid's huge Palace Hotel)—and so to Mexico City where, at 29, in 1952, he opened his first restaurant, the Focolare, which is still one of the capital's best. This venture he followed by opening the Jacaranda nightclub, a fabulous success from the outset, and so, in one leap, or pole vault, to the presidency of Nacional Hotelera, now affiliated with the ever-expanding Sheraton Corporation. Balsa Hotels, as the Mexico corporation is now called, comprises eight hotels, five in Mexico City and three in Acapulco. Those in the capital include the big, downtown *del Prado*, the *Hotel El Presidente*, on the corner of Calle Hamburgo and Calle Amberes, a frankly expensive "ultra" hostelry of 150 rooms, with drive-in garage and handsome pool; *Hotel Premier*, near Paseo de la Reforma, a 100-room place of very good quality but much lower rates; *Hotel Prado Alffer*, a luxurious 160-room downtown place on Calle Revillagigedo—don't let the street's six syllables throw you—that has every elegance and comfort, along with the city's largest and best drive-in garage accommodating 360 cars, yet with rates considerably lower than El Presidente; and finally, *Hotel María Isabel*, a big 600-room caravansary on Paseo de la Reforma's most important glorieta centered by the Independence Monument.

Western International Hotels, now linked with the Hotel Corporation of America, is strong in Mexico City, with the Alameda, the de Cortes, the Francis, the Majestic, and the Ritz. Hilton Hotels International is also represented, as is Intercontinental Hotels Corporation, the Pan American subsidiary. But before you get confused, let me make a recommendable rundown in alphabetical order.

The 17-story *Alameda*, on Avenida Juárez, is a place of real elegance and certain special charms. Among its charms I should list three of its restaurants: 1. *El Camichin* is a top-floor, top-flight restaurant open from breakfasttime to the small hours of the following morning. At night it offers high-grade floor shows at 10 and 12, but its magnificent closeup view over the Alameda across Avenida Juárez, is a show in itself. There is a swimming pool on this same (17th) floor. 2. *La Diligencia*, on the mezzanine floor, is a delightful cocktail lounge of old-fashioned atmosphere, to promote which the hotel has installed an old-style *diligence* (horse-drawn Continental stagecoach) on an open space of the street floor, where Plaza Corpus Christi adjoins the hotel. 3. *La Brasserie* is a French-style restaurant-café-snack bar on the street floor, bordering the plaza.

The *Alffer* is air-conditioned throughout; the lounge, bar and main dining room, up one flight, are the *dernier cri;* there's a large, lively coffee shop on the ground floor; each bedroom is enlivened, if you want it that way, by music-without-plugs; and on the roof garden there's a sun deck, a lovely reflection pool (not for swimming) and a 9-hole putting green, plus a luxurious banquet room, used largely for convention-type dinners, called *La Rondinella*. The major bar-restaurant in the hotel is the *Indra*, which is abundant with Bohemian atmosphere.

Hotel Ambassador, at Calle Humboldt 38, half a block from Avenida Juárez, on the opposite side from the Colón, is another air-conditioned place of 160 rooms, each with tub and shower and purified drinking water. The *Restaurant-Bar El Americano*, with garden setting, offers a fine international cuisine, under the direction of a Belgian chef. A feature of which the Ambassador is justly proud is its motor lobby, this latter being almost unique in Mexico City, though Monterrey's leading hotels have had motor lobbies for some time. The motorist drives his car right into the hotel's private 50-car garage and leaves it there as he goes to the registration desk. No nonguest may use this garage. I stayed in the Ambassador for part of a recent visit and found its service cheerful and prompt.

On Avenida Juárez, across Calle Revillagigedo from the del Prado, rises the tall *Hotel Bamer*, as well located as its larger neighbor. It has all the elegance and comfort of its near neighbor, the Alffer, and its lobby is adorned with an interesting globe. It has a fine restaurant, a popular bar and cocktail lounge and, of special interest in such a handsome location, a rooftop terrace.

Hotel Beverly, far out on Insurgentes at Calle Nueva York, in a pleasant residential area, is a place of moderate rates. If you're a motorist, you can park in the hotel's grounds, and whatever your transportation status you may swim in the heated pool in the garden. This is a family-type hotel and one of the best in its price range.

Hotel Continental Hilton, with 400 rooms and baths, is a place of outstanding luxury located on the important glorieta where the capital's two chief boulevards, Paseo de la Reforma and Avenida Insurgentes, intersect. The latter thoroughfare, to interpolate this fact here, is a city street 23 miles long, named for the *Insurgentes* of Father Hidalgo's time, referred to in Chapter 5. It is commonly called the longest city street in the world, but possibly Los Angeles' Western Avenue would challenge the claim. The Continental Hilton, to return to our subject, was rather severely damaged, especially in one part, by the earthquake of July, 1957, but restoration has long since been completed and this 16-story establishment has every comfort and elegant modernity that the Hilton name suggests. Its lofty *Belvedere Room* is one of the capital's most popular dine-and-dance places, with entertainment.

Hotel Cristóbal Colón (Christopher Columbus) is a downtown hotel of moderate rates, located at the corner of Calles Colón and Balderas, only a short block from Avenida Juárez. *Hotel de Cortés*, at 85 Avenida Hidalgo, opposite the northwest corner of the Alameda, is a colonial palace of modest tariffs. Its romantic appeal is great, despite the fact that it is on the edge of an extensive *former* red-light district, which sometimes—and quite needlessly—scares away tourists. One may walk across the street and find oneself in the pleasant paths of the capital's pleasantest park, whose other side is the shopping and social center of the city.

El Diplomático is a rather new 105-room place at Insurgentes Sur 1105.

Dean of all the downtown hotels, though a young dean (built in 1948), is the *Hotel del Prado*, on Avenida Juárez, opposite the Alameda. This place thinks of itself as an idea, quite as much as a hotel. There was a period during the war when American vacationists, denied access to Europe, poured across the Rio Grande in a ceaseless wave. Some hotels looked upon them as a soft touch and treated them as such. They picked up quick money but Mexico lost goodwill. The del Prado set itself to recapture the goodwill and sternly eliminate any tendencies toward "clipping." It has implemented its idea with sound, ungrasping service and reasonable tariffs.

How shall I cope with this hotel, this vast *city* of transient travel under one roof? Perhaps the only practical way is to hurl some facts at you. The del Prado and its furnishing cost nearly $10,000,000, and that was "way back in '48." It is constantly being refurbished. It contains 600 rooms with baths, no two alike, and 65 suites. Its huge lobby displays the famous Diego Rivera mural, *Sunday in the Alameda*. Massive Aztec jardinieres of stone accentuate one's sense of being in a park. There is a grand ballroom called *El Salón de los Candiles* (Chandeliers), a superb grillroom, a cocktail room called *Cantina Nicté-Há*, a *Bar Montenegro*, a breakfast room and a large dining room called the *Salón Versalles*. There is a bank, a travel office, a post office and, not least in interest, an extensive arcade of shops, eating places and services of every sort. There is a sun deck, with a real lawn looking over the Alameda, and a rooftop belvedere looking far off toward Mexico's volcanoes. Adjoining the main building is a large garage.

To return for a moment to the aforementioned Rivera mural, this tremendous painting of Mexican history and autobiography (52 feet long by 15 feet high and weighing 15 tons), was moved bodily from the dining room a few years ago in a nerve-racking period of 36 hours, during which the slightest mistake could have cracked and very seriously damaged it. This truly great engineering feat has enabled the public, not merely the hotel's diningroom guests, to marvel at this fascinating work, which can be pleasurably studied for hours. Public lectures on its intricate symbolism are given several times a week both in Spanish and English. I have been told that Rivera received $6,000 for the painting, and that the engineers who moved it received $16,000. Art appraisers estimate its present worth at about $750,000. The picture will be further discussed in Chapter 9, "The Spectrum of

Mexican Art."

The Emporio, at Paseo de la Reforma 124, is a lofty hotel of low prices, boasting a rooftop solarium.

Hotel del Paseo is a modern 12-story, 120-room hotel on Reforma, at Calle Milán, two or three blocks west of the Hilton. Its chief charm is the Panorama Restaurant and Bar on the 12th floor (orchestra from nine to two, nightly), with a magnificent closeup, or closedown, view of this fine area of the capital. There's a solarium up aloft also; and on the 4th floor there's a small pool, gaily lighted at night, with an adjacent coffee shop and snack bar. For what it offers, the prices of this good hotel seem moderate.

The *El Presidente* is among the most luxurious and well-planned hotels in Mexico City. For instance, as each guest arrives he is received like an awaited *guest* and seated at a table to register, not stood at a counter. Upon going to his room, and I mean any room, not the garden penthouse suites on the 11th and 12th floors, he enters through a private hallway and finds a bedroom and bath, together with an extra washroom, whose ensemble is as fine as anything of its kind in Mexico. A valet unpacks his bags without charge and in the spacious lighted closet the man's trousers will be folded over a long bar that can be raised and lowered at will, so that they won't have to be crowded on the same hangers as the coats. There's a good-sized private balcony with most rooms, and here the guest may have his meals if he wishes; since each floor has its own serving arrangements, he may have his breakfast, for example, almost in *moments* after placing his order, not after dragging minutes or a quarter hour.

And speaking of food and beverages, El Presidente has two restaurants and three bars, which is not unusual, but the type of restaurants *is* unusual. The main bar-restaurant, called *Zafiro* (Sapphire), is on the same level as the swimming pool. There is also a very small, very expensive, and more-than-luxurious dining room called *La Torre Blanca* (The White Tower). It can be entered either from the hotel or from the street (Calle Hamburgo) and is a sort of temple, with a circle of white columns surrounding it. Despite its diminutive size, permitting only ten tables, it has its own kitchen and à la carte menu. You may expect to spend a lot of pesos if you eat here, for it aims at the highest brackets and the most exclusive atmosphere in the city. The El Presidente also has a patio of fine shops and a 60-car garage.

Suites Emperador boasts "luxury that's different," and it seems to me a novel and interesting venture. It is located in the southern part of the city, about three miles from the center on a *rond-point* called Plaza Etiopia (Ethiopia), which Emperor Haile Selassie came to Mexico to dedicate. There are 70 "Emperor Suites," ten each on seven floors, and every suite is a completely equipped housekeeping unit, including a kitchenette with electric refrigerator and a full complement of utensils, silverware and necessary dishes. Each floor is named for a country (United States, Canada, Spain, France, Italy, Mexico and all South America) and each suite for a city. When you enter the elevator, you don't mention your floor by number you say, for instance, "United States, please," and if you forget just where your room is, you perhaps request "Washington." Or it may be New York, Boston, Philadelphia, Chicago, Miami, New Orleans, Dallas, Los Angeles or San Francisco. The whole hotel is ultramodern and really luxurious, from its street-floor lobby and its dining room (with open patio) to its rooftop solarium. The cost of the suites is very moderate, one reason being that the hotel's location is rather far from the center.

The Francis is a modern but not very pretentious place at Paseo de la Reforma 64. It is so near downtown that it could properly be considered a midtown place, as indeed could the Reforma, the Continental Hilton and all others that are not much beyond the Reforma-Insurgentes intersection. Maybe there's a saturation point somewhere in Mexico City's hotel development, but it isn't in sight yet.

Hotel Genève, pronounced in a variety of ways from French to Spanish (*Héneva*), is substantially farther out from town than the Reforma. It has its fans and addicts—lots of them—and it must be said that if it is less luxurious than many of those I have named, it is, by the same token, more family-type and relaxed in its atmosphere. It is a place where guests often stay for weeks or months and it has less of the transient feeling than do other quality places. The Genève's food is good.

The *Hotel Guadalupe* is fairly new, a modest but good hotel with low tariffs, located at Calle Revillagigedo 36. The *Hotel Guardiola*, at Madero 5 opposite the original Sanborn's, is even more modest and less expensive, while at the *Hotel Gillow* a double room costs, at this writing, less than five dollars. The *Hotel Lincoln* is another of those modest but recommendable hotels on Calle Revillagigedo.

Hotel Londres is a small but deluxe hostelry at Calle Londres 101, near Niza. It consists entirely of suites, each provided with a thoroughly up-to-date and complete kitchenette, including electric refrigerator, and each with a portable TV set. The top-price suites consist of a living room, a double bedroom, an extra studio room, kitchenette, bath and balcony. Somewhat in the same vein as the Suites Emperador, it names each suite for a foreign city, such as Amsterdam, Bruselas (Brussels), Burdeos (Bordeaux) and Argel (Algiers), and decorates each with a large-sized and interesting picture of its city. This place seems to me a good bargain, especially for those who can remain long enough to stock up and "housekeep" for a while.

A 19th-century mansion of a very wealthy family has been transformed into a hotel called, simply, *La Residencia*, at Calle Berlin 30, near the Vasco de Quiroga. It offers eight large double rooms "for a limited number of privileged guests," as its folder proclaims. It has genuine period furnishings, with many antiques and paintings, but it is by no means a museum. Its lounges, bar, patio and garden-restaurant are all of spacious dimensions.

Hotel Majestic fronts on that prodigious clearing in the city's older congested center called the Zócalo, this being the plaza on which the cathedral and the National Palace each has its enormous frontage, not to mention the National Pawnshop (*Monte de Piedad*). This hotel, a bit quieter than the Ritz and much more Mexican, is well placed for those who propose to take their educational sightseeing seriously. Most of the city's historic palaces, churches and museums are within easy walking distance, for this very square was the center of Tenochtitlán, the Aztec capital, and the center also of the Spanish-colonial city. Despite the capital's westward trend the Zócalo remains, for the masses of Mexican residents, the heart of the capital. From this throbbing metropolitan heart, trolley cars, busses and taxis by the thousand radiate to every part of the city. It reminds one, in this respect, of the Puerta del Sol in Madrid.

The dining room of the Majestic calls for a special note, for it is one of the capital's appealing places. High on the roof, it overlooks the teeming Zócalo and faces the National Palace and the cathedral. Had one been dining on this spot early in 1520, one might have watched Cortés with his own hands tear down the idols of the Aztec teocalli; and later one might have watched him lay the cornerstone of the present cathedral on the exact site of the teocalli. As has been mentioned earlier, the Majestic is under Western International Hotels management.

Hotel María Cristina, on Calle Lerma, near the Paseo, is a delightful place of residential type, with lots of space, lots of sunshine, a garden and good food.

The *María Isabel*, at Paseo de la Reforma 325, is tied with the del Prado as Mexico's largest hotel, but in grandeur it is an easy first, one of its features being the spectacular top floor (17th), which is devoted exclusively to nine supersuites. It is one of the most sumptuous and expensively modern caravansaries in Latin America (cost $12.5 million), all this being made possible by the wealth of Antenor Patiño, Bolivian tin king, who owns the property. The hotel is named for Patiño's daughter, whose romantic run-away marriage made headline news, but who tragically died in childbirth. I think it is fair to say that no hotel anywhere has more spacious, lavish and modern facilities for large conventions.

All of its many convention halls and rooms, great and small, have the latest equipment, including of course, the gear for simultaneous translations. There are Orozco murals in the lobby, the *Jorongo Bar* is a popular meeting place and the hotel's *Veranda Bar* offers nightly entertainment.

I cannot give the multitudinous details of this world hostelry, but four items may be tallied here: 1. Baggage is handled on the street floor and never clutters the registration area, which is a floor by itself one level higher. 2. Bedroom doors are all *recessed* from the corridors so that the hotel will not "look like a hospital." 3. The swimming pool is on the roof. 4. Fine supersuites, as mentioned above, are all on the 17th floor and are all of individual decor and inspiration. The Windsor suite is clearly British, the Malmaison French, the Salzburg Austrian, this with wonderful wood paneling, the Beverly American, and so on. The largest and grandest suite is the Marco Polo.

Of quite a different character and far lower prices than any of these big hotels is the downtown *Hotel Metropol*, at Calle Luis Moya 39. A relatively small but modern, well-run *thrift hotel*, its prices, rigorously held down, are guaranteed to give pleasure to the hard-pressed budget. Double occupancy in three types of rooms ranges from $7 (these with double beds) to $8 to $9.50 (the last-named with twin beds). Mexico City hotels of quality are not cheap today, nor are they expensive—even the deluxe El Presidente can sleep one person for $12, and two for $18—but when two can lodge for as low as six to nine dollars, many other dollars are released for general holiday fun.

The *Montejo* is a pleasant colonial-style place at Paseo de la Reforma 240.

Hotel Monte Cassino, at Calle Génova 56, off Insurgentes, is another of uptown's smart and accordingly expensive places, but I should say that its sophistication is tempered by a noticeably homelike ambience.

The *Hotel Ontario*, on Calle Uruguay, is modest and very reasonable.

CANDID NOTES ON HOTELS

The *Posada San Angelo* is a real country inn in the big city, dear to thrift-budget travelers and students. Here you may, if you like, enjoy an old-clothes atmosphere without any pretentiousness at all and dispose yourself for a siesta on a broad lawn in back of the Posada. What's more, it is able to maintain its present standard as one of the best places to eat in the entire Mexico City area.

Among downtown hotels of very good and comfortable type, but not aiming for luxury levels of elegance and prices, the *Prince*, with 125 rooms and baths, on Calle Luis Moya, a few steps from Avenida Juárez, has caught and held popular attention. Each room has filtered drinking water and also a radio, in case you wish to hear Spanish music or to improve your knowledge of spoken Spanish. As in the case of the luxurious Bamer, the Prince has only a small lobby, but in every other way, certainly including its low tariff, it is appealing. Its cuisine is outstanding for a place of such modest charges.

Hotel Plaza Vista Hermosa, at the curious address of Sullivan 1, set in a bit from the Paseo, is a most curious hotel. Wags call it "Mexico's only hotel with live television" because, although a lofty structure, it is built in a crescent shape so that every guest can look from his windows across the crescent at or into the windows of his fellow guests. The waiters in the bar-restaurant of the Plaza V.H. are dressed like bullfighters, and the chairs here are all covered with bullhide. A special feature of this hotel is its popular *Afro Nightclub*. Many of the capital's hotel nightclubs, including those in the Continental Hilton, the Reforma, the del Prado and the Alffer, have had to fold, at least temporarily, because of the high cost of foreign talent good enough, or famous enough, to pack in the customers, but the Afro continues—so far—to flourish.

The *Premier*, near Paseo de la Reforma at the corner of Calles Milán and Atenas, is a 100-room place of good quality, with fairly low rates.

Hotel Regis, on Avenida Juárez just west of the Alameda, is a large and well-run hotel, rather more of commercial type, with 400 rooms and baths, considerably less expensive than its more luxurious neighbors. Its ever-enlarging ensemble, which is said to aim at an ultimate goal of a thousand rooms, includes a swimming pool and Turkish bath, and its *Restaurant Paolo* and *Salón de Capri Nightclub* are deservedly popular. There is a huge garage behind the hotel.

Hotel Ritz, at Avenida Madero 30, continuing Avenida Juárez, is only a short distance from the American Express office, the main downtown Sanborn's, the main post office and the Palace of Fine Arts (Bellas Artes). If the del Prado and other leaders seethe with life, the Ritz roars with it. A famous fresco by Covarrubias, in the bar, depicts American and Mexican boating parties (at Xochimilco) mutually taking snapshots of each other. The same thing is done with human eyes in the Ritz bar. The Mexican element is more in evidence here than in the larger hotels but Americans often dominate the scene in lobby, bar and restaurant. The bedrooms of the Ritz are *cheerful*, and the hotel's tariffs are very moderate.

On Paseo de la Reforma at the corner of Calle Paris, is the *Hotel Reforma Intercontinental*, long a prime goal of American tourists. When Pan Am's IHC (International Hotels Corporation) took this hotel over some years ago, it gave it a wonderful reincarnation. It is said that a million *dollars*, not pesos, were spent on its rejuvenation and certainly it looks it. Its round, spacious garden-lobby, covered, is as cheerful as any lobby in the city, its rooms and baths are of high standards in modern comfort, its garden café and coffee shop, its various perimeter shops, vending almost everything you can think of, are appealing in their various ways and the dour, tip-hungry service of earlier days has long since been replaced by a smiling courtesy and quickness. Consider one item, laundry. Three times, on a recent visit, I sent laundry by the valet in the morning and got it back the same afternoon, without any unpleasant shock in the fair and moderate charges.

If you stay at the Reforma try, by all means, to secure a room on the Paseo side, high in the building's 12 stories, for you will then have a glorious view of the two famous volcanoes that are fixed "props" in the world's-stage picture of Mexico. *Popocatépetl* (correctly accented on the penult) means Smoking Mountain—and, as I have said, it smokes too much at times. Its altitude is 17,794 feet, being exceeded in all Mexico only by Orizaba. Its sister peak is *Ixtaccíhuatl*, meaning White Woman. The coif of the White Woman is only 16,200 feet above sea level but both mountains are perpetually covered with deep snow. The letter *x* in Mexico is pronounced in a variety of ways but inquiry has convinced me that in this particular name it sounds rather like our own *x*. The correct pronunciation of the mountain's name, as near as it can be put into phonetics, is *Iks-tak-see-watl*, without strong accent anywhere.

The *Hotel Romfel* is another one of those modern, modestly priced hotels on Calle Revillagigedo, at Number 35.

Hotel San Francisco is still another new downtown hotel of low tariff but good quality, located at Calle Luis Moya—opposite the Prince Hotel.

The *St. Moritz* is a pleasantly modern place of no great size on Calle Paris near the Hotel Reforma.

Shirley Courts, rather far uptown on Calle Sullivan, is an attractive place for motorists. Being a remodeled hacienda, it combines features of hotel and tourist camp. American-managed, it offers food that has home appeal to Americans.

Hotel Tecali, located at Calzada General Mariano Escobedo 736, well out beyond the end of Reforma, is a superior hotel of luxury suites suitable for a prolonged stay, if cost is a minor consideration. It also accepts transients. The name is that of a popular Mexican stone somewhat like onyx but of a light-brown color. A delightful feature is its cocktail lounge on the top floor overlooking Chapultepec Park.

Hotel Vasco de Quiroga, at Calle Londres 15, offers one of the best price bargains in Mexico City. Its luxury penthouse suites, each with double bedroom, large living room and open terrace, overlook George Washington Circle (with a statue of George). Its dining room offers excellent meals. One of the best, to my taste, is *carne asada a la Tampiqueña* (roast beef, Tampico style). The main bar and the hotel's restaurant, both made gay with various interesting wall decorations, are in the basement. The Vasco de Quiroga harbors the Mexican Folklore Center, a must for entertainment. The hotel's five luxury penthouse suites were decorated by the widely known interior decorator, Pamela Drake. Her studio, Decoraciones Pamela Drake, is at Calle Genova 2, Suite 106.

Hotel Versalles, relatively small and inexpensive is on Calle General Prim at the corner of Calle Versalles. Its rooms are air-conditioned and modern, and there is a radio in every room.

Hotels of minor importance have sprung up in all the better quarters of the city and many of them are fairly good thrift places. A handy booklet called *Lodgings in Mexico* is available from the Mexican Government Tourism Department, at 35 Paseo de la Reforma, or from the Mexican tourist offices in various American and Canadian cities. It gives all prices in pesos.

(Persons primarily interested in auto courts and motels, furnished apartments or furnished rooms will find a lot of them listed in John Wilhelm's *Guide to Mexico City* and also, rather more currently, in each issue of *Esta Semana* (*This Week*) and in the classified ads in the *Daily News*.)

Big-City Practicalities

The head porter, the travel clerk, the social director and all such functionaries in any of the luxury hotels thrive on tourist timidity, which is a self-imposed incompetence. Not one tourist in ten would run his business or her home on such a basis of personal helplessness, but it seems to be natural to travel that way. I have heard American women consult the mail clerk or the cashier on the challenging question of how to get downtown from the Paseo. I have heard American men consult the social director as

VIEW FROM SAN ANGEL INN, MEXICO CITY. THE SNOW-COVERED MOUNTAINS ARE IXTACCIHUATL (*left*), POPOCATEPETL (*right*).

THE CELEBRATED AZTEC CALENDAR STONE, GREATEST SCIENTIFIC "DOCUMENT" LEFT BY ABORIGINAL AMERICA. THE INSCRIPTION STATES THAT IT WAS FOUND IN 1790 AT THE BASE OF THE WEST TOWER OF THE CATHEDRAL IN MEXICO CITY.

CARVING OF THE TOLTEC TEMPLE OF QUETZALCOATL AT TEOTIHUACÁN NEAR MEXICO CITY. NOTE THE "PLUMED SERPENT," SYMBOL OF THE GOD.

Courtesy of Western International Hotels

DO IT YOURSELF BULL FIGHTING IS THE LATEST ADVENTURE AWAITING TRAVELERS TO MEXICO, AT THE RESTAURANT CORTIJO LA MORENA IN THE VILLAGE OF TEXCOCO, 25 MILES FROM MEXICO CITY.

Courtesy of National Railways of Mexico

PORTAL OF THE CATHEDRAL OF ZACATECAS, TYPICAL OF THE DECORATIVE EXUBERANCE SEEN IN MANY OF MEXICO'S 1300 CHURCHES.

A COOL SANGRÍA OR A TEQUILA COCKTAIL IS CALLED FOR ON THE PORCH OF THE HOTEL VIRREY DE MENDOZA IN MORELIA.

Courtesy of Mexican National Tourist Council

THE CATHEDRAL AND TREE-SHADED PLAZA THAT IT FACES TYPIFY THE OLD-WORLD CHARM STILL TO BE FOUND IN GUADALAJARA.

PARICUTÍN, MEXICO'S PHENOMENAL VOLCANO, WHICH BROKE THROUGH A MICHOACÁN CORNFIELD ON FEBR. 20, 1943 AND DIED IN 1951, IS THE ONLY NEW VOLCANO BORN IN THE WORLD IN THE LAST 150 YEARS.

ARCHITECTURAL CONTRASTS IN MEXICO CITY AMAZE ALL VISITORS. HERE, A CORNER OF THE PALACE OF FINE ARTS, COMMENCED LONG AGO BY DICTATOR DÍAZ, IS DWARFED BY THE 42-STORY LATIN-AMERICAN TOWER OFFICE BUILDING, WHOSE SUMMIT OFFERS A SUPERB VIEW.

Courtesy of Western Airlines

PHOTOGRAPHERS' DELIGHT IN THE "BUTTERFLY NET" FISHERMEN SEEN ON LAKE PÁTZCUARO.

PATIO RESTAURANTS ADD COLOR AND CHARM TO MANY MEXICAN HOTELS. THIS IS THE DE CORTES IN MEXICO CITY, ONE OF THE WESTERN INTERNATIONAL HOTELS CHAIN.

Courtesy of National Railways of Mexico

PATIO OF THE ANCIENT CONVENT OF SANTO DOMINGO.

Courtesy of National Railways of Mexico

MONTE ALBAN—TREASURE CHAMBER OF ARCHEOLOGISTS.

Courtesy of Western International Hotels

FROM THE ROOF GARDEN PATIO OF THE HOTEL MAJESTIC ONE HAS A FASCINATING VIEW OF THE ZÓCALO, MEXICO CITY'S MAIN SQUARE.

Courtesy of Mexican National Tourist Council

OUTSTANDING ARCHEOLOGICAL FINDS ARE IMAGINATIVELY DISPLAYED IN MEXICO CITY'S NEW MUSEUM OF ANTHROPOLOGY. HERE, IN THE OUTDOOR SECTION, A CLEVERLY DESIGNED WATERFALL CASCADES AROUND A HANDSOMELY CARVED MONOLITH THAT MIGHT ONCE HAVE SUPPORTED A TEMPLE ROOF.

Courtesy of Western International Hotels

THERE ARE BEACHES GALORE IN ACAPULCO. THIS ONE IS AT PUERTO MARQUÉS BAY.

to the exchange rate. This last, however, is not a fair example of helplessness, for the director was a lovely lady, with a fascinating name, Marguerite Smoke. What man with a dash of romance in him would fail to consult so charming an oracle so charmingly named? The exact topic of consultation matters little.

I have no fear of wrecking the livelihood of hotel staffs by presenting some big-city practicalities of Mexico, D.F. For those who like to know their way around, asking questions only when they must, the findings hereinafter may be of value; and it may be mentioned parenthetically that a good little book, presenting colloquial *Mexican* Spanish in the simplest form, is Charles E. Kany's *Spoken Spanish,* published by D. C. Heath & Company of Boston. With those travelers who prefer, while touring, to indulge the pleasant luxury of paying others to do everything for them, including the arduous job of thinking, this present roundup is honestly sympathetic.

Transportation within the central area of Mexico City is simplicity simplified. Taxis (*libres*) are *very* cheap, but may be hard to come by on weekends and at rush hours (early afternoon and midevening). Three pesos (24 cents) will give you a long haul. You pay the meter reading *PLUS 50 CENTAVOS,* by law; and you *should not tip*. The rate was once as low as one peso flat, but inflation changed this. An interzonal system was in force for a while, but finally satisfactory meters were installed and they are now almost universal. Chaffering on fares is "not unknown," to use a phrase dear to the late Baedeker, but with the cost so negligible in dollars, or rather in cents, few visitors indulge in this ancient sport of travel. As long as the peso remains at or near eight cents, the budget-minded will scarcely wish to wrangle, but for Mexicans it is a different matter. To them a peso is still a peso.

When taxis are taken by the hour, or to points outside the city limits, a definite bargain should be struck in advance, but it may be said that all such excursions are amazingly easy on your purse. Even the long trip to the airport usually costs only 10 or 12 pesos, though air travelers are presumed to be lavish spenders. Mexico is a land of oil and a land of very modest rewards for personal services rendered.

As this book goes to press, city fathers were in the process of ordering the withdrawal of some 6000 pre-1953 taxis from circulation and replacing them by spanking new cabs, in preparation for the 1968 Olympics. Bound to suffer in this modern sweep are many of the taxis traditionally nicknamed according to their color and design. The yellow ones are, or were, called *canarios* (canaries), the red ones *cardinales* (cardinals) and the mixed green-and-yellow ones *cotorras* (parrots). There are also some plain green ones with a row of sharp white "teeth" painted along both sides. These, quite naturally, are called *cocodrilos* (crocodiles), but whether bird or beast these cabs get you to your destination for next to nothing.

If you can't succeed in flagging a taxi, and sometimes your prolonged efforts may prove terribly frustrating, remember one saving feature of prime importance. On the two oft-named chief boulevards, Reforma and Insurgentes, and there only, hundreds of so-called *peso taxis* cruise up and down all day long, taking in a cabful of customers *at one peso each*, regardless of distance. If you stand at the curb on either of these great thoroughfares and look hopeful, the chances are good that very soon a taxi driver in the endlessly flowing *rivers* of cars speeding in both directions will signal to you by holding up *one finger*, signifying the one-peso fare expected. You signal back and he'll stop, for about two seconds, so you can pile in with three or four other customers. He'll let you off wherever you like, whereupon you give him one peso and he's gone with the river.

Local busses and trolley cars start chiefly from the Zócalo and fan out to all parts of the city in scores of lines. I should say that few Americans except permanent residents and necessitous students on thrift vacations ever use them, generally speaking, since taxis are so cheap. There are, however, three notable exceptions, namely three bus lines of special convenience between the uptown hotel sectors and the downtown centers. Even if you have an aversion to busses or are timid about using them in foreign cities you should learn these lines, for they may save you up to half an hour of worried waiting when you can't interest even a peso cab in your plight. Starting from downtown, here are the three specials, all of them so-called first-class busses: (1) From the Alameda, on Avenida Juárez, more or less opposite Hotel Bamer, a bus marked *Reforma-Chapultepec* traversing the whole length of the Paseo to the park at the base of Chapultepec Castle; (2) from the same starting point to and along *Insurgentes* (and so marked) to *San Angel* (or clear out to University City— *Ciudad Universitaria*—for an extra tiny payment; (3) from the Zócalo by Calle de Mayo to *Paseo de la Reforma* and *Chapultepec* (so marked). The best busses are identifiable by their cream-to-buff color and ask all of four cents for a ride. You can ride second-class busses for only 2½ cents. If a lot of first-class ones roll by you, all marked *completo* and refusing to pick you up, for they will take only as many passengers as they have seats, you may be driven to board one of these lower-bracket vehicles, which are an adventure from start to finish. They pitch and roll like tramp steamers in a high sea and are invariably so crowded that you must stand up and cling by an eyelash or two. Even the steps are usually packed, despite stern printed warnings that it is forbidden to stand there. Oh, well, let's be humble folksy now and then, if only to see how low-income Mexicans to whom a fare difference of 10 centavos is important must travel.

Letters, *telegrams* and *telephones* are topics of prime and obvious interest, and a bit of knowledge on this topic can save much wear and tear. Postage rates, despite several increases, are still very low in terms of dollar money. All the hotels sell stamps. Present rates—but these should be verified at the time of your visit—are as follows:

Centavos

Surface mail to U.S.A.
    Post cards   .20

Letters—for each 20 grams	.40
Air mail to U.S.A.	
Post cards	.80
Letters—for each 10 grams	.80

Telegrams to the United States are surprisingly inexpensive considering distances. Telegrams *within* Mexico are extremely cheap even when sent at special superspeed rates—which are *not* excitingly prompt at that. All telegraphic communications are handled by the National Telegraphs. International cable offices are located at Independencia 44.

Telephoning within Mexico *used* to be an adventure in exasperation. Nowadays, however, dial phoning for local calls is standard. Some hotels make no charge at all for local calls, while others charge from 50 centavos to two pesos. A call on a public telephone box (if your Spanish is good, and your dialing perfect) is but 20 centavos—1½ cents.

English-language publications are chief aids to self-sufficiency. Among Mexico City's newspapers, each of the large dailies, the *Excelsior*, *Novedades*, *El Universal*, and the new *El Heraldo*, has a page in English and each has good international news. The local columns and advertisements are likewise of practical interest. The smaller afternoon edition of *Excelsior* is called *Ultimas Noticias*, and the newsboys rush through the streets with it, at frequent intervals, like so much flak to stop you in flight. Newspaper Spanish is easy to pick up if you remember some of your school Latin or French. It is easy anyway. Try it. There are also two all-English dailies: the *Daily News* and the *Mexico City Times*.

A *Daily Bulletin* in English is issued in Mexico City and distributed gratis in hotels, shops and cafés. It has condensed news, stock-market reports, travel reports, entertainment notes and—most inviting of all—many advertisements of things to buy and of places where one may eat, drink and have fun.

Esta Semana (*This Week*) is a free weekly encountered everywhere and is a truly valuable publication for the transient. Its subtitle, *What to Do, What to See, Where and How*, proclaims only a part of its usefulness, for it also contains current timetables of airways, railways and bus lines, highway maps and city maps, fiesta and sports calendars, a shopping guide and information of a dozen other sorts about the capital and the chief cities. More than incidentally, its two-language articles and counsels provide a serviceable "trot" to build up your Spanish the painless way. By all means pick up and use this ubiquitous pocket weekly, or its rival, *The Gazer*. Both are badly printed on cheap paper, but they can help you, and who cares that they are frank organs of the tourist trade, with all the stops pulled out.

Health precautions are not of such overpowering interest in Mexico as in many other Latin lands, but it is decidedly wise to avoid the drinking water in small towns and to avoid lettuce, uncooked vegetables and fruit that cannot be peeled. D.D. (diarrheic disturbance) from drinking water or from rashness in eating is experienced by many tourists.

Be reassured, however, that in Mexico City at least all vegetables and fruits being received at the public markets are now cleaned, disinfected, and even preserved. You can see something of this process in the big *Jamaica Market* (pronounced Ha-my-ca). So far as water is concerned, most major hotels these days have purified water and post signs in the rooms stating so. All possible worry, however, may be routed by the simple and uncostly expedient of ordering Garci-Crespo table water, now known as *Peñafiel*, or one of the popular brands of beer, such as *Superior*, considered by some the best light beer, the popular *Carta Blanca* or the darker and stronger *Moctezuma XX*. If you pronounce the latter "Dose Eckees," meaning "two x's," the waiter will at least know what you mean. So far as food is concerned, one should always keep in mind that digestion is slower at high altitudes. It is, therefore, inadvisable to eat heavily in the evening or to exercise too strenuously after any hearty meal.

Smokes are important to many travelers and it is pleasant to know that by present regulations very liberal amounts of tobacco may be taken into Mexico duty-free. The printed regulations seem to put the amount at "2.2 pounds in any form," which means about 50 cigars or two cartons of cigarettes, *but* I have personally called up the customs authorities, with aid from a Mexican friend, and have been informed straight from headquarters, though any such advices are, of course, "subject to change," that "Americans may bring in four or five cartons of cigarettes, provided they are not to be sold." If you have failed to stock up before entering Mexico you may buy American weeds of nearly all popular brands within the country, though at prices up to twice as high as at home, but you may not find your most favored brand. Many Mexicans smoke locally made *Raleighs*, or a moderately mild brand called *Belmont*, and even pampered American palates generally admit that these are—not bad.

Imported brands of liquor are expensive in Mexico, and you may only bring in one bottle free of duty.

Incidentals—those little things of a big city that are the traditional budget-wreckers of travel—are really *little* in Mexico City, or they may be so if one watches them with half an eye. It has been already stated that most local trolley and bus fares are three and four cents, a shoeshine (called *grasa*—for "grease"), eight cents. Similarly, a glass of orange juice (*jugo de naranja*) in many a little streetside stand is but ten cents, and a toasted roll (*mollete*) and coffee in passable little Mexican cafés, about the same. A clear-view gallery seat for almost any concert or ballet in the Palace of Fine Arts, one of the most sumptuous theaters in the world, may be as low as 75 cents. And *flowers* are almost given away in this land of flowers. Even in Xochimilco, which is one of the capital's chief tourist traps, beautiful corsages of gardenias are about 50 cents and gardenias with orchids 75 cents. In the smart flower shops of the luxury hotels the prices soar like helicopters, but in the public markets where Mexicans "shop around" and where more and more Americans are finding vistas of fascination, the loveliest flowers cost so nearly nothing that one can hardly believe what one sees and hears. Inflation has not yet seemed to hit flowers (except in the hotels), and it is to be hoped that nature and the industrious gardeners will supply so many that this most typical of Mexico's attractions will remain the miracle it is today.

Seven Foci for Americans

The index and the shopping guide at the beginning of *This Week* may serve almost as a directory of current addresses you will need in Mexico City, though it is somewhat harmed by the omission of certain important shops and restaurants that apparently have not chosen to advertise. Seven special centers of interest for American travelers are of such outstanding importance that they may here constitute a practical directory of travel enhancement in Mexico City.

The new *United States Embassy* building is across the street from the Hotel María Isabel. The two, in fact, have linked underground foundations, so as to support each other in Mexico City's spongy soil. You should be sure to register here, for there are frequent social events open to visiting Americans.

The *United States Consulate* is at Paseo de la Reforma 305, and may be used as a mail address.

The *Pemex Travel Club* and the *Tourism Department's Information Bureau* are at the same address, Number 89 Avenida Juárez. Pemex will also hold your mail.

The *Benjamin Franklin Library*, in the *former* U.S. Embassy building at Insurgentes and Niza, is one of the most cheerful and attractive retreats in the city. Dedicated in 1942 under the auspices of the Coordinator's Office, the State Department and the Library of Congress, it is an institution in which every American may take pride. Its nonfiction books, especially those on Mexico, are of the most direct value to visitors, and its current fiction shelves are appealing. The reading rooms, open to all, regardless of membership, are light and pleasant, as against the vast gloomy halls that so often serve this purpose in Mexican libraries. A membership card—with the privilege of taking out books—may be easily secured. A resident sponsor is required.

Lectures and movies are offered gratis at regular intervals. The building, attractive in itself, is only five minutes' walk from the Paseo.

The *American Club*, now located on the upper floors of the Edificio Bearn, at 10 Plaza Degollado, one block south of Avenida Juárez, is a friendly rendezvous for Americans, and its restaurant and bar may be enjoyed by transients, even without a member's presentation card. Because of the plaza's hidden (though handy) location many short-time visitors never find it, but it is decidedly worth finding, as a shrine of good talk.

The *American Book Store*, at Avenida Madero 25, has already been mentioned. This focus, only two blocks from the original Sanborn's, is an eddy of home interest, with the newspaper and magazine sections usually claiming first place.

Shoppers in Paradise

Shoppers' ecstasy may develop into shoppers' fever in Mexico, D.F., although the U.S. Government has put a constraining leash on all out-of-the-country shopping by limiting your duty-free allowance to $100, *retail value*. The downtown main artery of the capital is a siren to pent-up shopping lusts, as is the newer uptown sector whose main stem is Avenida Insurgentes. It is wise to remember, however, that not only in the capital but also in provincial cities—especially Cuernavaca, Taxco, Puebla and Guadalajara—there are many shop windows that kindle the keen shopper's eye and set his or her arithmetic in motion. There are markets, too, and in some of them, including those of the small towns and villages on all the highways, wonderful bargains are to be had, for these places are not much aware of *turismo* and also they are still living in the age of barter. In the capital, the custom of bargaining is a thing of the past. Today, almost every store price-tags its goods. Nevertheless, be sure to ask the proprietor if you can have a discount.

Leather work, bibelots in glass, pottery and lacquer, furniture, modern or antique, native costumes, curios and, of course, *silver*, are the main items of shopper-interest in Mexico. If you are to include Taxco in your itinerary—and Mexico without Taxco is hardly to be imagined—silver purchases should wait at least until you have seen the Taxco shops and the artisans at work in such celebrated establishments as Talleres Borda and Los Castillo. Sarapes, which are blankets worn casually and charmingly by Indians, invariably arouse interest and they are offered by roadside vendors at almost every halt of every tourist trip, but many a shop in the capital also offers dozens of them at reasonable prices. Remember, when you buy a sarape, or a *rebozo* (shawl), that the more savagely colored items are designed that way to *give us what we suppose to be Mexican*. Actually, Mexican colorings are not crudely bright or violent but artistically restrained. The Toltec and Aztec relics often offered to pyramid-trippers for a few cents the relic, *may* actually prove to be genuine, or so I am assured by Mexicans in a position to know, but such trinkets happen to leave me chilly and I never could induce myself to buy any even at *seven to the peso*, a price once suggested to me by a vendor at the Acolman Monastery. I believe the Mexican government theoretically bans such sales of relics anyway, and also the exporting of them, so we may as well escape the topic and return to livelier scenes. The Mexican capital's main downtown street is still among the more exciting shopping streets of Latin America, even though deluxe specialty shops have tended more and more to move uptown. If it had one easily pronounced name instead of two (Juárez and Madero), it would probably be more widely known than Rio de Janeiro's *Ouvidor* or Buenos Aires' *Calle Florida*.

Three sure shots if you are seeking truly beautiful Mexican folk art are: the *National Museum of Popular Arts and Crafts*, at 44 Avenida Juárez, a retail store as well as a museum noted for its handblown glass, colorful pottery and leather goods; the *Bazar Cholula*, next door to the Hotel Genève; and the *Bazar Sábado* in the picturesque colonial neighborhood of San Angel, open on Saturdays only, as its name implies. Whether or not you intend to buy, do visit at least one of these shops. They are crowded with the sights and sounds that have lured you to Mexico.

The *Glass Factory*, at Calle Carretones 5, about ten blocks from the Zócalo, is also interesting to visit, to watch the artisans shape delicate figurines, animals, bowls and vases.

Piñatas, those effigies filled with gifts and candies and hung to be admired, then smashed with gay abandon at festival time and other special occasions, are to be seen at all the big markets. At Christmastime, the San Juan Market, with 10,000 piñatas hanging from its vaulted ceilings, is a joy to behold.

Perhaps the most important of Mexican art crafts is the weaving of textiles. Toluca, I feel, is the best place to shop for them. Copperware is one of the newest of the Mexican arts and crafts, Pátzcuaro being the country's copper headquarters. Uruapan is the center for lacquerware and wood carvings; Oaxaca, Guanajuato, Morelia, and the towns of San Antonio and Tlaquepaque outside Guadalajara for pottery. Of course, whatever you are seeking can be found right in Mexico City. Prices may be higher than in the towns of origin, but for many a traveler the convenience of choosing from a preculled assortment offsets the added cost.

The Calendar of Festivals in Mexico

The Mexican Government Tourism Department publishes a monthly calendar of fairs and fiestas. If you put them all together, you find that there are more than a thousand festivals throughout Mexico during the year. On a gala fiesta night, with the public buildings illuminated, the fountains plashing, and the streets pulsating with people, Mexico City is unforgettable. Traveling about, you are almost certain to bump into one or more in the provinces, as I did, for instance, in the village of Zimatlán, near Oaxaca (see Chapter 5). Dates of the major festivals vary, of course, from year to year. Among them are:

January 1–7. The *Chalma Festival* occurs in the Chalma Sanctuary outside Cuernavaca. To this shrine thousands of Indians make their pilgrim way each night of the year's first week, carrying torches, singing chants and doing odd dances.

February 1–8. The *Tzintzuntzan Fair*, held in the village of that name near Pátzcuaro (see Chapter 14), features the highly comic Dance of the Little Old Men, often reproduced in folklore shows in Mexico City, and it includes also a regatta on Lake Pátzcuaro staged by local Tarascan Indians. Tzintzuntzan was the capital of the Tarascan kingdom in pre-Columbian times.

Holy Week, in March or April. Taxco goes all out in celebration of this great pre-Easter period. The event in this town of tradition is of an exceedingly moving nature, culminating at midnight on the start of Easter Sunday in the famous "silver-built" cathedral of that lovely town.

During the Easter season an effigy called the Judas (pronounced "Hoodus") is much in demand. Usually taking the form of a skeleton, it is wired with firecrackers. The custom is to hang it from a tree in the garden on Holy Saturday and invite everyone present to write on it the name of a person he dislikes most. Then the fuse is lit and the Judas is blown to bits in a highly satisfactory way.

Mid-April. A *Flower Fair* (*Feria de la Flor*) is held at this high tide of spring in *Fortín de las Flores* (see Chapter 18), and surely no more favorable place for such a fair could be imagined, for flowers are so abundant there that they are included in the very name of that little resort town of Veracruz State.

May 10. On this date, a *Charro Festival*, with tournaments of brilliant horsemanship is held in Cuautla, a town of Morelos State near Cuernavaca. The riders all wear bright *charro* (horseman) costumes in honor of their historic revolutionary leader Emiliano Zapata.

Corpus Christi celebrations (the ninth Thursday after Easter) occur all over Mexico, including the capital city, where it centers in the Zócalo and the cathedral. Processions of children wend their way from all parts of the city to the cathedral.

July 25. On this date countless villages, especially in the central and southern states, have local festivals and the city of *Oaxaca* devotes a whole week to the fiesta, centering on the Cerro (Hill) del Fortín. Regional dances of considerable variety are the chief features.

August 1–6. An *August Fair* at *Saltillo*, near Monterrey (see Chapter 2), honors an image of Christ in the cathedral. At dawn on the first and last days of the fair, dancers togged out in vivid finery, including lots of little mirrors, go into action. The fair is as vivid as the dancers, its brightest feature being the "sea of sarapes" offered by local vendors.

First Week in September. In *Tepoztlan*, near Cuernavaca, a celebration is held in broad-minded honor of both La Virgen de los Remedios and the Aztec deity called El Tepozteco. A dance drama on a native theme concludes the fiesta.

October 12. *Columbus Day* is called the *Día de la Raza* (Day of the Race) all over Latin America, but the Indian element in Mexico quite naturally has scant interest in celebrating the day of the precursor of Spanish imperial oppression. The Spanish element celebrates discreetly.

November 1 and 2. *All Saints' Day* and *All Souls' Day* are important everywhere in Latin America. In Mexico, the most interesting celebration takes place on *Janitzio Island* in Lake Pátzcuaro (Chapter 14), where a candlelight procession makes its way to the village cemetery with offerings of food to the dead!

Children, during this festival, delight in spun-sugar skulls specially prepared with the name of each child-owner spelled out on the forehead. This is not considered macabre in Mexico; it is merely part of the fun they associate with death, for devout Mexicans consider death to be an entry into a far better life.

Nine Nights Preceding Christmas. On each of these nights, from December 16 through 24, Mexicans celebrate the *Journey to Bethlehem* in a traditional fashion that is known in other Latin lands but reaches its loftiest peaks here. The custom is described at some length in Chapter 10 under the heading "Evenings in All Keys."

CHAPTER 7

TOURISTS ON A WILLING LEASH

The Sightseers' Downtown

DOWNTOWN, for the sightseer, the shopper, the pleasure seeker, is a conveniently concentrated area. It means the dozen blocks from the Zócalo (with the cathedral and the National Palace) due west to the Caballito, which is the Little Horse. These terminal points are conspicuous in the pattern of Mexico. The Zócalo is officially named Plaza de la Constitución but no one ever calls it that. The origin of the popular name is variously explained. Some Mexican authorities believe that it is from the Arabian *zoc*, meaning market place, but the commonest explanation is that it means what it says in Spanish: *socle*. The socle of a proposed monument to Mexican independence is said to have been in ugly evidence here for years in the middle of the 19th century (it sounds strikingly plausible), so that ultimately the square took its nickname from the empty base. The monument was erected 60 years later on the Paseo de la Reforma, but the word grew into the language of the people long before that. It has found its way to all parts of the republic and the central square of most Mexican cities and towns, including even Taxco and Acapulco, is popularly called the Zócalo.

In this main and major Zócalo, Mexico took root. Here the Aztecs found the eagle feasting on a snake. Here they built their greatest teocalli and around it their capital city. From this area the celebrated Calendar Stone and many other great relics have been exhumed. Here Cortés founded the first Christian church and here was erected the first private residence of the conquerors' city. Before this clearing was a Socle, it was a glittering Bazaar called *Parian*. It was the first bullring in the Americas and was the gruesome torture chamber of heretics whose souls were being rescued by the Holy Office of the Inquisition. It is the place where Mexican independence was officially proclaimed and where Iturbide was crowned emperor. From Iturbide to the present time almost everything of national importance has happened, or has been celebrated, in this center of centers. Here, each year, in a dramatic ceremony, patriotism is rekindled by the reenactment of Hidalgo's Grito de Dolores. It can almost be said that if you know the history of the Zócalo you know the history of Mexico.

Even the Caballito—at the other end of downtown—first pawed the air in the Zócalo. This equestrian statue of Charles IV was cast in 1802, from a design by Manuel Tolsa, director of sculpture in the city's Academy of San Carlos. At the time of the rebellion it was threatened with destruction because it represented Spain, the hotly hated oppressor. For protection it was concealed in a great blue globe of wood and later dragged off to an obscure part of the university cloister where it was all but forgotten. In 1852 it was remembered and set up in its present location at the downtown end of the Paseo de la Reforma. Mexicans still have no use for Charles IV or any other Bourbon monarch but they love their Little Horse, and they are rightly proud of it as a Mexican masterpiece. The horse and its incidental rider are widely acknowledged to be one of the finest equestrian statues ever made. Amid the strutting regiments of such "cavalry" in all parts of the world it stands out with three others: the statue of Marcus Aurelius on the Capitoline Hill in Rome, that of Gattamelata by Donatello in Padua, and that of Colleoni by Donatello's pupil, Verrocchio, in Venice. It is amazing that a Spaniard of Mexico, an art director who has scarcely made the world's encyclopedias, should have achieved something in sculpture that ranks him with the greats.

An outstanding sight midway between "the two ends of downtown" is the view from the top of the 42-story *Torre Latino Americana* at the corner of Avenida Juárez and Calle San Juan de Letrán, opposite the Fine Arts Palace. The building is open every day, including Sundays, from 10 A.M. to 10 P.M. and one ascends by a main elevator and then a smaller tower elevator for a stupendous view—the adjective is weak—of the whole far-flung city in its dry lake amid the mountains, including noble Popocatépetl and Ixtaccíhuatl. Actually, the belvedere consists of three stories and on the open one at the very top are four strong telescopes aimed at the four points of the compass. One small peso gives you the use of them all. There is an excellent restaurant, the Muralto, also a little shop for films and post cards, and while you write the cards or take pictures, or enjoy a meal, you are regaled by soft music from records.

The Americas' Largest Cathedral

The Americas' largest cathedral is immensely impressive from the outside and equally disappointing inside. The façade, fronting on the open acres of the Zócalo, is a gray curtain of formidable masonry and stone traceries of prodigious width, totaling some 400 feet if one includes not only the cathedral's own façade but the adjoining ones of the Chapel of St. Anthony and the *Sagrario*, which means literally tabernacle or ciborium. The Sagrario is in the lavish churrigueresque style that one encounters everywhere in Mexico and that was mentioned in Chapter 5. At its worst it is a mere cloying jumble. At its best, if one is in the mood for rich fare, it is theatrically pleasant and this example is one of Mexico's best. A motif often noticed in Mexican churrigueresque (more clearly in Taxco than elsewhere) is the symbol of the shell. This was considered a Christian symbol and it also represented Kukulcan (Quetzalcoatl), so the old and new religions were neatly spliced by a simultaneous tribute to both.

The interior of the cathedral (374 feet in depth) has been completely renovated in its foundations and the whole prodigious acreage has been laid with a marble floor, which has done wonders, despite the cumbering of the nave, to make this famous edifice more cheerful to the eye. For several years the dust and turmoil were awful, since 25,000 tons of material had to be removed. As a note of archeology it should be mentioned here that the stones and idols of the original Aztec teocalli were used in the first primitive structure and every excavation for repairs or new construction unearths important treasures.

The nave, as in so many Spanish cathedrals, is virtually filled with the huge *coro* (choir), a priests' affair exclusively, with massive gates always closed to shut out intruders, whether of the worshiping or sightseeing variety. I have often asked in Spain and in Spanish America the reason for this "exclusiveness" and have never received a satisfying answer. It is maintained, they say, "for liturgical reasons." Historically, I suppose, the coro *is* exclusive, a sanctuary defended against the merely curious (such as tourists like us), a retreat within which the priests enter into solitude face to face with God alone. Its ancient opaque curtains became in time a rood screen, and then, in most churches of most lands, but not those influenced by Spanish tradition, a plain communion rail.

Many chapels are of interest. The one at the head of the left aisle features a "black Christ" of legendary fame. It grew black by "absorbing the poison" of a desperately ill suppliant.

The cathedral's treasures, together with those of the Sagrario, form a dazzling total in spite of all the depredations of the Rebellion, the Reform and the Revolution. Having complained of the cluttered interior I should hasten to emphasize the value of a careful survey under the guidance of an educated cicerone—but not with one of the dubious touts who cluster about the edifice and even inside it to importune the visitor at every turn. This cathedral is like a quicksand—but a pleasant one. Once planted in a study of it, however superficial one's intentions, one sinks deeper and deeper. This is, after all, one of the most significant religious structures in the New World. Its importance in Mexico matches its size.

Two Palaces and Two Museums

Two palaces and two museums capture the interest of even those who ordinarily sightsee only under protest. They are the National Palace, facing the Zócalo, the Palace of Fine Arts (*Bellas Artes*), adjoining the Alameda, and the *National Museum of Anthropology* and the *Museum of Modern Art*, both in the Chapultepec Park area.

The *National Palace* is one of the conspicuous examples of construction in tezontle material (see Chapter 8). This building is as architecturally plain as can be but its long low lines are good colonial and it makes a striking and restful contrast to the overdressed churrigueresque of the nearby Sagrario. One of Moctezuma's palaces originally stood here, but Cortés, running true to form, replaced it with one of his own. This was bought from the Conqueror's descendants 40 years later and transformed into the government palace. It has been rebuilt in whole or in part but much of the lower portion of the façade is a remnant of the Cortés original.

Dozens of salons are shown to the visitor, and, of course, the celebrated stairway murals by the late Rivera, who died in 1957, but the palace reaches its peak of interest only once a year, at midnight of September 15. At that dramatic moment the president of the republic steps to the balcony, above which hangs the Liberty Bell, and personally utters (*el Grito*) the Cry. This, as has been said, commemorates Hidalgo's original Grito de Dolores, shouted at the same day and hour in the year 1810, the cry that echoed for a decade until independence actually came to Mexico. The Zócalo is packed with tense thousands each year for this ceremony and the crowd takes up the president's cry, adding every noise it can think of, including the racket of innumerable firecrackers. Hundreds of church bells support the general bedlam and madness reigns. This is the Mexican counterpart of the coming of the New Year to Times Square and one must admit that Mexico's show is considerably more pointed than New York's.

The *Palace of Fine Arts* is a prodigious showpiece, but much more important to the culture of the nation it serves than are most such vanities. It contains a sumptuous opera house, a concert hall, a museum of popular arts, a gallery of paintings and several salons for current exhibitions of art works. Since the whole affair is operated by the state, some attractions, particularly lectures, are offered gratis, and everything, however grand and spectacular, is popularly priced. By ascending to the gallery (in an elevator) one may secure a seat for almost any performance of opera or ballet for a dollar though one's knees may be unhappy in the close-packed rows of the cheaper seats. The view, though distant, will be unimpeded. Rivera and Orozco frescoes are great drawing cards of the art galleries in this building and one of Rivera's works is his own reproduction of the very one that Mr. Rockefeller refused for Rockefeller Center—but paid for in full.

President Díaz began the construction of this steel and marble mountain in 1904. The Revolution finally completed it, but the cost in pesos was astronomical. When half done the whole thing sank crazily at one end, for all of Mexico City's foundation ground is hardly more than a mud pudding. Millions and more millions were spent to jack it up with concrete cradles and then the work went on. The whole interior was fashioned in the most luxurious style imaginable, with marbles of many colors and with magnificent hardwoods and costly metals. It gives one the impression that some fabulous American billionaire must have conceived it and that when he went bankrupt the United States treasury took over. The architect, it is said, gave his solemn and legal guarantee that the building would never sink again but it definitely is sinking. It has, in fact, already sunk some 12 feet below the surface of its surrounding streets, and it is quite possible that within a few generations only the great dome may be above the present street level. Still, this place of art, music and drama is a wonderful enhancement of your visit and mine. The building is heated in winter—something to mention in Mexico—and splendidly air-conditioned at all seasons. You will drop in here frequently if only to get cool or warm and to see the works of art. In the portion that is an opera house you may see the best shows in the world and hear the best concerts. The Tiffany curtain of spun glass, concealing the stage, is world famous. One hears of it in advance, almost to the point of tedium, yet it does not disappoint. It depicts a scene featuring snow-crowned Popocatépetl and Ixtaccíhuatl, and clever lighting effects bring sunset, moonlight and finally a pink dawn to the two peaks.

The *National Museum of Anthropology* may well be the world's handsomest museum. Of striking architecture and built at a cost of more than $20 million, it was completed in the autumn of 1964. The archeological treasures of Mexico are displayed part indoors, part out. You come upon the museum on the right-hand side of Paseo Reforma, about half a mile beyond the entrance (which is to the left) of Chapultepec Park. You can't miss it. It is marked by a 165-ton statue of the rain god, Tlaloc. The day he was moved into place, Mexico City was waterlogged by the heaviest downpour of the season! It happens that in 1963, in company with a group of archeologists and writers, I visited this same rain god in the quarry when he was "born," some 12 miles from the capital. It rained in sheets that day, too. Bringing Tlaloc to Mexico City was an engineering undertaking of some magnitude, for special roads had to be built and bridges strengthened.

The museum is laid out in the shape of a huge "U," divided into ten halls, each of which opens on the courtyard. At the far end you come upon the most important display—a 22-ton disk of basaltic porphyry, the priceless Calendar Stone of the Aztecs, which is not only a work of art but a marvel of astronomical science. It is 12 feet in diameter and 3 feet thick. Prescott gave credence to Indian stories that the stone, originally weighing 50 tons, was transported by the Aztecs from a quarry several hundred miles distant; but even if the story grew in the telling, its own message of a science patiently developed by generations of "untutored" folk is one that would be utterly unbelievable if it were oral instead of lithic. The glory that was Greece and the grandeur that was Rome never produced an astronomical table the equal in accuracy of that displayed by this stone.

Other prized possessions of the museum are the large statues of Quetzalcoatl and Huitzilopochtli. The former deity, Lord of the Morning Star, was definitely benign, but the latter, being chief of the Aztec gods, was perhaps the bloodiest and cruelest fanatic ever imagined by human worshipers. In reading the authentic accounts of the human sacrifices demanded by Huitzilopochti one wonders that man could ever have conceived so horrible a system or that priests could have put it into practice. The Sacrificial Stone in the museum makes it all too real, for we see the very cavity into which the victims' hearts were tossed, still warm and almost beating, after they had been torn out of living men, women and even small children in the name of religion; and one sees the "scupper" from which the blood flowed off in a steady trickle. The victims were often captives of war, but if these were not adequate to satisfy the god's lusty appetite, children were bought from poverty-stricken parents who were intimidated by the priests. The children were decked out in fine robes and flowers as they were led weeping through holiday crowds of spectators. Tears were a good augury and the priests were elated when there was a copious flow from childish eyes. In the case of war captives it was considered desirable to torture the victims at length and with all the ingenuity that could be devised. And after the heart had been finally torn out, the body was given to the Aztec who had captured him. It was then cooked, elaborately seasoned and served as the chef d'oeuvre of a dinner to which the proud host invited his neighbors, both men and women. Hospitality was competitive and at great dinners several roasted warriors were needed to grace a proper table. I think I have said enough, but it is only a tithe of the "whole truth" suggested by the Sacrificial Stone. One's admiration grows for the bravery of the Spaniards, not without practice in their own kinds of cruelties, who faced these horrors in a seemingly hopeless war of conquest.

Not only is the *Museo de Antropologia* handsome to look at, but it has an unparalleled collection of Mexican art from pre-Columbian times to the most modern muralists. Already, it has been compared favorably with the Louvre and other great museums of the world. It also houses some of the finest archeological objects uncovered at Teotihuacán. All in all, some 3500 artifacts have been assembled there. Incidentally, the museum has a fine outdoor and indoor restaurant and an automat. Prices are most reasonable for such fare as hamburgers (out of a vending machine!) and *tacos*.

The *Museo de Arte Moderno* is also new to Mexico City. An ultramodern circular building of dark glass, you will find it off to the right of the Boy Heroes columns just inside the gates of Chapultepec Park. Eventually, this museum will house a permanent collection of paintings by Mexico's four most famous contemporary artists—Diego Rivera, José Clemente Orozco, David Siqueiros and Rufino Tamayo. This is a most worthwhile project, since the works of these masters are widely scattered around the country. By bringing some of their works together in one place, a far larger public will be able to enjoy them. There is also a rotating exhibit of modern Mexican art.

Mexico these days boasts some of the finest museums in the world. Another notable one, specializing in Spanish colonial treasures, is the *Museo de Tepoztlán*, near Cuernavaca.

The Castle of Grasshopper Hill

The castle of Chapultepec, which name means Grasshopper Hill, is the symbol of the sightseers' Mexico, though it is also much more than that. The Aztecs had a temple on the eminence and they used the copious springs at its base for their main water supply. Cortés planned a fortress here and a later viceroy built one, but it was demolished by the United States forces that attacked it in 1847 under General Gideon Pillow. Some two decades later Chapultepec was invaded by the busy architects and builders of Maximilian and Carlota, who made it their residence, and that is why this castle's salons and boudoirs look like those of a French château. It was Carlota who ordered the building of the two-mile Paseo (later to be called Reforma) to connect the downtown area with the imperial residence. It leads straight as a die from the Little Horse to the Hill. The castle used to be the White House of Mexico, but Cárdenas, a superdemocrat, refused to live in it and had it converted into a museum in 1934. All succeeding presidents have followed his precedent and today the castle is the *Museum of National History*. Numerous souvenirs of Maximilian and Carlota are displayed, along with jewels, historical documents, magnificent woodwork and Gobelin tapestries. There's a push-button system that delivers recorded lectures on the place. Leaving the castle by the same road that ascends to it, you come upon a modern circular building which is also part of the Museum of National History. It is circular and contains dioramas depicting Mexican history from independence to revolution—with dramatic recorded commentary.

The forest of Chapultepec, surrounding the castle and lending glamour to this whole section of the capital, is one of the great and greatly romantic park-forests of the world, quite comparable in stateliness to the Bois de Boulogne and to Brussels' Bois de Cambre, with its tall beech sentinels. Mexico City's forest is distinguished by tall cedars which are arboreal cousins of the coast redwoods of California. Their name, in Aztec, is *ahuehuetl* (colloquially *ahuehuete*), meaning "Old-Man-by-the-River," and beneath their giant branches, among the statues and fountains of the park, students pace back and forth, studying vocally for their examinations. If the student has no examination, or doesn't care about it anyway, he has a girl instead of a book, and the two of them presently have a bench to themselves.

Americans who find a little monument in the woods close to the base of the rock, at its steepest front, may be sobered by the inscription which they read, for it proves an old truth, that there are at least two ways of looking at anything. The inscription on this monument reads: *13 Sept. 1847. A la Memoria de los Alumnos del Colegio Militar que Murieran como Héroes* [died like heroes] *en la* INVASIÓN NORTEAMERICANA. The names of the six victims of our "invasion" follow. These men were defenders of the hill and when their position became untenable they wrapped themselves in Mexican flags and leaped from the parapet to death on the rocks below. This act had nothing of the Japanese spirit of hara-kiri but much of the Latin spirit of drama. At any rate it showed how Mexicans regarded their "good neighbor" a century ago.

If you would see Chapultepec, castle, park and museums, as Mexicans see them, go there by bus (marked *Lomas de Chapultepec*, on Paseo de la Reforma), preferably on Sunday, aboard a packed second-class one—the first-class ones will be *completo* anyway—and roll to the base of the conspicuous hill. From there take a local bus marked *Servicio al Castillo*, which takes you up and finally back for a penny or two. All Mexico is there having fun and you are reminded of the Parc du Luxembourg or the Jardin des Tuileries in Paris. It is the very opposite of exclusive, but you have not come to be "that way," and you can take pleasure in being part of a huge, noisy picnic. The *charros* and *charras*, in glittering costumes, will be prancing showily on their beautiful horses and the brass band will be braying. The ponds will be full of boats and the boats will be full of very humble people, so happy that they are ready to cackle with laughter at anything or nothing. Let the fashionables roll by you in their snobbish Cadillacs and "Bweeks" and if they glance your way with lofty condescension, so much the better. You have achieved something paradoxical, since you, a foreigner, are far more authentically Mexican at the moment than are they.

The Luxury Section

The residential *avenidas*, as the motors see them, form a very attractive pattern of luxury in the southwestern part of the city. The central shaft of the pattern is unquestionably the Paseo. Extensive areas, recently developed, are models of loveliness and of artistic city planning. Architectural styles are varied, one of the popular ones being that borrowed from Mexico by California and returned to its place of origin under the name "Californian." The effect of the gleaming white plaster, with elaborately carved gray stone as trim, is undeniably entrancing in the Mexican sunshine. Neat streets are interspersed with tasteful plazas, whose fountains and clear pools make the ensemble seem like an exposition presented by a planning board for public inspection. One of the avenues in one of these developments bears the name Campos Eliseos, which one recognizes as the Spanish equivalent of Champs Elysées.

The wealth of this capital city is impressive as one rolls through mile after mile of fine avenues lined on both sides with the mansions of the rich. But also, it is clear that the city manages to support a middle class, despite the squeeze of low salaries and high costs of keeping up appearances, for there are many attractive *colonias* obviously inhabited by young, ambitious families, whose heads are hard-working business and professional men. Perhaps these thoroughly attractive but not showy suburbs represent the best evidence of young Mexico's progress along the hard road from independence to freedom.

Most neighborhoods have night watchmen called *veladores* who patrol the streets, announcing their coming and going by piping a flute. In Pedregal, one of the more elegant suburbs, the *veladores* wear blue cloaks and make their rounds on horseback. Nowhere is it wise to leave a car unlocked or unguarded, as hubcaps and radio antennas—and more—are favorite objects for thieves. Visit the Sunday morning Thieves' Market and you'll see plenty of them.

CHAPTER 8

STROLLS WITHOUT A CHAPERON

Tezontle Palaces of Old

MEXICO CITY is the only Latin capital in the New World, save to some extent Quito, Ecuador, which lends itself to unguided strolling as a supplement to the established tours. The downtown area, that of Aztec Tenochtitlán and of the colonial capital of Nueva España, is not of great extent and the extra rewards of random walks are certain and numerous. No guided tour can possibly do more than brush the surface of this city's wealth in romance. One is reminded of the old quarters of Paris, Rome, Venice, where palaces and churches are so thick that they jump into view unbidden in almost any street or *ruelle* or *rioterra*—which last, by the way, is a Venetian earth-river or filled-in canal exactly similar to many an earth-river in this very city. The old palaces of the Mexican capital have, however, a special and unique appeal because of the material—tezontle—from which virtually all of them are built.

Tezontle is a type of lava rock, almost as porous as tufa and consequently of a wonderfully soft appearance, though rough to the touch. It is durable but very light in weight, making it ideal for a city that rests on mud. The color is not a natural mineral color but a stain that was much esteemed by the Spanish colonials and that has been continued for romantic and artistic reasons by the moderns. I would call it murky rose but it cannot be neatly described in words and, moreover, it has a substantial range, varying from subdued pink to Burgundy, to maroon, and sometimes even to a dull purple. Always there is the murky or smoky tinge to it, which is not mere grime, though the weathering process and the assorted dusts, dirts and smokes of centuries darken it as they darken any material in any great city. It is, however, of smoky appearance when seen in fresh blocks in new construction. I do not know quite how it escapes being somber but it definitely does escape, and by a generous margin. Tezontle is cheerful and appealing. Perhaps the gray stonework, with its intricate carvings, saves it. In colonial times it was brightened by a creamy white trim for doors and windows, and in modern structures it is sometimes dramatized by contrasting white plaster.

Among the old *palacios* and *casas* constructed of tezontle—and most of them are within a half mile of the Zócalo—a very few have remained as public buildings or have been taken over by business concerns. The great majority of them are mere *viviendas* (tenements), inhabited in many cases by the poorest of the poor. Families with even a trace of means prefer less romance and more plumbing. Among the *palacios* still relatively intact three may be easily found by the stroller, not to mention the Hotel de Cortés (see Chapter 6) in which one may actually live.

The *Nacional Monte de Piedad*, facing the Zócalo just west of the cathedral, is the most conspicuous. In its modern capacity as the National Pawnshop, this calls for a special visit when in bargain-hunting mood, but the outside of the structure provides a good sample of colonial tezontle. This was the first viceregal residence and it is on the site of the "old houses" of Moctezuma, as a little plaque in the wall announces. (*Aqui Estuvieron Las Casas Viejas De Moctezuma Hasta 1521.*)

The *Palacio de Iturbide* is quite as handy, though less visible because of the narrowness of the main thoroughfare on which it fronts. It is at Avenida Madero 17, almost opposite the Hotel Ritz. Iturbide did not build this luxurious palace. It was built at the demand of an enormously rich and frivolous countess of the 18th century, the Condesa de San Mateo Valparaíso, and was acquired by Iturbide as his imperial residence in 1821. From 1855 to 1928 it was a fashionable hotel, used often for diplomatic guests and other celebrities. It was the center of capital life of the showier sort, until replaced by hotels in the modern style. Today it is occupied by numerous shops and business concerns. It should be noted in passing that the same wealthy Countess of Valparaíso owned the splendid baroque palace now occupied by the National Bank of Mexico on the nearby corner of the streets named for Isabel the Catholic and President Carranza.

The *Casa del Conde de Santiago de Calimaya* is easily the most exciting of the three tezontle palaces here brought to the reader's attention and it is the least visited because it is less easily found than the others, but it is near the Zócalo and richly worth finding. Walk from the southeast corner of the great square three blocks down Calle Pino Suárez and there it is at the corner of Avenida Republica del Salvador. It was erected by the first Count of Calimaya, who was a cousin of Cortés and who thus had access to any Aztec treasures that he might desire. A large stone tiger of somewhat insipid countenance, probably from the chief teocalli itself, is the building's cornerstone. There is much detail of carved stone and woodwork to study with admiration in this superb old palace and one may knock about the patio without interference from anyone. The building's tezontle façade is an added attraction, for it is pinker and warmer than most.

Almost anywhere in the very old sector of the city palace-hovels of great interest are to be seen. Look for them, for instance, on Calle Republica de Chile, on Calle San Ildefonso, on Calle Tacuba and especially on Calle Donceles, on the side opposite the Iris theater.

Churches Straight and Tipsy

The churches of Old Mexico City are even more numerous than old palaces and like them they rest on the mud blanket that was the former bed of Lake Texcoco. The majority, both of churches and palaces, have settled several inches into the mud, or, in many cases, several feet, causing considerable irregularity and tipsiness, but this shows up more in the churches because they are usually higher and most of them have domes and towers. Three churches call for special finding by the stroller, since none of them is so obvious as to be unmissable.

Nuestra Señora de Loreto, facing the like-named *Plazuela* off Calle San Ildefonso (the continuation eastward of Calle Cuba), is the tipsiest of all and is worth finding chiefly for that reason. It is nearly as far out of plumb as the Leaning Tower of Pisa and as one stands in the tiny square gazing at it, and particularly at the huge dome that tops it like an ill-fitting bowler hat, one almost expects to be a witness to its collapse, now a century and a half overdue. Manuel Tolsa, he who did the Caballito, built this odd church for the Jesuits, who wanted it in order to house a Loreto Madonna brought from Italy. To enter it one must descend several steps to a level four feet below the square and then mount several steps to the present floor. It is worth the risk, which is none at all unless a violent earthquake should occur while you are in it, and even this risk seems slight, since the church came through the big earthquake of 1957 without serious damage.

La Santísima Trinidad church can be seen a few blocks to the east of the Zócalo. It is on the corner of Calles Moneda and Academia. The Santísima—as it is commonly called—has one of the few notable churrigueresque façades of the capital's churches, and its side walls are of very ancient-looking tezontle. Its glazed tile dome and its exceedingly off-plumb tower combine with the florid façade and the red lavastone to make this church a combination of all that is Mexican.

Santo Domingo, one of the fine baroque churches of the city, is on the Plaza de la Corregidora (formerly Plazuela de Santo Domingo) three blocks north of the Zócalo as one walks up Calle Brasil (past the Monte de Piedad). The very charming square of the mayor's lady is a logical center for "left bank" wanderings (see later section of this chapter), but the church is a sight in itself, regardless of the square. It is a great remainder of the much greater monastery and central headquarters of the Dominicans in

CHURCHES STRAIGHT AND TIPSY

New Spain. This was the very wealthy order that operated the Inquisition and its main church is supposed to have cost $200,000, a fantastic sum for the year 1736 when it was completed and dedicated. The interior contains some fine churrigueresque that has survived all the anticlerical efforts of the Reform and the Revolution. The outside is dilapidated, like most old structures in this quarter, but it is still immensely impressive and, unlike most of the churches, it can be adequately seen, for the square in front of it is a long one and gives a fine vantage point for study of its enormous dome and its tall *campanario*.

The composition of this bell tower (whose famous original bells were removed at the time of the Reform) is worth setting into words, layer upon layer, though words are clumsy in dealing with such a soaring structure. There is a large clock on the plaza side of it at a level of perhaps 30 feet. Above the clock are three bells hanging in a vertical row. Above the bells comes a stretch of yellow tile work and then a bell chamber with a larger bell. The eye climbs up with the tower to behold a small cupola with more yellow tile work and, oddly enough, above this a tiled roof sloping up steeply to the absolute pinnacle, which is a cross against Mexico's blue heaven.

One need never take the churches of this city too seriously. No overpowering masterpiece will be overlooked if you miss them all, but they are an interesting company and the ones named above are but three picked almost at random from the multitude. Their struggle to remain standing in the ooze, which was once a reedy lagoon or at best an insecure group of low islands, gives one a sense as of wishing to help hold them up. However, they all survived a considerable earthquake in 1944 and the far heavier one of 1957, so they may reasonably look forward to a still riper and older age.

In the middle of the Paseo, you can't help but notice the golden Angel of Independence, spreading his wings from a 100-foot pedestal. During the just mentioned 1957 earthquake, he tumbled from his perch and smashed to the street below. But he means as much to Mexicans as does the Statue of Liberty to North Americans, so the angel was carefully pieced together again and restored to his lofty perch, just as before.

Three Marvels for Discovery

If the mood for unchaperoned strolls remains, the visitor may find various marvels of this historic city that are seldom seen by tourists since they are not included on the fixed city tours nor on most special church-and-palace tours. Leaving for a later chapter the great structures whose walls are covered with the work of the Mexican painters we may run down three unsung marvels of earliest days, though there are perhaps three dozen available for exhaustive searchers.

The *Hospital de Jesús Nazareno*, at the corner of Pino Suárez and Salvador, diagonally across from the house of the Count of Santiago (with the Aztec tiger cornerstone), is the oldest hospital in all the Americas. It could hardly be less than the oldest for it was founded by Cortés himself "on the famous site of paganism known as *Huitzillan* in the year 1527," as an inscription states. An endowment left by the Conqueror keeps the place up as a hospital and this in spite of numerous attempts, some by the government itself, to break the will. Huitzillan was the place where Cortés and Moctezuma first met, the former dismounting from his horse, the latter stepping down from his sumptuous litter. In the church of Jesús Nazareno, which adjoins the hospital, lie the actual remains of the Conqueror. For years this was doubted by many students, but dramatic proofs, osseous and documentary, discovered in 1946, established the fact beyond question. This city corner of Jesus the Nazarene is redolent of history, almost like the Zócalo.

A pronunciation note may intrude here to roil thoughts of history. The tourist who inquires for the "Hospital of Jesus" will evoke the blankest of looks from almost any Mexican, for it will not occur even to the average well-educated one that Jesus has any connection with "Haysóos."

Las Vizcaínas ("The Basques," a popular name universally used instead of the official one, *Colegio de la Paz*) contains a school for girls founded by three rich and philanthropic Basques in the 18th century. It is of enormous proportions, having a frontage on the Calle and the Plaza of Vizcaínas (just east of the broad Calle San Juan de Letrán) of about 500 feet. Its area, in case you like big figures, is well over five acres. There is little to see in the huge central court or the various smaller patios, but the whole rambling ensemble is, indeed, a marvel of Mexico. In many portions the *colegio* has sunk crazily into the spongy soil and this adds immeasurable charm to the picture. One forgets the neighborhood, which today is one of the most sordid in the city.

Fuente del Salto de Agua, two blocks south of Las Vizcaínas, is a fountain as attractive as its name (Water Leap). If it had as its motif a maternal wolf or a Neptune instead of twining snake columns, one could imagine it to be one of the fountains of Rome. The interesting chapel near it is popularly called by the name of the fountain.

Wandering on the "Left Bank"

Mexico City is one of innumerable cities ambitiously called by its boosters the Paris of its country or continent or hemisphere. The tag is less far-fetched than usual and in so far as it applies to this capital it applies also to the student sector, or Latin Quarter, or Left Bank. There is no river at all, but the atmosphere of the university sector is strikingly suggestive, in a smaller and less glamorous way, one must admit, and certainly without the bright cafés of the Boul' Mich or Boulevard Saint-Germain, of the beloved *quartier* of generations of students and Bohemians.

One really feels something of the Left Bank in the Plaza de Santo Domingo, and its radiating streets, the plaza being popularly called Plaza de la Corregidora, in deference to a conspicuous statue in it. The dour lady patriot sits in the middle of the plaza in bronze, looking august and a bit cross but no doubt hatching new plots by the minute to get rid of the hated Spaniards. One may find a bench near the mayoress, call a boy for a *grasa* (but he will be there at one's feet anyway, getting out his polishing paraphernalia), and let life unfold. Across the way is the University's *Escuela Nacional de Medicina*, affectionately called by the students *Casa Chata* (Flat-nosed) because of its snubbed or rounded front.

Three centuries and more of tortuous history, sometimes "torturous" as well, roll from this snub-nosed structure, or from the site of it. A part of the rambling Dominican convent first stood here but it was wiped out in 1716 by an inundation of Lake Texcoco, which was not then by any means the mere memory it is today. Then rose this present building to house the *Tribunal del Santo Oficio*, which was the Holy Office of the Inquisition, under Dominican auspices as in Spain. Tomás de Torquemada's contribution to civilization had already functioned for a century and a half in Mexico (two and a half in Spain) and required a building worthy of its importance and sanctity. One need not dwell at length on the horrible burnings alive—or the mere strangulation when the heretic's offense was slight. The stranglings took place on a corner of the Zócalo, but the burnings occurred regularly in the *Plaza del Quemadero* (Burning Place), a stone platform in what is now the Alameda, the fate of the victims having been previously determined in the Tribunal. The awful cloud passed with the torture and trial of the patriot hero José María Morelos, who was the Inquisition's last victim in Mexico. The Holy Office, after applying the torture preliminary to his removal for execution, declared him "an unconfessed heretic, an abettor of heretics, a disturber of the ecclesiastical hierarchy, a profaner of the holy sacraments, a traitor to God, to the King and to the Pope." Morelos, a sincere country priest, was none of these things except a disturber of the ecclesiastical hierarchy. That, one may be sure, he was, for the hierarchy relished nothing so little as a disturbance of its privileged status.

The building that La Corregidora faces, and that we face while the boy finishes the *grasa*, advanced to worthier uses with the coming of independence to Mexico and with the passing of the Dominicans. Manuel Acuña, the celebrated and so-Latin writer of *Pasionarias* (perfervid love poems), worked here and died here in 1873. He did, in fact, follow the line of his own poetry a bit too literally and took poison in this very building because a love affair had gone wrong. Thousands of Mexicans, who know his poems by heart, revere him all the more because he died, as one might almost say, in the line of duty. The whole Left Bank is still romanticized by that famous suicide.

The square of La Corregidora has much more than a university building to suggest Left Bank activities. It has interesting bookstores and art shops, with old prints and maps of Mexico, suggesting dimly the bookstalls along the Seine embankment. It has medical-supply shops and general student-supply shops and several curious old-fashioned printing presses that operate busily on the sidewalks. It has passing students too—lots of them at certain hours.

A special touch, not of the Left Bank but of Indian Mexico, is the row of *evangelistas* under the *portales* (arcades) on the west side. These are public letter writers and each is seated expectantly behind his ancient Underwood or dilapidated Oliver (I saw no Royals, Remingtons or Coronas but cannot explain the lack), ready to "take a letter" at the request of any timid Aztec or worried Toltec. He will undoubtedly touch up the letter gratis, inserting a bit of romantic fire here, if the love-making is too tame, weaving in some impressive legal phrases there, if it is a clumsy and amateurish business communication. These *evangelistas* look to us decidedly seedy, like garret poets who have tasted the dregs of disillusion, but to illiterate Indians, perhaps fresh in from some small village, they must look like gods. They sit there behind those mysterious instruments, play them like little marimbas and produce funny marks on paper, marks that will mean what the Indian has just said, marks that can be understood by a person who is far away. If it is a love letter the chances are that these strange marks will have to be set into spoken words at the receiving end by some learned person, for the addressee will not know what they mean. But, of course, Crisóstomo or José would know, if either of them is home from his studies at the *colegio*. It is all very wonderful. Compared with this the miracle of the radio is nothing. One hears that tiresome box blatting away in every village plaza, and that, after all, is mere talking and singing and playing—but words from a machine!

It may be of interest to you to know how much the typing of these letters costs. A peso (eight cents) buys a business letter; while a love letter costs anywhere from 50 centavos (four cents) to two pesos (sixteen cents), depending on the degree of passion you want expressed. There is a slight additional charge if you insist on correct spelling.

The Left Bank is by no means limited to the area of the Square of the Mayoress. It spreads along the north-south streets of Chile, Brazil and Argentina and the east-west streets of Cuba (San Ildefonso), Donceles and Tacuba. The last named is a street of bookstores and print stores, especially in the block directly back of the cathedral and at the corner of Argentina. At this latter corner one may look down upon some excavations of the Aztec city that are wide open to public view. The Left Bank is not something to "do" in a hasty walk. It is something to experience in various unplanned visits as convenience or mood directs.

Bargains in the Mount of Piety

Mexico's *Nacional Monte de Piedad* is an insistent magnet to such travelers who discover it, for the place is always seething with human interest, and sometimes one finds good bargains, even spectacular bargains. The odd name originated in Italy as *Monte di Pietà* and was established in Rome early in the 1500's by Pope Leo X, who was a son of Lorenzo de' Medici. The three gold balls of the pawnbroker are from the heraldic arms of the Medici family. The purpose of the Mount of Piety as a municipal or national institution is always in theory, and generally in practice, to save the poor from being mercilessly squeezed by usurers. A charitable paternalism was the honest purpose of the first example in Rome and the admirable idea spread gradually to France (Mont de Piété), Spain and the Spanish New World. Mount means bank (compare *monte* in certain card games) and refers to a public or government loan. Piété or Piedad originally meant pity, or charity, rather than piety; so Bank of Pity makes etymological sense after all.

One recalls that the institution has been abused in some cases, notably the famous *Affaire Stavisky* in France, where very seamy operations at the Mont de Piété in Bayonne were uncovered; but the average has been excellent and Mexico City's Monte de Piedad (there are others in Puebla, Guadalajara and other cities) is an excellent example. It was founded in 1775 by the Count of Regla, a philanthropic mine owner, and has been administered by the republic as a charity. The rich, however, seek it as much as the poor, to judge by the jewelry and fancy bibelots that are mixed with the junk. A relatively low rate of interest is charged and 90 per cent of the articles are said to be redeemed. But since some 50,000 separate articles, ranging from grand pianos to pocketknives, are often pawned in a single month, the 10 per cent residue provides a very substantial average of potential bargains.

Frequent *remates* (auctions) of unredeemed items of some selected type of merchandise are held at times announced by signs in the building, but these are avidly attended by keen-eyed professionals and the alien visitor may prefer to avoid such competition and roam at will, on an uncrowded day, looking for bargains under the glass cases of the main hall and in the various smaller rooms. These display rugs, antiques, optical instruments, musical instruments, books and so on, almost without end, though there are no pigs or parrots. Everything in the hall and in the lesser rooms is plainly ticketed as to price, and no bargaining is possible except in the competitive *remates*. The hours of the establishment are 8:30 A.M. to 2 P.M., whereas shopping hours are from

9 A.M. to 6 P.M. The hall, at the right as one enters from the Zócalo, is the general salesroom for jewelry, watches and other small items. The range of these, in value and price, is enormous, running from half a peso to at least 70,000 pesos ($5600), for I saw a diamond bracelet with the latter price mark. The items are no less interesting for their imagined history than for themselves. I noticed, for instance, a gold and enamel pin marked "Standard Oil Co. of New Jersey—10 years," and it was priced, so to speak, at a peso a year, for the tag read ten pesos. What unfortunate employee, I wondered, was stuck in Mexico to such extent that he had to let this go for the four or five pesos he presumably received for it? Or did some Mexican *ladrón* in a dubious bar lift it to turn it in for whatever he could get?

Once a month, the "Almoneda" takes place in several rooms of the Monte de Piedad. This is a general monthly auction of pawned items that were not redeemed in time.

I have a good friend, a resident of Mexico City, who once picked up a beautiful gold watch in the Monte de Piedad, with the impressive words *Cartier—Paris* on its face, for the nominal sum of 150 pesos; but my own shopping there was decidedly less successful, not to say less smart. Once when I was in the city a valued fountain pen with my name engraved on a gold band around it was lost or stolen. I was particularly unhappy because it matched an equally valued pencil that I still retained. A few days later I saw a pen precisely like mine in the Monte de Piedad. I examined the gold band through a magnifying glass but could not see any trace of my name. At any rate it was its twin and it wrote well for me. It was priced at seven dollars, but thinking this too much for a secondhand pen that might have been used for years, I told the pawn clerk I would think it over. I did think it over and went back next day to buy it. "*Vendido*," she announced briskly, pointing to the blank area in the showcase where it had been. I was too late and I have always regretted that I sought to appease the goddess *Frugalitas*. You will be wiser when you see something you really want.

Markets for the Myriads

Markets are among the brightest pigments in the metaphorical sarape that is Mexico. The fascination of them never palls, and most Americans—especially American women—who visit one of them once in Mexico City will go again and again. Between times they may decry their confusion, for every type of merchandise is offered, along with edibles, but they know in their hearts that their fastidious instincts will yield to the stronger instincts of trading and of watching the very heartbeat of life. "That is fancy talk," says someone, but wait until you see a Mexican market in full swing.

Prices will seem very moderate. You will recall, however, that no trader in any market ever expects to get the price asked. Do not insult him or her by paying promptly the figure first mentioned. The very least you can do with propriety is to hesitate, look dismayed and murmur "*Muy caro*" several times. It is more self-respecting to chaffer for a few minutes, if you can muster enough Spanish to do it. If not, just clothe yourself in the right amount of dudgeon and let the market man beat himself down— though not too far, for he needs your money more than you need his merchandise.

In a village market in the south of Mexico I once bought a little lava dinner bell in the form of a peasant woman wearing a long skirt. It rang nicely and pleased my shopping sense. I asked the price, expecting that it would be one or two pesos. To my astonishment the woman said "*Veintecinco centavos*" (25 centavos, two cents). I hastily bought it, feeling much pleased with myself. At another stand I tried some bargaining on another similar bell and was elated at my shrewdness in securing it for eight centavos. The woman gave me two tiny coppers of one centavo each in change from a ten-centavo piece. Later I showed off the bells at my hotel and found that a real trader had secured precisely similar bells at three centavos apiece. My ego was deflated, but remembering the pitiful poverty of the old woman who had sold me one of the bells for less than a penny in American money, I was not too sorry.

I have mentioned the remarkable inroads of sanitation in Mexican marketing and this is evidenced in a striking way by the capital's vast modern markets, which are wonders of the Latin world. These great bustling marts are at their best on Sunday morning, but can be seen in all their rich confusion any day of the week and, to my mind, they are among the most stirring sights of the metropolis. The market of *La Merced* is the largest, larger even than the immense air terminal! Its wholesale department sells fruits, vegetables, household articles and countless other things in carload lots. Its retail section is over a quarter of a mile long by 100 yards wide, with an additional couple of acres for meats and fish. It is located six blocks east and three blocks south of the Zócalo. The *decorations* for this and the other new markets are not the least of their attractions for they were designed by a talented lady named Elena Alvarez Murphy, whom I shall have occasion to mention again in connection with one of the capital's finest restaurants, La Ronda.

The *San Juan Market* is a modern four-building emporium, with sections devoted primarily to the retailing of foods, fruits, flowers and *baskets*, which last is perhaps the most distinctively Mexican part, and it is very easy to reach. Merely walk south on Calle Dolores, entering that street from Avenida Juárez at the eastern end of the Alameda, and you will soon be in the heart of it. Roses of many colors, gladioli, marigolds, lilies and orchids are only a few of the flowers deployed in the floral portion and in a tiny *plazuela* beyond. The massive fragrance of the roses fairly saturates the air. Fruits of every imaginable hue (including all those of tezontle), vegetables, herbs, articles of native craftsmanship in various materials—the endless piles of wares are pleasantly staggering to the senses. The gay display of piñatas at Christmastime is a joy to behold at the San Juan Market.

Lagunilla, six blocks north of Madero on Calle Isabel la Católica (whose name changes to Chile), seems rather more a bazaar than a market, for it is devoted chiefly to textiles and especially silks. Costumes of the style called *China Poblana*, which has become the national feminine costume of Mexico, are much in evidence, but the strange story of the "Puebla China-girl" belongs to the city of Puebla (and in some degree to Acapulco where the *China* landed) and perhaps you would rather not purchase her costume until you reach her city. (See Chapter 18.) In this market, as in many others, you will find flea-market areas where broken mirrors, rusty water faucets, early-vintage Gramophones and other "heterogenia" fight for space with statuary, paintings, genuine antiques and assorted bibelots, some of which may have real value.

Almost any populous street in the downtown part of the capital is a market of sorts and you need not hunt up one of the named markets to find things being sold in the traditional way. The whole western sidewalk bordering the Zócalo is a merchandise mart at all times. Before Christmas and before the *Fiesta de los Reyes* (Festival of the Three Magi; January 6), the booths and piles of toys and merchandise spread openly into the plaza, to the great annoyance of bus and taxi drivers. The broad sidewalk of the Calle San Juan de Letrán is another unofficial market.

Calendars seem to sprout from the sidewalks of almost *every* street, especially at Christmastime and in the early months of the year. They are huge pictorial affairs, often displaying pretty girls and most often *Japanese* pretty girls who are cycling or playing unconvincing tennis in extremely diaphanous costumes. Some enterprising merchant must have imported a shipload of these gaudy Oriental prints years ago, for they are hardy perennials of Mexico's street markets. One turns with relief to the living Mexican girls who are on every hand, neat and genuine little creatures, mostly of aboriginal blood and aboriginal grace.

CHAPTER 9

THE SPECTRUM OF MEXICAN ART

The Classics of San Carlos

MEXICO's major collection of classic paintings, by both European and native artists, is in the *Academia de las Bellas Artes*, a gloomy old building dating back 400 years, whose entrance is at 22 Calle Academia, two blocks east of the Zócalo. These classics include good examples of Murillo, Rubens, Zurbarán and one or two each of Titian, Velázquez, Goya and El Greco; and of the Mexican school there are several by the elder Baltazar de Echave and one colossal affair, the Virgin of the Apocalypse, by the celebrated Indian, Miguel Cabrera.

The authorities who administer this picture gallery as a part of the National School of Fine Arts do not make it an easy business for the traveler to see the treasured paintings. There is no sign to indicate the hours of admission, although it is open most of the day and part of the night. On my third try I was finally able to enter the building, but the place was as silent as a mausoleum. Presently, I heard the click of a typewriter, presumably that of Charon's secretary clicking off the current passenger list for the Styx ferry. I followed the sound upstairs to the *Biblioteca* and entered that august hall to inquire how I could see the paintings. "Go to the other end of the corridor and knock," said the harried typist, who proved to be a young man making a catalogue. "Nothing may happen for a while, but just keep on knocking." I followed instructions and sure enough nothing happened. At long last, a disheveled guard appeared and said rather sharply, "Not open until ten." Before he could shut the door in my face I whipped out my watch and showed him that it was then 10:15. He gazed ill-humoredly at the timepiece and was thinking up some other reason to refuse me admittance when I broke in firmly, "Please. This is my third try." A peso, not very subtly pressed into his hand, won him over and his humor rapidly improved. He even showed me the pictures himself and developed a gradual pride in so doing, for the collection is important. But he spoiled my contemplation of these masterpieces by rushing me along far too fast, as virtually all museum attendants do in every city in the world.

Rivera Gives Lessons in History

The mighty moderns of Mexico have attracted worldwide attention during the last quarter century, somewhat to the astonishment of Mexicans themselves. Basically, these men, starting with Diego Rivera, have done something new in the field of art. They have used their talents not as followers of a remote muse untouched by the practical problems of life but to advance, in open and unblushing propaganda, the theories in which they passionately believe, or have believed until success and the passage of time have slightly blunted their evangelism. These men are part and parcel of the Revolution. In the early twenties, when the "Mexican School" took form, the artists were outright Communists in their sympathies and in their practices. Rivera was one of the leading spirits in organizing the famous "Syndicate of Painters, Sculptors and Intellectual Workers." This fostered a cooperative shop to aid aspiring beginners and to distribute the work of seasoned members. It held earnest and thunderous meetings to denounce capitalism, bourgeois pursuits and traditional academic patterns of art. It published a very red newspaper called *El Machete,* which Rivera himself edited, in cooperation with Siqueiros and Guerrero.

The Mexican government discouraged this superrevolutionary syndicate and it broke up after a time, but the inner feeling of almost all the abler artists seems to have remained loyal to the syndicate's concepts. Art became something of a political football, since the reddest of painters must eat, even as the banker and the lesser bourgeoisie. Governments of the Revolution that were sincerely revolutionary, in the Mexican sense, gave the artists a decided boost in personal morale and in achievement. Those who were reactionary pressed their performance back into a mold of sycophancy. For a time the Communist Party controlled the Department of Education, which passed out the plums in the form of commissions for murals, and its patronage was as harmful as that of the unsympathetic reactionaries, for where the party line led, art must follow—and very closely too, or else . . .

The murals are, of course, the outstanding achievement of all the great moderns. They are always imposing, sometimes colossal, sometimes tedious, for one tends, in the course of time, to tire of being shouted at, however noble the theme of the shouting. Great murals are very conspicuous in Mexico City and one can hardly miss them. They are seen in the main entrance hall of the National Palace, in the University, the Bellas Artes Palace, the new Supreme Court Building, the larger tourist hotels and even on the stairway of Sanborn's, that attractive catchall of life.

Diego Rivera, whose death late in 1957 was headline news everywhere, still dominates the whole show so far as Americans are concerned. Orozco often shouts in louder tones and some of his bellowings are magnificent, but he is of notably uneven quality. Rivera was the pioneer master and he remains the most celebrated and the most interesting. To state the case in terms of popular fame, almost everybody in the States has heard of Orozco but *everybody* has heard of Rivera—if that means anything. When a bubbling tourist, pointing to some large but inconsequential historical painting in Chapultepec Castle, exclaims, "Oh, those must be by Riviera [*sic*]," she is placing the crown of laurel on the artist's brow. She does not know his work but she has heard of him and that speaks volumes for his fame.

Actually, the man Rivera was simple and natural in manner. He worked in a pink studio-villa, which was surrounded by a fence of ten-foot cactus spikes, directly opposite the old San Angel Inn in the Villa Obregón suburb of the city. He often dined in the sunny patio of the inn, and one Sunday noon I saw him there, unmistakably, dining with several friends. I called the headwaiter and asked if it was in order for me to meet the famous man. "Of course. I will call him to your table," said the waiter, as though he were speaking of a *sommelier* or a shine boy. Before I could stop the man he was off and presently he returned with the Olympian in tow. Mr. Rivera was as friendly and unaffected as could be. For something to say I asked him, possibly with more haste than care, if enemies were still throwing ink and acids at portions of his murals that excited their hatred.

"Not much any more," he said. "I did the National Palace painting over when they spoiled it. Then they spoiled it again and I did it over again. I think they get tired doing it now. No trouble lately."

This interested me especially because I remembered having seen that huge mural during one of the periods when it was disfigured by acid, leaving a large and ugly white stain. The damaged part represented the "immorality of the Church," as it does again in restoration. A priest holding a rosary kisses a voluptuous wanton and beside this scene is a tiny shrine of the Virgin of Guadalupe. This was a dagger thrust at the very heart of popular piety and it is said that some enraged Indian threw the acid. I would have liked to ask Mr. Rivera, who has been, in general, the Indians' great friend, why he did not select the rich man's Virgin of los Remedios for his taunt.

His *Sunday in the Alameda*, the great mural done in 1948 in Hotel del Prado, reached an all-time high in controversy, almost creating a small war. Its conspicuous placard, DIOS NO EXISTE (God Does Not Exist), though recalling a hectic moment of revolutionary history and thus perhaps defensible where placed, was another thrust at religion. It infuriated Catholic students, who rushed the hotel and scratched the words out. Then Rivera and his cohorts rushed the hotel in their turn. He repainted the slogan and even put it in *twice!* Siqueiros, it is said, jumped on a table in the dining room (boots on fine linen) and bellowed encouragement, along with praises for Stalin and Communism. Sure of countertrouble, the hotel made haste to board up the whole thing, but while this was being done some carpenter again scratched out the hated slogan(s) and made a scratch also clear across the face of Rivera, as a boy, in the picture. It thus became Rivera's turn again—but he could not get at his mural, since it was boarded up and stoutly padlocked. But now you and I may see this controversial legacy of art whenever we like, though its main point of controversy, the atheistic slogan, has been permanently expunged.

Far less violent than some of his colleagues, Rivera was always preaching about something, generally the aspirations of mankind. Occasionally, he roared at the top of his paintbrush, but he frequently relaxed to the point of doing something merely to please the taste of visitors, including the genus tourist. And it was even whispered in Mexico City that he had been caught, in his later years, doing little things for the sheer pleasure of achieving something beautiful or striking—in other words art for art's sake. If that was true, the revolutionary was slipping; but perhaps the artist was even advancing as age mellowed his spirit.

Personally, I enjoy Rivera's work most when it gives lessons in Mexican history, however impregnated with allegorical sermonizing. His most comprehensive effort in this line remains the National Palace mural on the stairway and others of enormous extent in upper corridors, these having been left incomplete at his death. The story of the Revolution depicted on the stairway wall is very powerful even though colored by his persistent scorn of the Church and his affectionate leanings toward Communism. Anyone who sees it will long remember the smug cruelty in the countenances of the rightists surrounding Díaz, who all face the same way the dictator does and all show their owners' concern to maintain *orden* (order). Similarly, one remembers the bright and devoted Revolutionists, each face directed opposite to that of Díaz and his group, each showing concern for the real values of life expressed in the conspicuous words (for those who cannot read facial expressions easily) TIERRA, LIBERTAD y PAN (Land, Liberty and Bread).

An equally striking lesson in history—and equally opinionated in its allegorical implications—is his pictorial account of the Conquest of Mexico seen in the loggia of the Cortés palace in Cuernavaca. That will receive comment in Chapter 17, but it should actually be considered as a companion piece to the artist's long historical "treatise" in the National Palace. The Cuernavaca masterpiece is, in fact, a sort of foreword to the treatise. The artist commenced it at about the same time, completing it before he completed the larger work. It was characteristic of Rivera that he generally had two or three great undertakings advancing simultaneously. At intervals in his very busy life he worked, as I've said, on some further historical murals of enormous yardage on the walls of the upper corridors of the National Palace, but if he could ever have completed it by his personal efforts it would have been a major miracle, for the plan seemed to demand several ordinary life spans.

The Rockefeller Reject in the Fine Arts Palace

The Rivera mural that naturally wins the most eager attention from American tourists is his copy of the one that he did for Mr. Rockefeller and which the latter destroyed at the request of many of his tenants who were irritated by the picture's glowing tribute to Russian Communism. Rivera reconstructed it for Mexico's Palacio de Bellas Artes in almost the exact form he had planned for the New York structure. You may see the controversial work on the west wall of the third floor, called second floor (*segundo piso*) by the Mexican system, which considers that one flight of stairs takes you up to the "first floor." It is verbosely called "Man at the Crossroads, Looking with Uncertainty but with Hope to a Better World." Whatever your social views you will not fail to feel sympathy for Mr. Rockefeller, honest capitalist and honest taxpayer. Lenin is conspicuously and very sympathetically featured in the mural, uniting various classes of mankind, and Mr. Rockefeller himself (though this may be a later and vengeful interpolation) is clearly but not at all sympathetically pictured having a good capitalistic time. As stated by Frances Toor, "In the group devoting themselves to the empty and degenerate pleasures of the bourgeoisie is the picture of John D. Rockefeller, Jr., the destroyer of the fresco in New York, with a glass of champagne in his hand." Careful scrutiny will show you that Mr. Rockefeller's other hand holds that of a lady and he kisses it gallantly. Beside him in the picture of "degeneracy," four women are engaged in excessively torrid dancing. Rivera sympathizers have condemned Mr. Rockefeller for junking the original mural, alleging that he had agreed to give the artist an absolutely free hand, but after all, the patron did pay in full for the work. If the artist has added this personal aspersion in the reconstruction, it speaks more for his fiery emotions than for his fairness. Mr. Rockefeller was a notably temperate, moral and upright man, as everyone knows.

The Search for the Painted Walls

The search for the murals of Mexico City will be greatly aided by a good guide who knows and likes the art of his countrymen. These works were mostly commissioned by the government's Department of Education and some of the most massive of them are in public educational buildings. These buildings, chiefly in the "Left Bank" sector of the old city north of the cathedral and sometimes of old colonial vintage, are confusing to one who looks for them on maps. The easiest way to find them is to sign up for a conducted tour.

The average short-time visitor will desire to see only two or three of these huge art buildings and to understand as much as possible of what he sees. Very practical help in understanding the pictures, but not in finding them, can be had in pamphlet form in the *Interpretative Guides* by the late Frances Toor, if these can

THE SEARCH FOR THE PAINTED WALLS

still be found.

The *Secretariat of Education* is perhaps the most important of all, as it is also the largest in "acreage" of mural decoration. In case you elect to hunt it up by persevering footwork, grip your map firmly and find the place in cartography before trying to find it in physical fact. It is at the corner of Avenida Argentina and Calle Luis González Obregón; this latter street is merely a single block of the important street that is República de Cuba to the west and San Ildefonso to the east. The corner is but three blocks north of the rear of the cathedral.

This huge building, once the church of Nuestra Señora de la Encarnación but totally rebuilt in 1922, has a three-deck double patio that you will think the largest in the world—and maybe it is. It seems impossible that so much wall space could be covered with frescoes of any meaning, but hardly a square inch escapes and one suspects that the artists felt a bit cramped, since even the stairway walls, none too well lighted, are equally crowded with messages to the world. The walls of the library, the theater, the administration offices and other rooms are also covered almost solidly with paintings. I entered the washroom marked *Caballeros* to see if there were murals there, too, but there were none. Surely that and its counterpart for *Señoras* will not be permanently neglected!

Of course, the prolific art work in this building is explained in part by the fact that it is the Holy of Holies of the Department of Education, through which almost all purchases of artistic labor by the Mexican government are funneled. But that does not entirely explain it. Mexican muralists love space and this is particularly true of Orozco, who did some of this work. Rivera fathered the thing and the great majority of the panels, totaling 142, are actually by him. Other artists whose work is found in various parts of the building include such able men as Montenegro, Siqueiros, Mérida, Charlot and de la Cueva. The themes of the patio murals concern chiefly the struggles and hopes of the Indians and of the workers in their age-long combat against exploitation. There is rich detail, and a very great deal of it, on such subjects as the village customs of the peons, their work and play, their fiestas, dances, marriage and death ceremonies. There is much, too, about mining and factory life, about transportation on land and on sea, about arts and crafts and science. In fact, there cannot be any phase or facet of Mexican life, past or present, that does not have at least a few paltry yards of space. Around the top floor there is a long ballad of agrarian life and it is interspersed, in dozens of banners, with little homilies. A couple that virtually translate themselves into English may be set down here as typical: *La Verdadera Civilización Sera la Armonía de los Hombres con la Tierra y de los Hombres entre sí;* and this: *La Tierra es de todos como el Abre, el Agua y la Luz y el Calor del Sol.* The whole agrarian ensemble is a forthright sermon or series of sermons delivered through a loudspeaker. If it seems to you crude, violent and exaggerated, and if the proportions of many of the Indians and workers and of the "props" around them appear to be curiously pressed out of shape, remember that the great artists who did this work knew just what they were doing. The last thing any Mexican muralist desires to do is to paint a pretty picture. He wants to *say something* in arresting or even caustic tone. The only trouble with this, from the spectator's point of view, is that after a few miles of such "talk" the eye grows weary, even as the ear grows tired of a six-hour oration. One would think these muralists had been engaged in a conspiracy to filibuster so that no vote on their merits could be taken.

The *National Preparatory School* is almost as important and almost as large, murally speaking, as the Secretariat. It is located only a stone's throw from the latter, being on the south side of Calle San Ildefonso (the same street, remember, as Calle L. G. Obregón), in the block between Argentina and Carmen. The building alone is one that would warrant stress—were there not so many—in the section devoted to tezontle palaces, for it is unusually massive and the red stain of the tezontle is especially appealing, being about the color of port wine. This building is often called, in parlance and on maps, the *Colegio de San Ildefonso*, which it formerly was, having been established as such by the Jesuits in 1749. It has funny little old windows and prodigious doors of carved wood, with attractive white marble and gray stonework to relieve the general severity.

Orozco was the chief decorator of this building, with almost all of the frescoes on the three-tiered main patio and its stairways to his credit, though Rivera is here, too, and several lesser but very good painters, including Siqueiros, Leal, Charlot and Fermín Revueltas. The name of Alfaro Siqueiros calls for more than passing mention, for he is really one of the important Mexican men of art; but he has at times been so tangled in the official violences of the Communist Party that his artistic work has suffered greatly. When it has appeared publicly it has generally, as in this building, been terribly mutilated by vandals and by more honest folk whose feelings have been unbearably outraged by the man's political activities. His work, some of it never finished and some badly defaced, is to be seen in the inner patio.

The historical paintings in this building, especially those on themes of the conquest, are of outstanding interest. One may, for instance, see Orozco's idea of Cortés, of the Conqueror's mistress, Malinche, and of his fiery colleague, Pedro de Alvarado (whose rash action brought the *noche triste* upon the Spaniards); and one may see (at the top of the main stairway in the larger patio) Jean Charlot's conception of the terrible occasion on which Cortés had the suspected Aztec porters slaughtered in the temple at Cholula. Other works of Orozco are seen in the new Supreme Court Building, in the Fine Arts Palace and on the landing of the staircase in Sanborn's. Others of Rivera are seen almost everywhere, including a movie theater on Insurgentes, the outside of the huge new stadium at University City and even within the waterworks installations in the Dolores quarter, beyond Chapultepec. These are done in mosaic work to withstand the weather.

Comparisons between Rivera and Orozco are inevitable, for

the fame of each is worldwide. The work of each is conspicuous in the United States as well as in Mexico. Rivera has been rather more prolific, but the spread of Orozco's paintings is also great. His famous *Epic of Civilization*, in the Dartmouth College Library, covers 3000 square feet and is called the largest coordinated "true fresco" in the United States. In general, Rivera was far the more serene of the two, and he maintained a consistent social ideology, based on Marx, which he "plugged" year in and year out. Orozco has been so violent and disordered as to be called a philosophical anarchist. Says George Kubler in his critique, "No doctrine animates his work; he portrays the endless variations of suffering and aspiration in compositional patterns which, unlike the centralized, stable designs of Rivera, insist on broken forms, contradictory movements and unresolved harmonies."

The New Mosaic Murals

Of late years many *mosaic murals* of heroic size (see above) have been appearing on various civic buildings of the capital and even on some private business buildings and theaters, a development that is more conspicuous, and therefore more startling to the eye, than even the outsized painted walls described above. For a sample you may have a taxi take you to the Communications Ministry (*Comunicaciones y Obras Públicas*). You'll be fairly overwhelmed by its immensity—it includes living quarters for hundreds of employees and a supermarket for their provender—and by the open-to-the-weather mosaic on one of its façades of the *World Story of Communications*, called the largest mosaic in the world, this complex and gigantic work being the achievement of several artists, one of the most effective being Juan O'Gorman.

And have your taxi, or better, a competent guide, show you the *Ciudad Universitaria*, on the capital's southern outskirts. How can I describe this University City? I can't, unless by quoting what a Mexican enthusiast said to me: "Since the pyramids of

THE NEW MOSAIC MURALS

Egypt nothing of such grandeur has been built on earth." See it, I urge, and compare your reactions with the above quote. See the kilometer-long Humanities Building. See the mostly-glass Science Building and the Atomic Research Building, with the vast Prometheus statue nearby. See the library, which is now the National Library of the Republic of Mexico, supplanting the dull and dingy *Biblioteca Nacional,* downtown. This new library is one of the most astonishing buildings that you will ever see anywhere, for its huge façade is one vast mosaic mural, designed on Aztec themes by Juan O'Gorman. Like the mosaic on the Communications Ministry, this one, too, is called "the largest in the world" and you will not feel like disputing either claim. Juan O'Gorman, since I'm on the subject, has done another big mosaic mural for the retaining wall back of the swimming pool of the Posada de la Misión in Taxco, which work, a dramatic story of Emperor Cuauhtémoc, has brought new glory to that picture town. Further mention of it will be found in Chapter 17.

Continuing your University City wanderings see—as if you could possibly miss it—the new stadium, its walls adorned with Rivera's mosaic murals, where 110,000 spectators may sit in seats *with arms* and, outside of which, 12,000 cars may comfortably park. See the athletic fields for every conceivable type of sport and see the multiple swimming pool, like nothing that even Hollywood has devised for any superfilm. It is said that some $50 million has been spent "so far" on this whole development and much remains to be done. The similar University Cities of Paris, Madrid and Caracas are peanuts, even mere birdseed, by comparison with this mammoth one of Mexico, D.F. If an ebullient Texan wishes to see something really BIG, let him come here and see this City of Scholarship and rub his eyes in disbelief!

If anyone from any state wishes to see something startling in *theater* construction, let him look up the *Teatro de los Insurgentes,* well out on the Avenida Insurgentes. It is a modern legitimate theater identifiable by a 60-foot mosaic mural on the façade, from a design by Diego Rivera featuring Cantinflas, that favorite and famous comedian of Mexico (see Chapter 10), whose show, *I Columbus*, was the first musical comedy presented here. You will note that in the design Rivera preaches one of his popular sermons, for it shows Cantinflas receiving money from the rich and distributing it to the poor. The tribute is a deserved one, for the comedian's generosity is said to be proverbial.

Modernity Gone Mad

It is inevitable that lesser artists of greater violence should follow in the wake of such a chaotic genius as Orozco. One of them, by name Jorge González Camarena, did two paintings for the lobby of the ponderous Guardiola Building (between the Fine Arts Palace and Sanborn's) and they are as conspicuous as possible, being directly over the elevators. If you view them, see if you are more successful than I was in reading their message. One depicts a colossal naked woman straight out of Brobdingnag. The other shows an equally colossal and equally undraped man engaged in some sort of desperate struggle. Possibly he is wrestling with temptation, but frankly I do not know what he is doing. In waiting for the elevators, and often one must use them, since various important offices are in the upper portions of the building, one feels inevitably as though one has wandered into some extraordinary sort of peep show. That is, Americans feel this way. Mexicans, including the numerous stenographers in the building, are accustomed to artistic extravagances and apparently consider the pictures run-of-the-mill.

On the last afternoon of one of my sojourns in Mexico City I wandered into the Fine Arts Palace and found that a special art exhibit, in the east room on the ground floor, was attracting attention. I entered and saw that a mixed collection of etchings and watercolors was on display. The inspiration was certainly not from the great muralists. It seemed rather from Salvador Dali than from anything of the strictly Mexican school, but it showed to what lengths of madness modernity will go in a country that is newly free and passionately proud of its freedom, when custom

MODERNITY GONE MAD

says, "Let art be unconstrained." Some few of the offerings were sane enough, even simple and pretty, but most of them were weird and many were markedly erotic. Avoiding description of the wildest ones, which would hardly be printable anyway, I will mention two middle-of-the-road watercolors, neither more nor less daring than the general average.

One presented a strumpet in diaphanous costume, walking under her umbrella through a rainstorm. To keep her "merchandise" untouched by the pelting rain, she had removed her breasts from her blouse and was somehow holding them above her head, just under the protecting dome of the umbrella. The other picture showed a figure that cannot be clearly described in words. It started as a female nude, brandishing a murderous revolver, but the head was that of a fierce male peon, heavily bearded, and the whole affair was part of a horse whose head was straining forward in wild fright, its teeth showing horribly. One can, if in a mood of broad humor, see a certain pungent wit in the first picture, but the second seems art from the lunatic fringe. Perhaps the usual revolutionary theme of the peon's fight for justice was intended but the picture turned out to be merely a crazy "gynandrohip," a Mexican Houyhnhnm gone berserk.

CHAPTER 10

METROPOLITAN FUN

"See You at Sanborn's"

You do not actually need to *say* the words above. Merely enter one of the big Sanborn's restaurants, perhaps that downtown emporium-of-everything, the old, original Sanborn's, at about five o'clock and you *will* see him or her. Sanborn's is all things to all tourists and, likewise, to an increasing number of wellborn Mexicans. The original establishment is now supplemented by six highly successful branches: in the arcade beneath Hotel del Prado, at the corner of Paseo de la Reforma (Number 45) and Calle Lafragua in the building that houses the U. S. Consulate; at Salamanca 74; at Niza and Hamburgo, near the Geneve Hotel; at Insurgentes 421 and alongside the María Isabel Hotel. The restaurants at Reforma 45 and at the del Prado never close.

It is the "Old Sanborn's" that presently concerns us and this, be assured, is quite as much a sight of the capital as it is a place to buy and to eat and drink, for it is housed in an ancient private *palacio* called *Casa de Azulejos*, or House of Tiles, built of blue and white majolica. You'll find it at Madero 4, only a stone's toss from the Palace of Fine Arts.

As a building, quite regardless of its uses, it is famous, and the story of it, no more apocryphal than most popular tales, is a part of the story of Mexico. Briefly, the casa appears to have been built (but not of tiles) by a wealthy colonial nobleman, about the year 1600. His son did much to develop trade with the Orient and won from the Spanish king a resounding title—Count of the Valley of Orizaba. At that point the family stock ran low, for the count in turn had a son, Don Luis, who grew up as a restless spendthrift, never sticking to any task that was given him. "*You'll* never build a house of tiles," the count taunted him, which is as if an American father of today were to say to his son, "*You'll* never cut any ice in the business world." The taunt stuck and Don Luis, acquiring the ancestral house in the course of time, did build a house of tiles, or rather he rebuilt the ancestral house, covering it with the beautiful blue and white tiles of Puebla that have been admired by all visitors to this city for the past 300 years. It became, in 1890, the property of the severely exclusive and aristocratic Jockey Club, which used it as headquarters for about two decades until its antithesis, the Revolution of the People, took it over in 1910 as the "House of the Workers of the World." Then, after a short time, it became Sanborn's, when two able and energetic American brothers of that name bought it and developed the establishment we see.

Sanborn's sells almost everything under heaven that a tourist could wish to buy—silver articles, perfumes, leatherware, straw baskets, sarapes, antiques, drugs, novelties, postcards, and so on and on; and its restaurant-tearoom, located in the former patio of the palace, now glassed over, is a most alluring rendezvous.

Cheerful is the word for Sanborn's. The waitresses wear Mexican costumes as in the Monterrey branch of the house, the blouse being orange, yellow, red or green, the skirt being striped and long, the cap or coif being a gay "runner" pinned to the hair and hanging down the back. The babel of talk and laughter in the thronged room is incessant from eight in the morning, when it opens, until nine-thirty in the evening, when it closes. The "chocolate doughnuts" that one may purchase with coffee, tea or chocolate, make a pleasant accompaniment for gossip, for earnest argument, or even for a bit of business, in the manner of Vienna's bright cafés. Sanborn's is the downtown center of the metropolis, a center of relaxation for many travelers who book in the hotels of this area, abetted by the newer Sanborn's on the Reforma. Almost everything in the downtown portion of the city is mentioned in relation to this nucleus. "You know Sanborn's, of course [identifying the one meant]. Well, starting from there—"

Eating Around the Capital

Mexico City is definitely interesting to gourmets. In all Latin America it is second, in this respect, if even this exception is now valid, only to Buenos Aires, though it may not equal Buenos Aires in beef dinners and neither city, taken as a whole, is within gunshot of the widespread excellence of Paris. Epecurean émigrés from Paris would find few places in Mexico's capital to remind them of the *best* Parisian fare, but the food is excellent in some establishments and good in many. Meats are abundant and of tasteful, though not of Argentine quality; fowl, especially chicken and turkey, will be found everywhere; and there is an ample variety of vegetables and an amazing array of fruits. The raw materials of good eating are lavishly maintained in establishments patronized by travelers, but the cooking may sometimes be uninspired. In the capital's restaurants the variety of decor, and that indefinable something that makes "atmosphere," as against pretense, is outstanding and it is fair to say that many places serving indifferent food do have special character or special patronage to add interest and offset culinary lacks. In all this we are, of course, considering *international* establishments and food, Mexico's broad heritage from Europe, tinctured by the natural desire to appease American tastes. There are two distinct "philosophies of food" throughout the country, Spanish-Mexican and Indian-Mexican. The Indian-Mexican restaurants and their offerings will be mentioned later.

Americans, unless they are of the most fashionable late-dining set, find meal hours in Mexico a bit awkward. The "noon" meal is ordinarily between two and three-thirty (though the government's startling edict reducing the siesta period from three hours to one hour partly Americanized the capital's eating habits). The evening meal (but not at Sanborn's and other American-type places) begins at nine or nine-thirty. If you enter a fashionable restaurant at eight-thirty you may be almost alone in it.

Sanborn's, in the House of Tiles, is a convenient starting point for most *downtown* gastronomical explorers, since it is the first place outside of the hotel restaurant that anyone is sure to find, but I should emphasize that *uptown* restaurants, meaning separate restaurants and not the dining rooms of the big hotels, have of late years completely eclipsed the older ones downtown. Following the pattern set in describing hotels, I will present the downtown eating places first.

I hope I shall not be hailed as a heretic before some inquisitorial tribunal if I state that I personally find Sanborn's food rather mediocre except for the good breakfast fare. I go there—and very often—because I love the animation of the place. I think it is the most attractive center of sociability in the whole of Latin America; and its breakfasts are inspired. A costumed waitress brings the morning paper (upon request) and life becomes instantly very pleasant. The coffee is outstandingly good and the ham and eggs, hot cakes, toast and marmalade wonderfully homelike. The patio-under-glass radiates pleasant life and hums with conversation, even if you have "helped open it" at the crack of dawn. The noon and evening menus provide a *plato del día* (plate dinner), a *comida corrida* (table d'hôte dinner) and various items à la carte, both international and Indian. The prices are moderate.

Now let's emerge from Sanborn's and review other eating-out possibilities in alphabetical order.

First, though, I urge you: try Indian-Mexican food. If you have ever dined at La Fonda Del Sol in New York City, or Señor Pico in San Francisco, you already know, of course, that it is delicious. For those of you not so acquainted with Mexican food, try any sort of tortilla as a starter, since this has been the Indians' staff of life for some 6000 years. It is a pancake made of corn that has submitted to a thorough soaking in limewater (hence the gleaming white teeth of all Indians) and has then been ground into a paste and slapped to the proper thinness. A *taco* is a tortilla "roll" filled with chopped meat or fowl, or maybe cheese, and then fried; an *enchilada* is a taco drowned in chili sauce and other hot condiments and sprinkled with grated cheese; a *quesadilla* (which is the street-stand "hamburger" of Mexico) is a tortilla filled with the same items as the taco, or maybe with pumpkin seeds, and then deftly formed into a sort of turnover, which is fried in lard. The *tamal* (tamale) is a tortilla rolled around meat or nuts and raisins and then placed in cornhusks to be steamed for hours. *Chile con carne* is not a Mexican dish at all but a Texan imported into Mexico to provide something that Americans will think of as "typically Mexican." The *tortilla tostada* of the Café-Restaurant Tacuba won my personal blue ribbon. It is a flat, toasted-and-fried affair lavishly covered with chicken and beans and a spicy salad.

Beans (*frijoles*) are as basically Indian as tortillas and one encounters them in a variety of forms, but oftenest as a brown-mauve paste that looks but does not taste like chestnut paste. Rice (*arroz*), boiled and then fried, generally accompanies the beans.

A special dainty that rouses the curiosity of bold tourists is the *gusano de maguey*, which is a slug, white in color, that has fed himself fat on hearts of cactus. A slug is closely related to a snail, which is, after all, a mollusk that carries his house on his back. Any dictionary will tell you that. So a Mexican gusano may properly be considered as highbrow as his cousin, Escargot de Bourgogne.

More substantial dishes than the above are equally exciting but cause no shuddering. Two need special stress, for they may be had in any large restaurant that prepares food in the native style. They are *Mole de Guajolote* and *Huachinango à la Veracruzana*. Mole is a truly delectable curry sauce, generally dark brown in color and composed of pumpkin seed, chili, chocolate and 16 varieties of spices. Always one is told that the spices must number *sixteen*, so I suppose it would be ruined if there were 15 or 17.

Anyway, it is delicious and as served on a base of guajolote it is the national dish of Mexico. It has been so since Moctezuma served it to his guest, Cortés. Guajolote is traditionally, though not necessarily, turkey (*pavo* is the common word for turkey), and the bird is amazingly catholic in appeal, for emperors have loved it yet it is definitely the meat of the commoner. "After all, a turkey is only a glorified buzzard," explained a Mexican friend of mine. Mole de Guajolote, whatever its lineage or social quality, is a delicious dish; and if you see on any Mexican menu any dish with the word mole in it (as *Mole Poblana*, which is mole in the style of Puebla) order it and be rewarded.

Huachinango à la Veracruzana is a fish classic quite the equal of the fowl classic that has aroused my lyric outburst. It is red snapper sautéed with olives, pimientos and, of course, a collection —perhaps less than 16—of warm-to-hot spices. This, though, is rather more Spanish-colonial than Indian.

Pescado blanco is another wondrous delicacy, but you may have to wait for a sample of it until you reach the shores of Lake Pátzcuaro or Lake Chapala, for this "whitefish"—and it is actually translucent and almost transparent—is an exceedingly delicate creature and can be transported only with difficulty. A popular story relates that President Díaz once sent a tankful of live pescados blancos to Edward VII and the king liked them so very much, and said so, that the Mexican dictator felt obliged to send him a fresh tankful each year. It was so extraordinarily difficult to achieve this with success that it caused something like an annual crisis in Mexican foreign policy, but perhaps it did at least offer a practical and interesting problem to the dictator's Científicos. I did not blame King Edward when I sampled this fish, so marvelously dainty and esculent, in the restaurant of the *Posada de Don Vasco* of Pátzcuaro village. I wish for you the same treat.

Fruits beyond numbering and naming enhance any Indian feast of Mexico. *Aguacate*, a black-skinned variety of avocado pear, is one of the most delicious. This is sometimes called a vegetable but it does, after all, grow on a tree. *Papaya*, with its orange-yellow lusciousness, is familiar to all who have been anywhere in the tropics. To the cool plateau of Mexico it is brought from the hot south or the *tierra caliente* of the coastal belts. *Guayaba* (guava) is less esteemed for itself, eaten raw, than for the wonderful paste, called *guayabate*, that is made from it. Guayabate is a sweet staple of many Latin-American lands, including Mexico, and of course guava jellies and jams are familiar in the States. *Zapote*, of the dark variety (there are several others), is a special fruit for which I have developed a particular weakness. Its skin is green, its pulp an alluring "dark pink," the flavor is indescribable, so I will not describe it, except to say that it is slightly on the sweet side. And, finally, since this is the land of cactus, keep on the watch for two cactus fruits (which, however, you may not like) called *tuna* and *pitahaya*. The tuna, which is cool and pleasant when the prickly coat has been peeled off, is from that branch of the cactus family (*nopal*) on which the eagle was standing as he devoured the serpent.

Candies of kinds hardly known to most Americans are common in Mexico. *Biznaga* is the most typically Mexican and, therefore, the most favored. It is candied cactus, pale green-white in appearance and delectable. San Antonio and other Texas cities now offer it to delighted tourists on their way to Mexico. Candied yam (*camote*) and candied pumpkin (*calabazate*) are also popular; and various fruit pastes, mostly coming from the Morelia region, are as full of allure as of flavor.

The adventure of eating in Indian Mexico offers great attraction to the untimid visitor. With a little meal-to-meal advice from one who knows his gastronomical way, it can be vastly enjoyed and the palate need not be scorched to a crisp.

Now to names:

Ambassadeurs, located at the beginning of the Paseo (Number 12) and hence on the edge of downtown, would be willing, I think, to confess itself the best restaurant in Mexico, and the claim would find many to support it. Of French influence, quietly perfect and sure of itself, this restaurant would be deluxe

EATING AROUND THE CAPITAL

in any city in the world, including Paris.

Angelo's (Florencia 39) is a restaurant to aim for if you like Italian food, especially ravioli, done to the *commendatore's* taste. *Restaurant Austria* (Insurgentes 1162) specializes in Viennese fare.

For *American food*, Sanborn's seven places are "axiomatic," though its offerings are by no means *solely* American. So is the *Pam-Pam* place in the del Prado arcade. *Hotel Bamer's* two restaurants feature first-class American fare, and the coffee shops of various hotels can also give you almost anything American. At the *Reforma's* counter I've enjoyed *Pollo en Canasta*, which is not a card game but Chicken-in-the-Basket. The *American Club*, at Plaza Santos Degollado 10, is as American as it sounds, and so is its restaurant, which you may enter freely even without a member's note of introduction.

Bellinghausen (Londres 95) is *echt Deutsch*, simple and inexpensive. It has had a good bourgeois charm for more than two decades.

Czardas (Atoyac 93, close to the Paseo) offers gypsy music to go with its beef Stroganoff and Hungarian goulash.

Cardini's, at Madrid 21-A, behind the Hotel Reforma, is a spaghetti house.

Chipp's, at Calle Genève 59, opposite Hotel Monte Cassino, doesn't derive its inspiration from any special race but serves first-rate international food. Its lighting is dim but not religious, its atmosphere rather elegant. Chipp's is more popular for dinner than for lunch.

Caballo Bayo (Bay Horse), out near the racetrack, is a good place for Mexican food. Incidentally, I may mention here that race fans will find a good general restaurant at the racetrack itself.

Chalet Suizo, at Niza 37, seems as genuinely Swiss as Grindelwald or Kandersteg. Portions are very generous.

Café Tacuba, at Calle Tacuba 28, is the capital's great temple of Mexican-Indian food. It is also, rather paradoxically, a shrine of Spanish-colonial culture, with somewhat self-conscious Mozarabic architecture and all the properties suitable to a Spanish-court dining room of the time of Columbus. One of its rooms is like an old sacristy and another resembles a chapel. The latter is called Salón de la Virgen and has an aristocratic-ecclesiastical touch in a painting of the *Virgen de los Remedios*. The establishment's other paintings include two of special interest, being portraits of Borda, the 18th-century silver king of Taxco, and Sor Juana Inés de la Cruz, the fabulous nun-poetess.

Casa de Virrey (House of the Viceroy), in a colonial mansion on Calle Revillagigedo, very near Hotel Alffer, is in part a garden restaurant. It specializes in beef and lamb dishes in the style of Argentina.

Circulo Sureste, at the corner of Calles Bucareli and Lucerna, in an untouristy sector, is a humble-looking place that specializes in well-prepared Yucatecan food, starting traditionally with *Tacos de Cochinita Pibbil* (suckling pork in a taco, or tortilla, with a spicy sauce) and concluding with *Merengue Yucateco*, a very sweet pastry affair. A main-course favorite here is *Calamares en su Tinto*, being squid-in-its-ink, with rice.

Circulo Vasco (Basque Circle), authentically Spanish and not concerned with looking so to tourists, is on the third floor of Avenida Madero 6, adjacent to Sanborn's.

Coffee shops abound in Mexico City, not only places like Sanborn's chain of them, and the lively *Pam-Pam*, in the del Prado arcade, but in many of the leading hotels. A good and spacious downtown one is that of *Hotel Alffer*. Deluxe, in every way, is the *Restaurant del Lago* in Chapultepec Park. Located beside a lake, as its name implies, it is glamorized nightly by illuminated fountains.

Delmonico's, at Londres 87, specializing in American food, lives up, in commendable degree, to its famous borrowed name, for it is one of the city's very best eating places, locally famous for its broiled steaks. Often indulging an exhibitionist mood it is ready to serve skewered meats aflame from a brandished sword,

EATING AROUND THE CAPITAL

but this trick is too well known nowadays to cause much excitement. Delmonico's fashionable bar-lounge has brought it more than local fame, for it features flaming, sparkling and smoking beverages—one, named Paricutín for Mexico's volcano, has a sparkler inserted in it—but the pièce de résistance is its marvelous dry martini. In the preparation of this cocktail, frozen (not merely ice-cold) glasses are used and the Noilly Prat is injected with an atomizer!

The *Derby* (Reforma 400) is still another luxury place, but with a special pink-coat atmosphere in its decorations and in the costumes of its doorman and waiters that appeals to the international horsey set. Its walls are done in an interesting black-and-white Derby motif.

Restaurant El Paseo, not to be confused with the hotel of the same name, is on Paseo de la Reforma, a block from the Hilton as you go toward town. It makes merry in the evening with a piano bar. A specialty of the house is *Fondue Bourguignonne*, a delicacy long known in Europe and now, more and more, invading the Americas. The guest "dips his own" steak tidbits into a pot of near-boiling fat.

El Refugio, at Liverpool 166, is tiny and unpretentious to look at, but is one of the best for authentic Mexican food. It is located in the fashionable Genève district, a block behind the Genève Hotel.

Flor de Lis (Spanish for Fleur de Lis), at Calle Huichapan 21, is a Mexican *merendero* (lunchroom) owned by a tamale factory, which also does a big catering business. Needless to say, its tamales are about the best to be had.

César Balsa, named in an earlier chapter as the president of a great hotel chain, came up the ladder on rungs of virtuosity by serving fine food, and one of the best and most interesting restaurants in the capital, not to mention an outstanding supper club, is his. The *Focolare*, Hamburgo 87, is his enormously successful restaurant in which a fleet of violinists maneuvers all over the place rendering, but not rending, good music of many nations.

The atmosphere of the place is gardenish, with lily ponds and vines here and there, and stairways designed as much for beauty as for use. The food, broadly European but with a little extra emphasis on Italian dishes, is absolutely tops and the prices are up aloft, too, though they're not a whit too high for what is offered.

Gitanerías, at Calle Oaxaca 16, makes the evening lively with *Spanish* music. A *purrón* of wine is the feature here, the Spanish word meaning a sort of beaker, with a spout. It may take a bit of practice to manage a purrón.

If, some day, you're in an exploratory mood, wandering about the ancient quarter centered by the Zócalo, give thought to the unpretentious but good *Hostería de Santo Domingo* (Mexican and general menu), on Calle Belisario Domínguez, near the Santo Domingo Church. Two thin dollars will buy a satisfying meal here.

Jena, at 110 Calle Morelos, corner of the Paseo, only a little beyond the Ambassadeurs, is as good as the best, or very close to it. This is the restaurant that caters Eastern Airlines' "Famous Restaurant" flights from Mexico City. A luxury place, it charges accordingly. Its tablecloths display a map of Napoleon's victory at Jena, but the management claims German ("really Austrian") leanings. Pronounce the restaurant "Hay-na" and you will be understood. Fine European fare is featured here. Duck with orange sauce is one of the specialties.

Konditori, at Génova 61, brings Copenhagen to your table, especially with its well-made Danish pastries.

There are numerous "La whatnot" restaurants in the capital.

La Fonda del Refugio, on Calle Liverpool between Florencia and Amberes, is a very good place for *Mexican* food.

La Góndola, at Calle Genève 10, suits its fare to its Venetian name by specializing in excellent *Italian* food.

La Jacaranda, at Génova 44, is a supper club named for a jacaranda tree at one end of the establishment, with a multitude of brilliant sea-blue blossoms. At the other end, in a small and lovely garden seen through a plate-glass wall, there is a "dancing waters" affair similar in artistic effect, though of smaller dimensions, to the dancing waters in certain German cities such as Hamburg and Berlin. The waters, illumined with various colors from hidden lights, dance in rhythm to the music of an orchestra, and only the determined iconoclast could fail to find the effect magical. La Jacaranda offers no floor show, but it has two orchestras that are first-rate and absolutely tireless. The music never stops, from midevening to early dawn. Lights are extremely dim and I am reminded of a Tokyo dance hall that advertises "Our policy is to keep the lights so low that patrons literally have to *feel* their way around."

La Lorraine, at San Luis Potosí 132, is a newish place in an old town house, proud of its fine French wines. The onion soup and homemade pâté are magnificent here.

La Cava, at Insurgentes 137, is called by some "as good as Ambassadeurs," but it asks a lot less money.

Every visitor who eats around, sampling a good many of the capital's fine restaurants, has his own personal favorite that he's ready to defend with conviction, so I, as a part of everybody, will assert that my favorite, regardless of location uptown or downtown, is *La Ronda*, located at Calle Génova 39. I'm even ready to court argument by stating that I think it the absolute equal, in quality of cooking and serving, of the very best three-star restaurants of Paris—but with this difference: Of the Parisian temples of gastronomy the omniscient *Michelin* says, with truth, "Here price has no meaning," but in such a Mexican shrine of fine food as La Ronda, you should do all right for five or six dollars, not ten or fifteen, as in Paris today, or New York, for that matter. On soups—try the mushroom soup with many slices of mushrooms in it—salads, meats, seafood and desserts, this place seems to me flawless, as now operated by its skilled restaurateur, Mario Polidori. And its decorations, highly original but not bizarre, were done by Elena Alvarez Murphy, who has already been mentioned in connection with the city's fabulous new markets. Many people consider this lady Mexico's finest and most imaginative artist in interior decoration.

Lady Baltimore, across the way from the original Sanborn's, is a crowded American-Mexican stronghold, where light meals and light chat are enjoyed.

Loredo, at Hamburgo 29, advertises that here "the riches of the sea are converted to a delight for your taste." Well—they really are.

Luaú, at Calle Niza 38, is a genuine Chinese restaurant, small but good, specializing in Cantonese dishes.

Manolo's, at Calle López 1, just off Juárez, despite its Italian sound, is of the world worldly. It is quite as much at home in French, Spanish and American food as in Italian.

Mauna Loa, at the corner of Calles Hamburgo and Florencia, very near Hotel El Presidente, is owned by an American resident, Nicholas Noyes, and managed by another American, H. Lindsay (Lin) Gatty, a son of the late famous flier Harold Gatty, who flew around the world with Wiley Post way back in 1931. The restaurant is a 250-seat showplace featuring Polynesian (*including* Hawaiian) motifs, drinks and soft music, and offering American, international and Cantonese cuisine. Its decorative gimmicks are a great array of Polynesiana and other items from "all over." You'll see a little grass hut, a big waterwheel, some outsized gods and goblins, some Japanese floats and a shallow pool in which three pink flamingos stalk pensively about. Oh, yes, there's even an Australian wallaby hopping around in a little garden outside. You may think this array too "busy," but don't let it fool you into thinking the place is a tourist trap or the food merely showy. It is considered by many as good as the absolute best and the restaurant's popularity, ever since its opening in 1958, has been immense. The problem is not a question of the quality of the cuisine but of finding a table so you and those with you can partake of it. Approximately 80 per cent of the patronage is Mexican society folk and they are mighty particular about their food. If you want a charcoal-broiled steak or a lobster thermidor, you can have it, or if you're brave enough to order such Chinese classics as bird's-nest soup and hundred-year-old eggs, you can certainly have these—I did, and got a great kick out of the exotic delicacies—but if you're in a more "celestial conservative" mood, you'll find a great list of Cantonese specialties. Important to many a guest is Mauna Loa's entirely stainless-steel kitchen, to which everybody is invited for inspection.

Probably the most exciting restaurant in Mexico City *for location* is the aforementioned (Chapter 7) *Muralto*, on the 41st floor of the 42-story Torre Latino Americana. It is deluxe and very expensive, but the magnificent view to the four corners of the metropolis and far beyond to the mountains, including Popocatépetl and Ixtaccíhuatl, would warrant still higher prices. There is a bar here too, and on the 42nd floor there is the famous "observation deck."

Normandia, at Calle López 15, only a slingshot from the Fine Arts Palace, is an authentic bit of France in Mexico, serving dependably delicious Gallic food and fine wines.

Among newer *French* restaurants is the *Normandie*, at Calle Niza 5 and Paseo de la Reforma. This is under the same ownership as the Normandia, which chooses to spell its name in the Spanish way. The Normandie, one flight up from the street, has a splendid view of one of the Paseo's landscaped glorietas. Its food is definitely French, but of its two hard-working orchestras, supplying music for dancing till four o'clock in the morning, one is French, the other Mexican.

Ostionerías (oyster bars) are numerous in Mexico City and they offer their natural specialty, *Ostiones Cóctel*, at amazingly low prices, about 20 cents, even in presentable and cheerful places. One of the best ostionerías in the city is just where you would expect to find it, adjoining the Senate Building, and it boasts of securing its oysters from Guaymas, which has been for centuries a celebrated source of bivalves. This oyster palace is across the street from the National Telegraph Office, just north of Calle Tacuba. The name of the street—take a deep breath—is Calle Santiago Felipe Xicotencatl. And right here I might mention that when you order oysters on the half shell, in good Mexican restaurants, you ordinarily receive a *full dozen* of them, not a stingy six, as so often in the U.S. and other lands.

Passy, at Amberes 10, just off the Reforma, is a restaurant partly open to the sky, very homey and attractive, with an *intime* atmosphere in its side rooms. It is French.

Parador, at Niza 17, calls itself "a corner of Spain in Mexico." It is only a few steps from the Benjamin Franklin Library (see Chapter 6), and usually there's a cozy fire burning.

Restaurant Périgord, at Avenida Yucatán 33, back of Hotel Roosevelt (on Insurgentes), serves fine Gallic specialties in two or three simple upstairs rooms. (I recall its wonderful Burgundy snails and then its *coq au vin*, with imported French *vin rosé*.)

Prendes, at Calle 16 de Septiembre 10, is a bare place without any smartness of style whatever. It has, in fact, only one thing to offer, namely *food*. To Prendes I have often returned for that very thing. So many others go there on the same quest—first families of Mexico, old residents (of all nationalities), tourists who have been "told" that it has not always been easy to find a table, but the opening of many new restaurants uptown has lately cut in very noticeably even to Prendes' trade. Seafood built the reputation of this place, yet just now—today—I enjoyed here a steak the equal of any I have had in Mexico. It was the *Beefsteak Especial Prendes* and the fact that it cost me not very much more than a dollar detracted nothing, I suppose, from my enjoyment of it. Somehow, this place keeps its prices much lower than other quality establishments. It asks at least a third less than the "confessed" leaders. Prendes is very popular with men, but many women go there, too. Beer may be had on draft, and the word for a big bumper is *tarro*. This plain house of good food is easy to find on the street that parallels Avenida Madero, one lift south.

Quid, at Puebla 154, is a master-restaurant for charcoal-broiled steaks and lots else. Soft music fills the air till two A.M.

The *Rivoli*, at Hamburgo 123, next to El Presidente Hotel, is *very* expensive and *very* good, two of its mouth-watering specialties being *Chicken Chichén-Itzá*, baked in a big banana leaf and smothered in herbs of Yucatán, and, for dessert, genuine *Sachertorte*, a famous chocolate cake of Vienna.

Rincón de Goya, at Toledo 4, regales its guests with Spanish music and dancing, and, of course, Spanish food.

The three *Santa Anita* restaurants are all recommendable for Mexican food. They are located at Avenida Insurgentes 1089 (just beyond the bullring), downtown at Calle Humboldt 48, and at Mariano Escobedo 716.

Tibet Hamz is a conspicuous Chinese restaurant at Juárez 64, opposite the Alameda. Actually, it serves international as well as Chinese food and in addition to its regular tables it has a long counter section for quick service. The waitresses wear pink Hong Kong dresses with a very modest split.

Viena (or *Vienna*), not far from Hotel El Presidente, is tops for *Wiener Schnitzel*, goulash and other Austrian dishes, as well as for luscious (and fattening) Viennese pastries, often topped by *Schlagobers*, which means whipped cream.

Villa Fontana, at Reforma 240, is a very European restaurant, enlivened every evening by "violin strollers" who wander about the place as they play. This place is rather more popular for preprandial drinks than for dining. Many make it the "first stop" on a long evening.

The Sign of the Tilting Glass

Mexico City is as gay, at least in the sense of the tilting glass, as any city in Latin America. Here, as Rivera's frescoes would say, "the empty and degenerate pleasures of the bourgeoisie" flourish mightily.

Tourist drinks in Mexico are international rather than of-the-country, with the single exception of *tequila*, which is passably popular but so very inexpensive that sporty spenders are ashamed to order it. "It is done," however, in the city of Guadalajara, near which the drink is made, and in Taxco, where a famous tequila cocktail called the "Bertha" is an established feature of life. The most popular tequila drink, however, is the "Margarita," served in a salt-rimmed glass and made with Tequila Sauza. Tequila is made from a form of maguey (century plant), which is not in the strictest sense a cactus but is always so considered. The fleshy lower leaves are roasted, crushed and then left in large casks to ferment. The juice is distilled later by a complicated process. The liquor, as ultimately refined, has a taste that is all its own but which some consider to resemble Bourbon. The Bertha, made with lime juice and honey, looks like a Tom Collins but tastes remarkably like a Daiquiri. The analogy is interesting in more ways than one, for if Cuba has made a lady out of rum, certainly Mexico has made a lady out of maguey juice. It is safe to say that if tequila were to cost six dollars a fifth in Mexico, as it does in New York, and if a Bertha were to cost a dollar instead of 25 cents (or maybe 50 cents in smart bars), it would be ordered a great deal oftener by tourists. No one who stands treat wishes to be thought "Scotch" and therefore it is quite impossible to order a round of drinks that cost only 25 to 40 cents apiece. The solution is to buy tequila in New York, where it is exotic and costs enough, and to buy imported gin and *uiski* in Mexico, where, similarly, it costs plenty.

The distilled *mezcal* and the fermented *pulque*, both made from types of maguey, are hardly for tourist palates or stomachs, though millions of Indians take passionate pleasure in them. Mezcal, like tequila, is colorless and it is perhaps even more potent. Oaxaca is the center of its manufacture and consumption. If you try it there or elsewhere, be sure to drink it in the accepted fashion, which is also the way to drink straight tequila. First, you shake on the back of your left hand (assuming the right to be your drinking hand) a dash of "salt," which is actually made from maguey slugs with a bit of chili. Toss off the fiery drink at one gulp, as if it were Swedish *aquavit*. Then suck a bit of lime, which is invariably served with tequila, and hurl the slug salt nonchalantly from the back of your hand onto your tongue.

As for pulque, the peon's "likker," it is simply too raw for Americans, except as a bold experiment. Fresh pulque, not thoroughly fermented, is the liquid called *aguamiel* (honey-water), the common drink of rural Indians. As finally fermented and served in city bars—and pulque may be sampled *only* in lowbrow *pulquerías*, not in regular bars—it is a murky and, to most Americans, a rank and offensive liquor. One drinks it for no other reason than to be able to say one has done so.

Bars in the metropolis of Mexico are more numerous, if possible, than are restaurants. Those of the chief hotels, both downtown and uptown, especially such dim (un)religious dens of social and amorous tippling as the *Montenegro Bar* in the del Prado, supplementing the same hotel's *Cantina Nicté-Há*, are unfailingly popular. Others in the front rank of popularity are the old *Ritz Bar*, with the satirical fresco by Covarrubias; the *Indra Bar* of the Alffer; the *Bamer Bar* of the Bamer; the *Jardin Bar* of the Reforma; the *Mayan Bar* of the Continental Hilton; the superlative *Zafiro Bar* of the El Presidente; and the *Jorongo Bar* at the María Isabel.

One may offer a note of comfort to those who, from principle or from health considerations, desire to avoid strongly alcoholic drinks and yet do not wish to miss all the fun. There is a mild, delicious and thoroughly Mexican beverage called *sangría*, being a mixture of claret and lemon juice. It "giveth color in the cup," yet it is not incandescent like the cactus drinks.

Mexican ladies of good family are still supposed to think of bars as they think of cigars—"for men only." You will read cautionary remarks to that effect in some guidebooks. But it is obvious that our American free-and-easiness has just about broken that taboo to smithereens in the capital and the chief tourist resorts. One now sees women in almost any first-class bar and not all of them are American tourists. Nor are they international adventuresses and diabolically clever spies.

Evenings in All Keys

Evening entertainment of the loftier sort centers largely in the magnificent Palace of Fine Arts. Here one may enjoy spectacles of every sort, ballet being a prime diversion. Music also centers here, ranging from that of the *Orquesta Sinfónica de México* to performances by ballet troupes and world-known soloists in every branch of musical art. Mexico scraped the bin of its national exchequer to provide this wonderful setting for the fine arts, and lucky are you and I to find the Palace ready for our patronage, always at very moderate cost.

Luxurious modern movie houses, frequently offering current Hollywood films, *which often talk English*, not Spanish as in Spain, are abundant in Mexico City, some of the leading ones being the plushy *Roble* and the *Chapultepec* on the Paseo; *Las Américas* (with the exterior mosaic murals by Rivera), well out on Insurgentes; and three older downtown places on Avenida Juárez named the *Regis* (specializing in foreign films), the *Alameda* and the *Variedades*. Major CinemaScope productions are usually shown at the *Diana* and the *Mavacar*.

Of the capital's legitimate theaters only the "vaudevillainous" *Iris* (Donceles 36), the *Lírico* (Avenida Cuba 48) and the higher-grade *Teatro Fábregas* (Donceles 24 A), which offers musicals and ballet, may attract Americans with little or no knowledge of Spanish. It is to be hoped that the Iris or the Lirico may announce that the world-famous Cantinflas is billed. This limp comedian, with a line of double-talk that invariably convulses Mexican audiences, has often been seen in the Iris. I saw him in a drunken sketch called *Posadas Cantinfleras* and despite the fact that his tricky talk flowed rapidly over my head, I thought him a true genius. The man has, to a marked degree, the gift that everyone recognizes and no one can define, personality.

The word *posada* (literally "inn") refers to a peculiarly Mexican custom, though it is seen in some other Latin lands, and if you are in Mexico just before Christmas you may likely experience it in one form or another to provide an evening not seen in its fullest flower elsewhere. On the nine nights preceding and including *Navidad*, which is "Nativity" (Christmas), Mexican families imitate the journey of the Holy Family from Nazareth to Bethlehem, by going to the house of a friend (and the next night to another friend, and the next night to another, and so on and on), knocking and asking for "lodging," which is always granted—by prearrangement—in the form of a party. In these modern times, in the fashionable capital, each "lodging" develops into a dance and a big time, but it includes a religious procession with candles —which is taken lightly as part of the festival. The climax is the breaking of the *piñata*, a large, flimsy, paper-covered contraption that is suspended from the ceiling. Various persons, blindfolded, take swings at it with a stick and at last someone hits it mightily, and a shower of candy, nuts and little presents of all sorts falls to the floor. Of course a grand scramble ensues and fun is had by all. If you do not participate in a posada of purely Mexican stamp you may at least enter into the somewhat synthetic version that is offered during the Christmas season at various nightclubs.

A "must" to take in is the *Mexican Folklore Center*, in the auditorium of the Vasco de Quiroga Hotel, at Londres 15. Shows are held Friday evenings at nine o'clock. Costumed folk dances of Mexico's various provinces, and also some terrific Aztec dances, keep the evening popping for a good two hours and the performance is both artistic and authentic. The elaborate costumes and fabulous headgear are handmade. For this quite overwhelming show the tickets cost, *at this writing*, but 12 pesos (96 cents). If you want a full dinner while watching the show it costs an inclusive 49 pesos ($3.92). How this remarkable entertainment can be staged for such returns is a mystery to me, but a highly pleasant one. It must be noted here that the Folklore Center is very popular and often every table is taken, even though the room seats 350 persons, together with a balcony, where meals are not served. You should, by all means, make advance reservations through any travel agency. For this service there is a cover charge of ten pesos per person, but that 80 cents *includes a drink*, hard or soft.

The Clubs of Midnight

Nightclubs in Mexico City have been more vulnerable, more sporadic, more "subject to change without notice" than those of any other large city I know and the fact is that, by and large, visitors do not come to this high-altitude metropolis to sit up late and watch floor shows.

Los Globos, at Avenida Insurgentes 810, is a nightspot specializing in Cuban dances and songs, and offering, at present, the city's biggest and most pretentious floor show. It has become so popular that advance reservations are almost essential. *La Bodega* is a Spanish wine cellar with gay Spanish show at Calle Abraham González 3, which is a short street connecting Calles Atenas and Lucerno, very near the Paseo.

The *Afro Club,* in a sort of annex of the Hotel Plaza Vista Hermosa, is active and well patronized. Of nonhotel nightclubs, the earlier mentioned *Jacaranda,* where very good dance music is offered but no floor show, flourishes steadily and impressively. *La Terraza,* far out on Insurgentes, is considered by some knowledgeable night prowlers to be as good as the best; and two others on the same long avenue, *La Fuente* and *Los Flamingos* have their followings. *El Eco,* on Calle Sullivan, is a jam *boîte.* Of the older nightclubs, the *Capri,* in the Hotel Regis, has shown remarkable durability and it is still very good. Another that has weathered the shifting winds of tourist patronage is the *Astoria,* at Nuevo León 16, which advertises its "aristocracy of atmosphere."

And that, I think, is quite enough to report on Mexico's conventional big-city night life. Other facets of the night that are anything but conventional will now have their turn on the midnight stage.

Explorers at Tenampa

The lower levels of night life ramify amazingly. I was advised by a knowing Mexican to take a taxi on some Saturday evening to *Tenampa* and see what I should see. So I murmured the magic name to a taxi driver and presently found myself in a lowbrow little square marked Plaza Garibaldi. The most conspicuous thing in the square was a small and dingy-bright café neon-labeled TENAMPA. In it were several groups of gaily costumed street musicians of the type always called *mariachis,* oddly from the

French word *mariage*, because originally they were players at wedding feasts. They were twanging their guitars and tossing off the last bumpers of beer preparatory to taking their talent out into the night. One such group, eagerly sniffing gratuities, came to my table and serenaded me with such a din that my ears rang. An artist in crayons rushed up and did a hasty caricature of me, peering at me the while in the manner of Paris café artists. The resultant masterpiece he generously thrust upon me, asking four pesos for it. I was too weak to refuse so I gave him the money and also the portrait.

Finding the Café Tenampa very far from fragrant, I presently withdrew and walked about to see the sights of the night. I found, for one thing, an exceedingly lively and not-bad nightspot called *Guadalajara Noche*, whose dance band was enhanced by a trumpet player of amazing virtuosity. Soon I had had my fill of the Guadalajara night and left the place, my ears still ringing with the din, to wander about the area and look in at several *carpas*, which are tent shows set up in the side streets. These are typical of popular life everywhere in Mexico. You enter the tent, pay 50 cantavos per act and watch the crudest, liveliest, most variegated show imaginable. Pulque tenors vie with impersonators and joke-smiths and all of them vie, rather unsuccessfully, with glorified girls who stamp the helpless stage and trot about as if they expected the audience to think of it as dancing. Miss Brenner had a word for the carpas. She called the shows "sincere," and they are just that. There is no question that every performer is in dead earnest about the whole thing; as artists they are doubtless very kind people, earning what they can for their needy dependents. I saw a lot of acts, so they earned about a quarter of a dollar from me.

Two other gay spots, assuming that they survive for a while, are *Mexico Tipico*, somewhat like the Guadalajara de Noche, and *Pigalle*, of Montmartre inspiration.

Mexico City, they say, has done away with the red-light district and certainly things are now almost totally closed up, so far as the "street strollers" go. There are still a few dance halls, but whatever the character and motives of the individuals in the motley throng the dancing appears to be quite unwicked. The grimy establishments, some with very fancy names, are densely packed with unwashed humanity having a good time. I could profitably have worn a gas mask. In one very pretentious "palace," with something like two acres of dance floor, a Mexican youth startled me by taking me under his wing—very kindly and impulsively, I must say—and going the rounds to find me a partner. He was not commercially minded, nor were the girls "on the make." In fact, his generous search proved unsuccessful. Every girl—and most of them were Toltecs or Aztecs—was already doing very well and needed no gringo caballero. Perhaps you will have better luck—or worse.

CHAPTER 11

SPORT AND SPEED

The Sunday Bullring

The bullfight, called *corrida de toros*, takes place at four o'clock on Sunday afternoons, meaning, amazingly, *on the dot of four*, and it is the event of the week to many thousands of Mexicans, the event of the trip to many tourists. The period from October until Lent is the high season, when the best bullfighters of two hemispheres are seen. Admission prices range from a minimum of 6 pesos to whatever tourists will pay. Reserved seats at 20 to 50 pesos are snapped up like special bargains and sometimes even the hotel porters can hardly secure for importunate guests seats at any price. There is an official ticket office on the street called Izázaga, leading east from San Juan de Letrán, and it is worth finding if your patience is quite inexhaustible, if your olfactory organs are hardy and if you would like to go to a lot of trouble to save considerable money. Here seats may be bought as unrich Mexicans buy them, by standing in a queue and working your way at the pace of a dying snail up to the ticket window. Sunny-side seats (*Sol*) may be as cheap as 6 pesos, shady side (*Sombra*) as cheap as ten pesos.

The urgent and unflagging demand (many a Mexican stenographer and shop girl annually invests her slender savings in a season ticket) seems to me one of the phenomena of life. Having seen in Spain enough bullfighting to satisfy me, I cared little whether I saw a *corrida* in Mexico; but once, at a few minutes before four on a big Sunday, I made my casual way to the bullring and was lucky in picking up from a scalper a rush ticket for the shady side at a mere 20 pesos. I was presently seated just as the first bull came thundering into the arena. I had paid about a third as much as most of my friends and my seat was perfectly placed so that I could see the whole show without too close a view of—blood. Granting that there was extraordinary luck in this, I proudly claim that there was also a modicum of calculation back of the luck. The Mexican aficionados, who go in multitudes to the bullring every Sunday, consider 20 pesos a lot of money. On the other hand, the tourists seem to consider 20 pesos extremely little for so superlative a spectacle, and the society Mexicans, who wish to be seen in the smart section if at all, avoid the rush seats, regardless of sun or shade, as if they were highly dangerous to health. So it often develops that the 12- to 20-peso Sombra seats are too dear for the multitude, too cheap for society and tourism. They happen to be just right for me, and possibly for you if you wish to try the "system," remembering that luck may not favor you.

I find it hard to be fair to bullfighting. I know that there is skill, high bravery, even genius in the performance of a first-rate fighter. It *is* thrilling to watch the fighter weave his supple body to right and left, scarcely moving his feet while a ton of animal savagery, keyed to kill, thunders past him a dozen times, the stiletto-sharp horns grazing his satin-clad thigh each time. It *is* thrilling to witness the frenzy of fifty thousand aficionados shouting their rhythmic *Olé! Olé!* like a monster metronome in time with the fighter's movements. But even so, I must confess that I do not like the sport. I am not a fan. The fact that it is a performance repeated six times at every corrida without perceptible differences (except to the student of the art) makes it boresome to many mere onlookers. And the fact that a dullwitted animal can "win" against a brilliant man only once in a thousand times makes it—to me—something less than a sporting proposition. Also, my heart aches for the poor old hacks that once were horses and become dead meat on Sunday afternoons, and for the bulls themselves when their turn comes to vomit blood and stumble down to death. I repeat that I am not fair to bullfighting and any true aficionado will rightly and hotly resent what I have just said. Also, he will think me stupid.

A curious bit of comic relief to this discussion is the word *toreador*. There is no such word in Spanish. Georges Bizet invented it for the opera, *Carmen*, because he happened to need a four-syllable word for the rhythm of the famous "Toreador Song." Americans took it up so naturally and insistently that it finally has begun to force its way into dictionaries.

If you have an urge to try bullfighting yourself, inquire about Western International Hotels' unique new restaurant, *Cortijo La Morena*. Located in the village of Texcoco, 25 miles from Mexico City, it is a bullring restaurant devoted to the idea that every man has a secret yen for at least one moment of truth. The management provides matador costumes and capes, and instruction in the art of the ring by a professional bullfighter. Then you—and the bull (a baby bull)—are turned loose in the small arena. For those who would rather watch than fight, the colorful restaurant has tables encircling the ring, and there is also entertainment by mariachi musicians and flamenco dancers. There is, happily, no bloodshed. All the baby bulls return to the corrals very much alive. La Morena, a replica of Mexico City's first bullring, also has an interesting bullfighter's museum.

The Lightning of Jai-Alai

The lightning of jai-alai (*pelota*) was, for several years, "heat lightning." The Cárdenas regime banned the game all over Mexico because gambling is an integral part of it, as of horse racing everywhere. The Avila Camacho regime retained the ban for a time, but in his middle-of-the-road fashion relaxed enforcement of it to some extent. Then came the Alemán regime, more to the right and far less dour than that of Cárdenas. The ban was lifted completely and *juego de pelota*, as it is known in Mexico, was wide open again and conspicuously advertised, even in the hotel

Bulletin. The chief *frontón*, or playing court, is called *Frontón México* and is located close to the Revolution Monument. (Incidentally, the official ticket office for the bullfights is back of this frontón, at the corner of Calles Ariga and Edison.) There are several frontónes where *girl* players hold forth. They use rackets instead of the classic wicker cestas, but don't assume that this makes it a mild or soft game. The señoritas are fast and furious and this feminine version of jai-alai is great fun to watch. One frontón specializing in girl players is the *Frontón Metropolitano*, rather far out in the western part of the city.

The game's origin seems obviously traceable to the Maya-Aztec game of *tlaxtli* or *tlaihiyotentli*, whose ancient ballcourts are such stimulating sights today in Chichén-Itzá, Copán and elsewhere; but there is also a Basque game that claims to be its parent, and most of the good players are actually of Basque origin. Perhaps the two old strains were united in wedlock to produce the modern jai-alai. The name means "always fiesta" or "always gay" in the Basque language and it is pronounced, for all practical purposes, like "high ally." The average evening's play consists of two *quinielas*, which are individual contests among six players in rotation, one of whom must win six points, and two *partidos*, or team games, like doubles in tennis. These team games are furiously fast as the blue pair (*azules*) is pitted against the red pair (*rojos*). The game consists of 25 or 30 points and it lifts you to your feet a hundred times to yell applause with the crowd.

Futbol *and* Beisbol

A surprising feature of Mexican sport in very recent years is the success of American football (in competition with ever-popular soccer) and baseball. As one of 7000 spectators I saw my first game of football in Mexico City 25 years ago, and was amazed by its speed and general excellence. The contestants were the University of Mexico and Politécnico, a college of the same metropolis, and the university's team was coached by an all-American, Bernard A. Hoban, of Dartmouth College. I was so interested in it that I managed to meet all the players and I later became well acquainted with some of them. In that initial period of the sport they were forced to cope with difficulties that would simply have stopped an American college team, used to high standards of equipment and plant, but they forgot all such lacks in the excitement of a fighting game whose spirit was as good as the best I ever saw. Almost all of them had odd and candid nicknames: *Franki* (for Frankenstein, because he was so ugly); *Changa* (Monkey, because he resembled one); *Manzanita* (Little Apple, because his face was round and red and shiny); *Ochi Chornya* (because he had some Russian blood); *Madame* (whose last name was Récamier); and *Flash*, a poor chap who was so slow that he had never quite made the first-string team though he tried hard every year.

The game ended in a 7-7 tie, the university team coming from behind to push the ball down the whole length of the field in the last three minutes of play. The crowd in the stands yelled itself hoarse and I honestly believe that those 7000 Mexicans thought they had had as exciting a Saturday afternoon as they could possibly hope for in the bullring the next day. Attendance at the big games is spectacular now. In the vast stadium at University City, and in the splendid Aztec Stadium built for the 1968 Olympic Games, up to 110,000 spectators avidly watch the big games, the biggest of all, as I have said, being the annual match between Mexico University, with its present enrollment of some 78,000 students, and its chief rival Politécnico. This development of an alien game in an eager "bullfight land" is one of the current phenomena of international sport. If you are in Mexico in the football season, which is roughly the same as ours, you will give yourself an outstanding treat by watching our great American game as borrowed by a Latin neighbor.

Baseball, now organized into a professional league affiliated with the American Athletic Association, is perhaps less popular than football, but it is gaining every year and the quality of the game is quite as astonishingly good as is the quality of football. I watched a big game (for four pesos admission to the best section; this was in Guadalajara) between the Patiño nine and the local Jalisco nine. It was good going every minute, and with the exception that the field was of dust instead of turf and that there was no fence over which a Mexican slugger could hope to knock the ball for a home run, it was startlingly like any good American game. These teams were of only minor standing but the playing seemed quite as good as that seen in the ball parks of our bush leagues. The umpire (*arbitro*) wore a blue serge suit and a cap twisted around backwards. Pop bottles were much in evidence and, of course, a few stronger bottles. There was a drunk (*boracho*) in the stands who made high comedy by insulting the umpire, by making numerous speeches and by giving affectionate *abrazos* (hugs) to every man around him.

The players, from *el pitcher* to *el filder*, used the American baseball terms, even to the numerals, as did the umpire. "Strah-eek one," he would bellow, and then "Strah-eek two"; and if the pitched ball was wide or low or high he would shout "Balla balla." If the batter made a third strike he would roar his official *Out*. But if he finally connected and made a long hit that enabled him to circle the bases the crowd (assuming it to have been a batter of the home team) would drown out any futile words of *el arbitro* with its own delirious shouting of *Jonrón! Jonrón!* That, you recognize, of course, as Home Run!

Hipódromo de las Américas

One of the least typical but most popular of sports attractions for the tourist is horse racing. It flourishes mightily in the Mexican capital as it does in Rio, in Buenos Aires and in Santiago. Races generally take place on two weekday afternoons (at present Thursdays and Saturdays) and on Sunday noons—in order to be over well before the bullring's demands at four o'clock. Tickets are, of course, on sale in the lobbies of the leading hotels and race talk fills the air on race days.

The track is rather far out in the fashionable perimeter of the city beyond the park of Chapultepec but it may be reached by the ordinary Paseo busses. Tourists who go to play the horses are, however, seldom so plebeian as to use them.

This track and its appurtenances make an ensemble of modern luxury, as one would expect, for the Jockey Club is its social temple and this remains the most exclusive club in Mexico as it has been since the Díaz decades when it occupied the Casa de los Azulejos. Mexican racing is managed by an official Racing Commission rather than by a national code and the august members of this commission meet in the august club. It is possible to lose a good deal of money (the stern shadow of Cárdenas vanished long ago) at the Hippodrome of the Americas, but it is possible also to see superb horseflesh in action and to enjoy, without much pecuniary damage, one of the gayest and liveliest scenes in Mexico.

CHAPTER 12

WONDERS OF THE CITY'S OUTER BELT

The Shrine of the Indian Madonna

THE church of the dusky Virgin of *Guadalupe* is a must on all tour programs because of the historic and romantic interest attached to her veneration. Our Lady of Guadalupe appeared on December 12, 1531, to an Indian named Juan Diego (John James) who stood on the hill called Tepeyac, a few miles outside Mexico City. Miraculously she left her likeness stamped on his *tilma* (mantle), a primitive garment of maguey fiber worn at that time over the shoulders and knotted in a manner quite different from the modern sarape. This tilma, with the miraculous image, is now guarded as a very sacred relic in the magnificent basilica that was erected two centuries later at the base of the hill. Originally, Our Lady of Guadalupe was of Iberian and rather aristocratic quality in old Spain, but her tender courtesy induced her to change her countenance and complexion. To Juan Diego, and to many millions of Indians since his day, she was an *Indian* Madonna, as any sacred portrait of her reveals. She was and is the national patroness of Mexico, for it was under her inspirational banner that Father Hidalgo rallied his ragged forces in 1810 for the War of Independence.

The suburb of the Mexican capital, where the miracle occurred and where the shrine now stands, came to be called Guadalupe Hidalgo and any American schoolboy will recognize this name, since it was given to the treaty by which our Mexican War came to an end in 1848. In Mexico's modern era the sacred suburb is officially and clumsily called Villa Gustavo Madero (he was the only revolutionary brother of Francisco), but the old name still lingers on in popular parlance.

The shrine of the Indians was long the most important pilgrim shrine in the Western Hemisphere and tremendous fiestas took place each year on December 12, but Mexico's more or less agnostic Revolution dampened these celebrations and it is doubtful if they will ever again reach the old proportions, though the fiesta has come back to some extent. On the eve of the Great Day, I once saw it, felt it, smelled it and it proved to be still—or again—quite overpowering, as it would be to any visitor from the States, unused to great hordes of primitive Indians. I saw one pious mestiza who was apparently kneeling her way—as many pilgrims formerly did—from the Zócalo to the basilica, a matter of *four long miles*. Her knees were horribly lacerated and bloody but she had at least half a mile yet to go. Indian watchers were continually throwing down garments in her path and I supposed it was from compassion, to soften the going. But no. I was informed that her knees were considered holy because of the torture inflicted on them and that any garment kneeled on by the pious woman would absorb holiness, along with a bit of blood, and would bring blessings to its owner.

The sights and smells in and around the great square before the basilica when I first saw it—but *not* now (see below)—were of savage and kaleidoscopic color. Hundreds and hundreds of little booths were set up and from at least half of them lurid eatables and drinkables were being sold. Numerous carpas were in full blast and I discovered that because of the Great Day and the crowds the admission price was doubled or trebled per act. I think I paid an entire dime for a single act in one tent. Its climax was a large and plushy *encantadora* who concluded each song by pulling a candy from her dimpled bosom and tossing it out into the audience. She danced, too, as a cow would dance, I thought, and the Indians loved it. They kept shouting something that sounded suspiciously like "Take it off, take it off," but she was only in a mildly teasing mood and took nothing off. In an adjoining tent I saw a *Gran Sensación: Fenómeno Humano: Pulpo Humano*. The poster outside had shown what *Pulpo* meant. It was an octopus; and the octopus had a human head, sure enough. The repulsive creature undulated in a glass tank and from its center emerged the head of an Indian girl. To entertain the audience the face smiled through the water and to add further to the general amazement the girl from time to time stuck out her tongue tauntingly. It was all a miracle in the eyes of the Indians, but not so great a miracle as Juan Diego's mantle, with the self-portrait of the Virgin painted on it.

This wonder, which is enshrined in the center of the basilica's high altar, is very real even to many devout Catholics of Mexico's more privileged classes. Highly educated persons have earnestly explained to me that the colors are obtainable from no known pigments and that it is utterly impossible for skeptical science to duplicate the luminous painting, especially the rays that the figure sends forth to right and left. And when efforts have been made to "touch up" the rays with fresh paint, the tilma has steadfastly "rejected" the paint.

The picture is six feet long by two feet wide and is displayed on festival days behind thick plate glass in a frame of solid gold. Beneath the venerated objects kneels Juan Diego himself, sculptured in marble, and near him Bishop Zumáraga, who finally came to believe in the Indian and his story. The basilica is a grand and grandiose affair, worth seeing purely as a spectacle of ecclesiastical construction. During the annual fiesta, when I was among those present, its nave was enlivened by the flags of the 21 Americas. After gazing at the traditional sights and flags for a time, I made my way out into bedlam, picking my path through many hundreds of Indians who were rolled up in their blankets and sleeping soundly on the stone floor just outside the portal. They were freshening up, I suppose, for bigger doings. The fireworks would start soon after midnight and would continue until dawn. There would be dancing in the square, too, hour after hour, and then more worship in the basilica. They would not even think of starting on their toilsome homeward way until evening of the next day.

I must, in fairness, report that in recent years the space in front of the basilica and around it has been amazingly cleared of the cluttered commercial incrustations of four centuries, and the edifice is now revealed as a dignified shrine. This change was a crying need, for Guadalupe is today unquestionably the most important pilgrim shrine in all of Catholic America. Now unencumbered, it is visible for several miles as one approaches it on the long, wide boulevard called Calzada de Guadalupe. In the immense plaza now fronting the big church there are 21 tall flagpoles that display, on fiesta days, the flags of the 21 Americas. There are also two large blocks of masonry on the plaza, their sides decorated with carved representations of the eight different primitive cultures that form the aboriginal cultural background of modern Mexico.

Floating through Xochimilco

The floating gardens of Xochimilco (here the *x* is pronounced *s*) no longer float, as they actually did in earlier times, being manmade rafts of earth-covered reeds. They have been anchored by the lovely poplar trees that rise from them. The glamour of this world-celebrated suburb of Mexico City is authentic, even when seen on Sunday, its fearfully overcrowded day. I may confess that I first visited the place in a strongly debunking mood, quite determined to be disappointed. A place talked about and written about and photographed so incessantly must, I thought, have become an unmitigated tourist trap, a tedious sort of false-Venice, dressed up with guitars and flowers. Never has a mood of mine been more promptly and thoroughly shattered by the impact of reality. Xochimilco *is* full of tourists and guitars and soft-drink vendors and sarape vendors. It overflows with them; but one simply does not care. Its soft loveliness is so genuine, its romance so imperturbable and sure of itself, that it could hardly be spoiled even by a resort promoter.

The name Xochimilco means Place of Flowers and in this place humble gardeners grew them for the grandees of Tenochtitlán. The flowers are still so abundant that they dominate the whole scene. Some millions of them are offered for sale each Sunday and if you invest six or seven pesos you may buy a marvelous corsage of gardenias or enough carnations to decorate two or three rooms. The boats that are lined up at the wharf to take you on a canal trip are outlined in flowers, and their names, such as *Lolita, Juanita* and *Viva El Amor*, are solidly wrought in flowers. Marimba bands float by and beside you and Latin music fills the air, along with floral fragrance. The drink vendors and flower girls talk Aztec to each other and the dim mystery of this speech is entrancing, but they will sell their wares in any language, including one that they suppose to be American.

A fascinating tour offering by the travel agencies is the combination of Xochimilco and the bullfight, offered every Sunday.

Pyramids Like Mountains

Mexico has at least six preconquest pyramids but by very far the largest is the Pyramid of the Sun at Teotihuacán, some 30 miles northeast of the capital. Its dimensions are exceedingly imposing, the nearly square base being 720 by 760 feet and the summit being 220 feet above the broad plain. In climbing it one is sharply reminded of the altitude of the plateau from which it rises, for one puffs like the well-known grampus, and this goes for youngsters as well as for not-so youngsters. Nearby, to the north, is a smaller Pyramid of the Moon, and in the opposite direction is *La Ciudadela* (Citadel), an amazing quadrangle of ancient masonry running a quarter of a mile in each direction and containing, among other treasures, a very remarkable Temple of Quetzalcoatl with numerous carved representations of the feathered serpent and of his symbol, the shell, so common also in Christian symbolism.

The vast structures of this whole *Zona Arqueológica*, as it is called, are all pre-Aztec. They are generally considered to be wholly or mostly Toltec, though some archeologists claim that at least the Sun Pyramid is very much more ancient than the Toltec era. Aside from the expert and intricate carvings, the outstanding interest of this Zone and of the lesser zone and pyramid of Tenayuca, nine miles north of the capital, lies in their revelation of the scientific attainments of the Toltecs. Their knowledge of structural "engineering" amazes all students of the epoch, and their knowledge of astronomical measurements, so precise that they could figure exactly when the sun's rays would touch any given point on any given day of the year, fairly baffles the mind. In some respects they were far ahead of their contemporaries in Europe.

A period of crisis, from the religious angle, recurred every 52 years (1143; 1195; 1247; 1299), when the high priest of Quetzalcoatl mounted the pyramid and watched the Pleiades pass the zenith. When this transit had been accomplished "in safety," a huge beacon was lighted on the top of the chief temple and this signal was picked up by watchers on various hills who lighted similar beacons. Thus the good news was quite literally "flashed" throughout the country that the favor of Quetzalcoatl could be expected for another 52 years.

The Mexican pyramids and their adjoining temples warrant unlimited study, since they are of unlimited importance in the picture of American antiquity; but every casual visitor, even if he has seen the larger pyramids of Egypt, finds them exciting. And the simplicity of seeing them, involving only an hour's drive, is not the least of their practical assets.

Half-day tours offered by the travel agencies combine the pyramids with Guadalupe.

Toluca Arts and Crafts

Toluca, Mexico's highest city (8760 feet), is not of special interest in itself (it is rapidly becoming one of the leading industrial cities of the republic), but it *is* of interest to shoppers and bargain-hunters, because of the little villages surrounding it, villages where half the humble homes are devoted to the making of bright basketry, sarapes, cross-stitch bags and all sorts of embroidered articles for table use and for personal adornment. These villages are half lost in extensive meadows and marshes, and it is not practicable to see them without an experienced guide or a personal friend who knows his way about. The spirit of the skilled workers, at least in former times when it was quite unsullied, is reflected by a tale that a craftsman named Pancho in the Santa Ana community told me. He said that the F. W. Woolworth Company once asked him to make or procure several thousand small straw mats of a type that would presumably sell fast in the States. Reluctantly he agreed to comply, but insisted that the price for so many would have to be higher rather than lower *per piece*. The dime store could not be made to appreciate the typically Indian psychology of this and the deal finally fell through. "I get so *bored*," said Pancho firmly, "if I do the same thing so many times!"

Those travelers who visit Toluca on their own rather than with a guide may reasonably satisfy their bargaining instincts by browsing in the city market, which is one of the liveliest in Mexico. Friday is the best day, the day when tours from Mexico City run out here, but any day will do. The Toluca market sprawls over several blocks, and consists of hundreds of stalls presided over by Indians from the surrounding countryside. Nowhere else in Mexico are you likely to see such a vast collection of hand-loomed sarapes and rebozos, pottery, baskets, jewelry and toys. You're expected to bargain here, and the easiest way, if your Spanish is none too fluent, is to point to an object and ask *Cuanto?* (How much?). The seller will say a price. You should suggest another. He will shake his head. You should shake *your* head, turn your back, and start to walk away. Automatically, almost, the vendor will lower his price. Smile. Shake your head again. He will continue to lower the price. Be firm! Buy only when it's obvious he will go no lower. Bargaining is *not* niggardly

TOLUCA ARTS AND CRAFTS

in Toluca. It's expected of you. It's part of the fun for the vendors.

The motor approach to Toluca by Highway 15, the famous Pacific Highway, over the lofty *col* (10,380 feet) at Las Cruces, is enough in itself to justify the trip. It is magnificent in its variety of scenery and it offers several side trips of unusual character. One is to the *Desierto de los Leones* (Desert of the Lions), which is noteworthy for being no desert and having no lions (the name was a pun on a family named León). It contains gardens, cloisters and a curious underground labyrinth, once the retreat of allegedly convivial Carmelite monks. This is, however, a mere picnic ground (on Sundays and holidays) for metropolitan myriads. A far bolder trip is that to the summit of the *Nevado de Toluca*, an extinct volcano almost 15,000 feet in height that dominates the Valley of Toluca from every angle. The Aztec name of this mountain is Xinantécatl, which means Naked Man, and a cold nudist he certainly is, for snow crowns his rugged brow at all seasons of the year. There is a gravel road that leads to the rim of the volcano's crater and directly to the crystalline lakes of the Sun and Moon. This trip, made easily from Mexico City in a day (including the Toluca City visit), is vigorous rather than actually venturesome, and warm clothing is a necessity. It reminds the traveler once again that the advertising cliché is well within the truth when it proclaims Mexico the Land of Contrasts.

A very *easy* motor trip may be made from Toluca to *Valle de Bravo*, which lies some 40 miles to the southwest. That small mining town is one of three colonial jewels designated by the government as National Monuments; Taxco and San Miguel de Allende being the other two. The region round about it will become—if plans carry through—one of the major resort areas of Mexico, with excellent hotels to draw and support turismo. The *Refugio del Salto* (Waterfall Refuge), three and a quarter miles from town, is an appealing mountain inn of quality, located close to a lusty waterfall.

Another fascinating jaunt, about an hour beyond Toluca, takes you to the town of Ixtapan de la Sal, one of the most notable of Mexico's 12 spas. The *Hotel Ixtapan*, there, calls itself "America's Shangri-la," and, in parenthesis, "The Fountain Inn." There is a Fountain of Beauty (for women) featuring Turkish, Russian, Oriental, solar and medicinal Baths, massage, a gym, a diet dining room and a beauty salon. There is a Fountain of Health (for men), with steam baths, massage, facials, electrotherapy and a barber shop. There is a Fountain of Youth, with four large pools and 20 private pools. The Fountain of Fun encompasses a golf course, ten riding horses, rides in old-fashioned carriages, a theater, five more swimming pools, a shooting range, tennis courts and orchestra and mariachi entertainers. And there is a Fountain of History, being 11 dancing water fountains depicting the history of Mexico, before a background of 150 Italian mosaic murals. All this is offered for a minimum of $12 per person, double; $18, single; meals included!

CHAPTER 13

EXAMINING THE HEART OF MEXICO

Mexico is a fifth larger than the combined areas of Texas, New Mexico, Arizona and California, our four abutting states, but of its three-quarters of a million square miles, some 10 per cent, surrounding the capital in all directions, contains 80 per cent of all that attracts the average traveler. From the practical angle this in itself is interesting. It means that without undue exertion or expense the average man or woman can not merely "do Mexico" but can see enough of the country in two or three weeks to have a fairly adequate, if superficial, picture of it. If only two weeks are available one may logically devote one of them to the capital and the other to a single well-planned provincial trip.

Of these there are four of superlative quality, not counting the highway approaches from the States, which have been briefly discussed in Chapter 2. All are *travel areas*, capable of being seen in a number of different ways, according to taste, rather than mere rubber-stamp tours; and all are within the heart of Mexico, that 20 per cent of the country that is italicized in terms of travel. I shall assume that your eyes are now on a map as well as on this text, without bringing on permanent strabismus. The four major trips, or areas, will be mentioned in the order in which they are to be treated in subsequent chapters.

1. *West to Guadalajara, Puerto Vallarta and Mazatlán.* (Chapters 14 and 15.) The natural route is the remarkable Pacific Highway (Route 15) that leads through Toluca, Zitácuaro and the historic city of Morelia. Before that city is reached, a short branch road to the left leads to the superlative spa of San José de

Purúa (there are quickie overnight and three-day tours just highlighting this spa), and beyond the city another short branch leads to the lake and town of Pátzcuaro; farther along the main stem there is still another branch road that leads to Uruapan and the "late volcano" of Paricutín; and finally, after 422 of the most scenic miles in Mexican travel, the highway reaches the western metropolis of Guadalajara. Every mile of the highway and the branches named is paved. A week is about the minimum time in which all of this can be enjoyably done. Allow at least a couple of extra days for flying from Guadalajara to Puerto Vallarta (only 45 minutes), or to Mazatlán, or to both.

2. *Northwest to the Towns of Independence.* Querétaro, San Miguel de Allende and Guanajuato are romantic towns that were the sinews of Mexican independence, and have a special appeal. Each has good hotels or inns aglow with personality, and major improvements in the highways permit travel agencies to offer a seven-day Guadalajara circle tour, merging all the attractions (except Puerto Vallarta and Mazatlán) mentioned above with the Independence Towns.

3. *South to Cuernavaca, Taxco, Acapulco* (Chapter 17). This is the classic of Mexican provincial travel, the one that everybody looks on as a sheer necessity. And it *is* a necessity. All things considered—romance, beauty, variety, simplicity—it richly deserves the unrivaled popularity it has won. The highway is paved all the way, which is 264 miles, and except for a short turnoff to Taxco, it is a broad speedway, with modest tolls. There is excellent air service between Mexico City and Acapulco, shuttle flights all day long, the flight taking less than an hour. There are all-expense tours that turn around at Taxco, and also ones that conclude at, or return to, Mexico City from Acapulco. Prices are remarkably reasonable, a four-day Cuernavaca-Taxco-Acapulco-and-return-to-Mexico City tour, for example, selling, at this writing, for $58.

4. *Southeast to Puebla, Oaxaca, Fortín* (Chapters 18 and 19). This is an area that can be seen in various travel combinations. All

the goals can be most comfortably reached by car. The distance from Mexico City to Oaxaca via Puebla is 355 miles and from here a glamour road leads to Fortín, a masterpiece of engineering through land the Mexicans call "the valley of Shangri-la." It's a side trip from the highlands into tropical orchid- and gardenia-clad jungles. Mexicana provides frequent air service to Oaxaca, as does Aerolíneas Vegas from Acapulco and Puebla. Some of the packaged tours utilize air travel, and there is also a not-bad railway service.

It should be repeated here that a paved road runs clear across Mexico from Guadalajara on the west to the original Pan American Highway on the east (at a point between Valles and Mante), making it practical and pleasant for the motorist who has reached the capital by way of the highway from Laredo to circle the heart of Mexico, finally returning by the northern portion of the same artery.

The four main regions of interest mentioned above are packed by the travel agencies into neatly arranged tours, sometimes cramming two regions into a single week, and if you have no car of your own and do not wish to struggle with Mexican timetables you will presumably allow romance to be thus predigested. As a matter of fact, the great majority of non-Spanish-speaking travelers still find it easier to let personal independence yield to professionally planned tours, but with the steady improvement of motoring conditions and with the enormous development of plane services, "impulsive travel" is gradually gaining its great and thrilling place in the Mexican sun.

Also of strong and increasingly popular interest are packaged tours (or go-on-your-own) to Yucatán (Mérida, Chichén-Itzá, Uxmal) and Cozumel Island in the Caribbean. You should allow yourself ten days, at least, for a trip in this direction.

CHAPTER 14

WESTWARD TO THE FIRE BELT

The Luxury Spa of San José de Purúa

MEXICO's leading spa—I think the adjective could not now be challenged—was born about the same time that the volcano Paricutín was born, in the winter of 1943. Its advance has been phenomenal and still continues. There are many spas in Mexico, but this one is the pride of them all. For several years of its infancy it had so few rooms available, as against the instant and enormous popularity it won, that it was as shy as a corporate Garbo and did all it could to avoid being advertised, but the establishment has greatly grown and its attitude has consequently changed. It maintains an office in Mexico City, and provides an excellent daily limousine service from capital to spa, a distance of 118 miles, a three-and-a-half-hour drive.

To present a fact or two, the altitude of this spa is 4300 feet above sea level. It has grown in guest capacity from a small spa to a large one, many of its accommodations being in separate cottages.

Its waters have curative value in the treatment of many ailments, including certain forms of diabetes and heart trouble, a point that I mention very lightly because I personally have always, in Europe and elsewhere, avoided with enthusiasm those places where elderly and ailing folk "take the waters." Somehow this is different. One does not feel that one is in an outdoor hospital or old-people's home.

San José de Purúa is a marvel of marvels, something straight out of a dream and quite impossible in any sort of actual world.

The main building of the hotel, designed in an odd arc with a high bridge leading to the *comedor* (dining room), is located on a narrow shelf of land on the side of the extremely deep gorge of the Tuxpan River. To beautify the setting, and also for utilitarian reasons, the management early planted no less than 15,000 orange trees on the gorgeside, and along with these some coffee trees. There are three large swimming pools with warm radioactive water gushing into them all the time directly from the cliff. It oxidizes in the open air within a few minutes and turns to an odd *café au lait* color, so that the pool is always brown. However, it is no whit less clean than any spring fresh from the earth, and the curative properties are said to be extremely potent.

There is also a large and more conventional pool within the very hotel area. The spa features free massages and mud packs; also excellent food, miniature golf (a putting green), and horseback riding.

The chief attraction of San José de Purúa for those who are not trying to cure something is the worship of the sun. Many decorative young things, and middle-aged and old things, too, spend many hours of every day in their bathing suits on the well-lawned perimeters of the pools, toasting in the sun and building up a tan that is several shades browner than the water and almost as brown as an Indio's skin. This sport is particularly popular in the bright winter days from December to March, when every day is built to the sun god's order.

Colonial Charm in Old Morelia

The approach to Morelia along the motor highway is beautified by wild flowers, wild birds and wild mountains. The latter reach their "thousand crests" in the panorama called *Mil Cumbres*, which, as an individual spectacle, surpasses any one thing on the Original Pan American Highway. At whatever time of day you pass this point you are certain to see cars in the little parking ground and mountain-gazers at the curving parapet. These thousand peaks compose some of the wildest country in Mexico and much of it is absolutely virginal. Ordinary motor maps reveal not a single town or village to the southwest. A few hermit communities do exist in this 300-mile stretch to the Pacific, but to the average Mexican virtually nothing is known of the whole great region.

Among wild flowers the most insistent note, and a very pleasant one, is sounded by the flowering bush called pipirigayo. The blossoms are a luminous red and the five-syllable bush is a Mexican variety of myrtle. Tamer notes, but no less beautiful, are those of the peach and pear orchards, which are in bloom even in late January. The birds are colorful, too, especially cardinal birds and bluebirds, which are seen everywhere along this Pacific Highway.

Morelia, with several fine hotels, notably the colonial-inspired *Virrey de Mendoza* and the modernistic *Alameda*, both in the heart of the city, abetted by the much lower-priced *Roma* and by the *Villa San José*, a charming inn on the edge of the city, overlooking it from high ground, is a lovely old-new city, capital of the State of Michoacán. The town dates from 1541 and by law all new construction must conform to the colonial-type architecture. This is the native town of José María Morelos and proudly it changed its name—in 1822—from the original Valladolid to Morelia. Two relics of the patriot are shown to visitors, the House-Where-Morelos-Was-Born and the House-Where-Morelos-Lived. The two are not the same house, for the elemental reason that Morelos' mother was out when labor came upon her and she could not get home in time, so she entered the nearest house she could find—and had her baby there. The actual Morelos house is now open to the public as a museum. The patio was an open-air stable in Morelos' time and it is full of old-world charm. Moss is on the cobblestones and piety is in the air. Over the watering trough is a little statuette of the Virgin, for the simple priest who was to become a military genius sought to guard his horse from every evil that the devil could devise.

The charm of Morelia is a many-faceted thing. The bougainvilleas give off the brightest gleam and are almost dazzling in their lush brilliance, but many an old palace, church and convent soften the picture with a venerable patina that only centuries can give to old masonry. If you see some with gargoyles in the form of cannons pointing their muzzles out from the roof edge, it indicates that these were the homes of conquistadores, for this was the arrogant symbol of those who conquered Mexico. And if you see above the cannons a row of bicuspids—as the toothsome architectural term has it—the symbol indicates a conqueror who was of noble lineage. A fine structure having both is the State Library, at the corner of the main street (Madero) and the little street called Nigromante.

When you enter the cathedral note the inner doors—six in all—of magnificent tooled leather, called *cordobanes;* and do not miss the quaintly conceived old painting back of the high altar, which shows Christ ascending to heaven from a hill above Morelia! The town is plainly identifiable beneath the rising figure.

Shoppers will delight in the beauty of Morelia's earthenware toys.

By the Waters of Pátzcuaro

The branch road that leads from the highway at Quiroga in 15 marvelous miles beside the Lake of Pátzcuaro to Pátzcuaro town is exciting all the way. It takes you first to Tzintzuntzan, which musical name, meaning Hummingbird Place, is self-pronouncing, with the accent on the penult. This was the very ancient capital of the Tarascan Indians, and their descendants are seen all about it and for many miles in both directions on the highway. You may recognize the women of the tribe from their heavily pleated red skirts, which are said to require ten yards of material. You may recognize Tarascan names from the *tz* double consonant (as in the above name and also Pátzcuaro and Janitzio), which dominates their language as *x* dominates Aztec. And the sites of old towns you may recognize by the peculiar T-shaped stone temples called *yácatas*, with imposing rounded fronts. There is a good one on the hillside near the present village of Tzintzuntzan. The name Tarascan itself, since we are in their land, is not without interest. It means son-in-law! The story—and quite true—is that in early days, the Indians, dazzled by the Spaniards' splendor, eagerly offered them their daughters in marriage and in so doing said repeatedly to the cavalier concerned, *"Tarasca, Tarasca,"* as if to make the arrangement stick. The Spaniards, hearing the word so much and not aware of its meaning, called the Indians themselves Tarascans.

Pátzcuaro town, on high ground above the lake, is supposed to have been founded in 1324 by a Tarascan chief, and this gains credence from the fact that recently, in the course of some excavations in the main plaza, a Tarascan tomb was discovered and it proved to be full of treasures in gold, jewels and fine pottery. These finds, considered of prime importance, have already made their way mostly to the National Museum of Anthropology in Mexico City. But if a Tarascan chief, maybe the very one who was buried in this tomb, founded Pátzcuaro, the man credited with giving it its modern form was Bishop Don Pasco (or Vasco) de Quiroga, for whom the beautiful and sumptuous tourist inn called *Posada de Don Vasco* is named. (There's another good inn, *Posada de la Basílica*, but the Don Vasco, which is under Western Hotels management, is the easy leader.)

In the little town itself there is not much to see except a colossal mural, *The History of the Tarascan People*, in the town library. This fine work is by Juan O'Gorman—he and his wife Helen are in the picture, as any guide will point out—and in size it threatens Orozco's supremacy, for it is fifty feet in height! Oh, I forgot. There's another sight to see in Pátzcuaro, unless progress has snuffed it out before you get there, namely the local prisoners in their jail. This fronts on the main plaza and you may see the jailbirds seated comfortably in their second-floor "apartment" looking out on life. It must be jolly to be a prisoner in Pátzcuaro,

BY THE WATERS OF PÁTZCUARO

for you are in the center of social life and you can chat with passers-by and enjoy the band concerts from a box seat. When your wife or sweetheart passes she will toss cakes or candies or smokes up to you, as will any friend worthy of the name. You fare well and have even a sort of distinction, as though you were a dignitary dispensing wisdom from your dais.

In the midst of the gleaming lake of Pátzcuaro rises the *Island of Janitzio* crowned by a huge statue of Morelos. I do not think in all my wanderings I have seen a more absurd affair than that statue, though it was perpetrated by one of Mexico's able sculptors, Guillermo Ruiz. The gossip is that the statue started out to be *colossal*, but funds or material ran out and so the top part of the figure was, so to speak, *condensed*. From feet to waist the patriot-priest is of truly heroic proportions, but from his waist to the top of his head he is definitely dumpy and his right hand is very oddly cramped as though he had been in the act of making a gesture when he was caught by a rheumatic twinge and was forced to give up the idea. But the statue has its uses, for you may go to Janitzio by a much-coughing putt-putt that passes for a motorboat, and climb to the monument and then to its summit for a superb view that you will always remember.

Janitzio, with its steep streets, its primitive ways and its strange butterfly nets for fishing, is a marvel of picturesqueness and one regrets that it should have been made laughable by a well-meant ineptitude of art. The island has a most amazing story, for it was the last stronghold of true Tarascan life and capitulated finally to civilization as recently as 1922! It is said that up to that time the islanders spoke *only* Tarascan and had picked up no Spanish at all, for they rarely left their island and they were dour and unfriendly to Mexican visitors. It was a case of exaggerated timidity but also the people of the island took pride in the fact that the conquerors had not yet conquered *them*. The Janitzians have a strangely Mongolian cast of countenance and until 1922 they seemed almost as remote from Western civilization as if they were on a mountaintop in Tibet. They did not know the meaning of a bath. They did not even know coins and their uses. Then a boy from the island made his way to Pátzcuaro and worked for a Mexican family as houseboy. The national government seized the opportunity to engage the young fellow as a sort of liaison officer. The authorities are said to have paid him two pesos a day to establish contact with his fellow islanders and break down their hostility. In the end the plan was successful and all the islanders now speak more or less Spanish, not to mention a trace of English, for they have become decidedly tourist-conscious and they now know very well—down to the tiniest tot—what coins are for!

Friday is Market Day in Pátzcuaro. Indians wearing their colorful native costumes come from miles around to sell their fine crafts. Copperware from the village of Santa Clara del Cobre is the most outstanding, but you also see much pottery, straw dolls and figurines and curious fish-shaped silver ornaments.

When Uruapan Took the Veil

Some 160 miles short of Guadalajara a paved branch road strikes off from the Pacific Highway due south into the volcano country, reaching the city of Uruapan in 45 miles. This has always been the Fire Belt of Mexico, but in February, 1943, it became, for a period of eight years, the country of THE Volcano, *Paricutín*, exciting the wonder of two worlds—the scientific one and the sightseeing one. Volcanoes are notoriously temperamental. For unpredictable moods and vagaries they outdo the traditional opera singer and for instability they surpass a Hollywood marriage. When Paricutín died down in 1951, it spelled doom for Uruapan's tourist boom. Individual tours may still be taken to the defunct volcano and its nearest city, but mass touring there would seem to be a thing of the past. Nevertheless, a little reminiscing may be in order here, for with extinct volcanoes "you never really know."

Scientific opinion says of the eruption that it was probably from a "fire pocket," known to science as a magma chamber, rather than from any deeper portions of the earth, yet the length

THE BIRTH AND DEATH OF PARICUTÍN

of it, continuing without serious interruption from 1943 to 1951, proved a big surprise even to experienced vulcanologists.

The show I saw there was the one most thrilling sight I have ever witnessed in my life. Uruapan, the takeoff town for it, both suffered and benefited, perhaps in equal measure, from the newborn fuming giant. Before the eruption it was an exuberant floral paradise in its own right, a traveler's Eden, as it is now, but for all the long years of the eruption it was forced to submit to a gentle rain of volcanic ash whenever the wind was from the west. On the other hand, it suddenly enjoyed an utterly unexpected tourist boom, which did not die down until the volcano itself died down. *Hotel Progreso, Hotel Mirador* and two private homes made into good inns, *Mi Solar* and *Quinta Flores,* did a volcano-office business, at least during the high tourist seasons. The town was incredibly dreary-looking during the first few months of the volcanic activity, everything being covered with a thick shroud of ash, but as the citizens of Uruapan adjusted themselves to their new "weather," they learned to cope with it by frequent and energetic scrubbings. The *Hernardez,* the *Victoria* and the *Tivoli* are among the recommendable hostelries at present.

A chief industry of the town has long been lacquerware, and almost every traveler takes home some beautiful samples of it, chiefly trays, gourds and small boxes. It is, in a strictly literal sense, *lousy stuff,* for the lacquer is an oily gum made from plant lice called *axe,* gathered by Indians during the rainy season. When applied to the desired article and when properly and quite interminably rubbed by patient hands to make it impermeable, this form of lacquerware is exceedingly durable. The designs generally represent birds, animals and geometric figures of Chinese and Indian inspiration. Clever wood carvings, created locally, are also featured in the shops.

The Birth and Death of Paricutín

Mexico's Huge Baby, christened Paricutín from the hamlet where it was born, received more world publicity than any other baby of its time, with the possible exception of the fabulous five-that-came-at-once, the "first successful Quints," of Callander. Paricutín was unique in being the *only* volcano of any significance born since science reached an advanced stage where every cry, every tantrum and ever shuddering tremor of the young hellion could be heard, watched and measured with accuracy. The baby was photographed, too, not only by eager tourists with their movie cameras, but by scientific cameramen for an hour-by-hour record and by skilled professionals representing the leading illustrated magazines.

Fame, of men or mountains, is ephemeral. A few years ago it could have been said with truth that Paricutín was so well known that it needed no introduction, yet now the mountain and its name are half forgotten. One Dionisio Pulido and his son were plowing their field for the spring planting of corn—than which nothing could be more Mexican—when their crude ox-drawn plow turned up a wisp of white smoke, and the startling vision was accompanied by odd rumbling sounds in the earth. The place was two miles outside the Michoacán village called Paricutín and the date was February 20, 1943. Father and son and even the stolid animal broke and ran, as from the devil. Pulido hastened to tell the priest of his own village and then the headman of Parangaricutiro, another village slightly more important and slightly farther distant. Everyone thought the man crazy, but he had only to lead them to the spot and let them see for themselves. Within a matter of hours the wisp was a column of ash dust and within a day there was a true volcanic cone 30 or 40 feet high. A week later it was five times as high, and a month later 15 times as high. Despite some variations in intensity, it went on with a persistent power that puzzled the experts, for most such babies of Vulcan, begotten in Mexico in past centuries, have died in infancy after a few weeks.

To make my own lay report of Paricutín, as it looked then: I made my way by car from Uruapan with a tour group to Parangaricutiro and there we hired mules to carry us up to a ledge

THE BIRTH AND DEATH OF PARICUTÍN

from which visitors were permitted to view the spectacle. My *mulita*, a fine mouse-colored beast of rare ambition, insisted on taking the lead of the cavalcade in which I started and presently I found myself far ahead, alone in a gray world that was silent save for the increasing rumble of the volcano. This rumble was like two sounds that do not, however, resemble each other. One is that of surf on a gravelly beach; the other is that of a heavy cart passing over cobblestones. Up and around and over and through ash-dead fields and ruined forests for an hour or so the good gray mule carried me until we reached the end of the line. Then the animal stopped determinedly, for she had finished her stint.

I was on a shoulder of ash-carpeted hillside, perhaps half a mile from the volcano's cone, and the sight was awe-ful. At intervals of a few seconds prodigious puffs of steam ash burst from the crater as a gas bubble broke down below, and these seethed upward to join the great umbrella that filled half the sky. Each dark ascending pillar was intershot with myriads of "sparks" that glowed even in the daylight. These sparks were, of course, lava bombs two or three feet in diameter.

The greatest show on earth went on and on and on. I was so utterly enthralled by it that I scarcely noticed when my companions arrived; it seemed almost sacrilegious when someone suggested that we sample the sandwiches we had brought along from the hotel and try the coffee that an Indio was brewing for us in a nearby shack. Darkness settled slowly down and with every minute the show improved in spectacular effects. "Oh, OH! Look! And look at *that!*" Everybody was exclaiming and nobody felt apologetic about it, for the sublime grandeur of the thing forbade correct and urbane small talk. When full darkness came, Paricutín was at its incredible best, with rockets of every huge sort hurling their burdens of sparks upward with primitive, savage, unstoppable force. It seemed the perfect illustration for one half of the ancient riddle: "What happens when an irresistible force meets an immovable object?" There was no immovable object unless it was the pull of gravity, which finally broke the force of even the most powerful bombs and dragged them back to mother earth.

At last we had to go back and it was like taking children away from a circus. We looked back over our shoulders a hundred times, and I was sorry, on the return trek, that my mule insisted on being so speedy. As she took me into the forest, hidden from the volcano by a spur of the hill, the going became pitch-black, but she minded it not at all. She plodded on, losing the path now and again but always finding it quickly.

At the hotel in Uruapan that night my shower worked and the water was hot, and I was very glad, for hide and hair were saturated with fine ash.

CHAPTER 15

GLAMOUR AT GUADALAJARA

Delights of Plaza and Portales

Mexico's second city, whose population is over a million, is a sheer delight to the taker-of-things-easy. There is a lot to see, but sights, as such, are not so exigent as in the capital. It is entirely defensible to do nothing except enjoy the relatively placid life of the place, loafing in its plazas and devoting unhurried hours to shopping, actual or window, under its numerous arcades. The Plaza Mayor of this city, with its cathedral and Government Building as beautiful ornaments and its leisured life as the main attraction, seems to me one of the two most thoroughly delightful plazas in Mexico, the other being in Oaxaca.

Guadalajara, named for the ancient Arabic town in Spain which originally spelled its name *Wad-al-hadjarah* (river-filled-with-rocks), is a rich, distinguished, erudite city, but it is not a hard-driving city and one cannot quite imagine the brisk decree of "no siesta," imposed some years ago upon the capital, ever being seriously applied here. The people of the well-to-do sort— and there are many—live well and dress well but they are in no hectic rush to pile new wealth upon old. The women, by the way, are widely reported to be of special beauty. Many and many a city makes this claim in travel-propaganda booklets, but Guadalajara has, I think, no need to publicize such pulchritude. Take a seat in the plaza some evening while the band is playing the waltzes that are always in vogue here and "look them over."

If I have seemed, in the above, to dismiss Guadalajara as unambitious I should make haste to correct the picture, for a lot of progressive developments have occurred and are still occurring. The city serves as the hub of a very large cattle, dairying and agricultural region, it is the banking hub of all western Mexico, and it is the only large Mexican city that is on the high plateau yet close to the sea, being but 75 crow-flight miles from Manzanillo, an increasingly popular goal for amateur fishermen and a new port of call for the cruise ship, *Patricia*, and is also conveniently close by air to the popular beach resort of Puerto Vallarta, and the small port of Cuyutlán. Eventually, a good highway will be extended to the coast, and when that happens Guadalajara will receive a further fillip.

The city has a splendid airport, a fine railway station and a towering intercity bus station. The Municipal Building is another source of pride to the citizens, and surrounding the entire city is a belt boulevard called *La Circunvalación*. An abundant water supply blesses the city, too.

Guadalajara has a unique corps of guides on motorcycles, whose duties are to give all possible aid to tourists within the city, including general information, maps, lists of hotels and restaurants, and even assistance with flat tires and minor motor troubles. This idea is expected to be adopted in other major Mexican towns where the complexities of traffic often befuddle the newcomer behind the wheel.

Far and away the leading hotel in Guadalajara is the *Guadalajara Hilton*, dating from 1965, a high air-conditioned tourist palace of 250 rooms, many with private balconies, enhanced by a rooftop supper club called *La Rondalla* and a swimming pool. Also of high quality is the *Camino Real*, under Western Hotels management, with all rooms air-conditioned and *two* swimming pools. It is a bit out from the center of town, being at the corner of Avenida Vallarta Poniete and Avenida del Niño, but it's a real charmer, one of its features being nightly violins and mariachi music in its cocktail lounge. The *Hotel Fénix*, a link of the Hoteles Azteca chain, is a highly popular veteran (from 1912), which has spared no efforts to keep up with the times. It is a first-

DELIGHTS OF PLAZA AND PORTALES

class tourist-and-business hotel of 250 rooms, with its own spacious garage. The rates are extremely moderate, doubles with bath being under $11. A new place of thrift rates is the *Roma*, also an Azteca hotel. It has a rooftop swimming pool and a panoramic view of the city. The *Gran*, with an attractive patio bar and pool, the *Morales* and the *del Parque* are other good hotels. There are also several good motels, including the *California Courts*, at 2525 Avenida Vallarta in a residential section of the city, and the *Campo Bello Motel*, two or three miles south of the city on the highway to Mexico City.

Guadalajara has a number of rather good restaurants, among them that of the above-mentioned *Motel Campo Bello*. Separate, nonhotel restaurants include *La Copa de Leche* (The Glass of Milk), on the central Avenida Juárez; *Focolare; Tekare; Cazadores; El Colombo; La Cabaña; Carnes Azadas Tolsa;* and, for German food, *El Parador Germano*, at the corner of Calles López Cotilla and Maestranza.

Night life, except in the chief hotels, is sparse in this big city. *Montparnasse*, on Avenida Vallarta, is recommendable, as are the *Tekare*, the *Fuente Trevi* (Trevi Fountain) and the *Navy Club*, which last has dancing but no floor show.

On the loftier level of entertainment is the historic *Degollado Theater*, where Italian and Mexican opera companies present grand opera, chiefly in the autumn, and where the Guadalajara Symphony Orchestra gives its excellent concerts. For musical middlebrows there are pleasant open-air band concerts in Plaza de Armas and in Revolution Park.

Guadalajara receives far less attention from sightseers than it deserves. There are some most unusual things to see and enjoy, but motorists are always hurrying to some other place, and visitors arriving by plane, train or motorcoach are often content merely to stroll the sunny streets and plazas, enjoying whatever they happen to find. Among the long-established sights I have enjoyed, three are of outstanding appeal: the *State Museum* (cheerful patio), displaying Spanish and Mexican paintings, along with popular arts; the *State Capitol* (*Placio del Gobierno*) and the *Hospicio Cabañas*, the first two being close together in a Civic Center around the Plaza Mayor and the Hospicio about eight blocks to the east. The State Capitol is seen almost inevitably by most visitors, for in enjoying the plaza one automatically enjoys the building's superb façade, a typical example of churrigueresque, and then one strolls into the spacious patio. This patio is as beautiful as the façade. It is a two-tiered court with fine stone arches that are embellished with tezontle. Orozco is "all over the stairways" on walls and ceilings and these paintings are among his most stentorian works. Survey Morelos as he surveys you from the ceiling of one of the stairways and see if you can avoid a sense as of shrinking away before that huge "patriot glare."

The Hospicio is a place to be measured in acres, and also, if you are in an impressionable mood, in heartbeats, for human interest pulses high within its walls and in its 25 patios and flower gardens. It is an orphanage for several hundred homeless children and it also houses a girls' industrial school and a home for aged women. One of the old crones attached herself to me and showed me the Orozco murals (you knew, of course, that there would be some enormous ones here), but the heartthrobs were the children! Anyone who can watch them at play and at work, without moistened eyes and tightened throat, is sentimentally impermeable. On the occasion of my first visit one group of very young kiddies occupied an immaculate tiled patio and they lay in a circle on their backs looking up at the Guadalajara sky while a teacher sat in the center telling them patriot stories of Mexico. Another group was of six-year-old boys, each in a cranberry-colored sweater, and these youngsters had been set to swab down a great tiled corridor. Each had a wet mop and they did their job with savage gusto and a great deal of horseplay. I saw one boy charge off at a mad tangent for a distance of twenty yards, using his mop as steed of battle. I suppose he was galloping down upon a company of Spanish royalists. Still another group of children, all under ten, composed an orchestra that was being led by an earnest maestro. The music was astonishingly good and I listened in amazement.

If you think an orphanage sounds grim and pathetic try this one and see if it calls for a revision of the standard picture. Guadalajara is inordinately proud of her Hospicio and well she may be, for unfortunate children expand in its cheerful atmosphere like the flowers in its brilliant and innumerable gardens. Incidentally—and it really is incidental in this case—the view of the Hospicio from the center of the town and that of the town from the Hospicio form a two-way delight matched by few civic vistas in the whole republic.

Among other sights of the city one should not neglect the imposing monument to the city's hero sons (*Estatua de los Niños Héroes*), a tall shaft erected in 1956 on Avenida Chapultepec, nor the gleaming boulevard named *Avenida Las Américas*, with 20 bronze busts, one to each block, of leading historical figures of the 20 "good neighbors" of Mexico. Colombia, for instance, is represented by Simón Bolívar, the revered liberator of that country (and Venezuela, Ecuador, Peru and Bolivia) from the Spanish yoke; Argentina by her great patriot-general, José San Martín; Cuba by her martyred revolutionary leader, José Martí; Chile by her valiant soldier, Bernardo O'Higgins; and our own country not by Washington but by Abraham Lincoln, for it is quite understandable that Mexico, ever conscious of her own long struggle for freedom, should feel a special veneration for the President who freed our slaves.

Temptation at Tlaquepaque

San Pedro Tlaquepaque (pronounced Tlah-kay-páh-kay) is a pottery-makers' suburb of Guadalajara and a place of relaxation for the city's multitudes, as well as for the lesser tourist multitudes. It is only two and a half miles from the center of the city, so you can easily get there on your own. There are also regular tours.

Shoppers' fever rages in this little town, for there are hundreds of good things to buy and about a dozen places where one may buy them. The word for pottery is *alfarería* and one sees the product and the word on every hand, but there are also many temptations in woodwork, textiles and fine embroideries. Two large places on the entrance thoroughfare are *Pedretti* and *Sahagen*, but equally good, if less conspicuous, shops are numerous on the far side of the plaza. The one called *Tonal Art Store* is internationally known. Tlaquepaque is one of the chief provincial magnets for all those travelers to whom shopping is a major attraction of Mexico.

Open-air cafés abound and if they are far from fastidious they are at least lively, for itinerant mariachis are so numerous that their competing ballads drench the air with Latin rhythms, and the mariachis of this city, by the way, are reputed to be Mexico's best. It is earthy and noisy and very pleasant in this potters' village. Mexico has a good time here and so will you.

A Day for Lake Chapala

An easy and very scenic holiday from Guadalajara is that blue ribbon of Jalisco State that includes the *Salto de Juanacatlán* and the *Lago de Chapala*. The *salto* ("leap" or waterfall) is a Mexican Niagara that is actually the second in size of all waterfalls on the North American continent, being about 500 feet in width and 75 feet in height. One marvels that there can be this much water in Mexico, but the answer is that Juanacatlán is formed by the Río Santiago, which is the effluent of Lake Chapala. That lake is Mexico's largest, some four times greater in surface area than Switzerland's Lake Geneva.

Juanacatlán is reached by a five-mile road branching to the east from the Chapala highway. The latter pushes on to the resort and lake (both called Chapala) some 35 miles distant from the city. In the resort there is a small but charming garden inn, the *Villa Monte Carlo*, with a swimming pool of thermal-spring water. Chapala *is* a beautiful lake and it has many devoted fans. Its shores lure artists and writers not only from Mexico but from foreign lands, which have fine lakes of their own. It lured Neill James there in 1943 and in the lakeside village of Ajijic she wrote her charming vagabond narrative *Dust on My Heart*. She lived there and owned the *Posada Ajijic*. On the west end of the lake is another pleasant little village called Jocotepec. An important craft here is heavy hand-loomed sarapes, seen to advantage on market day (Sunday). There is a small and quite charming inn called *La Quinta*.

From Guadalajara to Chapala there is an hourly service of good busses. There are also regular tours. Whether you go on your own or not, you will wind up in a place with a familiar ring. Yes, it is the Zócalo! Little Chapala, somnolent beside its inland sea, has a central "socle" because in Mexico City a monument once remained unfinished.

Two or Three Days for Puerto Vallarta

If an escapist, old-clothes beach retreat lures you, a place where motorcars have to cross a swift stream, lined on both banks with scantily clad women washing clothes and themselves, to reach the resort's Las Delicias bathing beach, a watering place where travel sophistication is still on the defensive (though it is beginning to make "dangerous inroads"), then Puerto Vallarta is your goal. You can fly there direct from Los Angeles (and soon from other major metropolitan cities), and the place is a regular port of call for the winter cruise ship, *Patricia*. Hotels are springing up with enthusiastic abandon. *Posada Vallarta* is currently the best. Designed in Mexican-colonial style, it has 125 rooms and 12 suites, all air-conditioned, every room with its own terrace and view of the sea. Other attractions are its two dining rooms, its tennis court and its private beach. The most casual *Los Arcos* offers international cuisine, and the thatch-roofed *El Pueblito*, directly on the sea, features carefree dining, dancing and entertainment in the Mexican manner. The 135-room *Hotel Tropicana*, on the main beach, and the smaller *Posada de la Selva*, with pleasant swimming pool and terrace, are other up-to-date places of special interest.

Still another new place is *Los Cuatro Vientos*, with its restaurant called *Chez Elena*, in the center of town, but on a hill with panoramic views of town and ocean. All rooms here are suites and have private terraces, and the management boasts of "natural air-conditioning," temperatures being up to ten degrees cooler than at beach level.

Las Campanas Bungalows are also appealing, for the establishment consists of ten bungalows, each with private terrace and bay-mountain views, nestled in a walled garden on a hillside behind the parent *Hotel Oceano*. Old standbys are the *New Hotel Rosita* and *El Paraíso*, directly on the mile-long *Malecón* (sea dike), whose charm comes from not striving to be what it isn't.

If you're looking for maximum privacy, the *Lagunita* may be for you. It's at Yelapa, reachable only by launch from Puerto Vallarta. There are 18 cottages with panoramic views of sea and mountains, private beaches (note the plural), fishing, hunting, horseback riding and an unspoiled, unhurried atmosphere.

Snuggling close to the hills behind it, and seeming to withdraw timidly from the rolling surf, Puerto Vallarta is traced by half a dozen streets running close together north and south, from a river called the Cuale Creek. Beyond the Cuale and to the south of town is an additional bit of a city, where the favorite beach, *Playa Delicias* (Beach of Delights) is located. This beach was originally named *Playa de los Muertos* (Beach of the Dead) after a bloody battle that took place there back in the 1850's. Running along the shore of the bay, within the city limits, is the favorite meeting place for young men and women—the above-mentioned Malecón—a concrete walk that can be most bewitching under a full moon.

More of the Pacific Coast
Barra de Navidad and Mazatlán

Located close together south of Puerto Vallarta, about 25 miles northwest of the port of Manzanillo, just within the borders of

Jalisco Province (200 miles southwest of Guadalajara, by road) are the developing resorts of *Barra de Navidad* (Christmas Sandbar) and *Tenacatita*. They both offer superb beaches, and the first-named also has a lagoon running behind it that provides private boat docks. There are many cottages here, but, alas, no really good public accommodations as yet. At Barra de Navidad, *Melaqua Hotel* is fairly pleasant, but so far there's nothing for the transient at Tenacatita except lots of natural beauty.

Much more aggressive is the development of Mazatlán, to the north of Puerto Vallarta, reachable in 145 miles by the Pacific Highway from Guadalajara. It is developing as a tourist resort so fast that it would be little short of astonishing were it not that such development is long overdue.

Its five-mile beach is flawless and its tropical temperature is cooled by almost unfailing breezes, usually straight off the sea. In the center of town, yet also directly on a curving beach (the sea sucks out much of the sand here each spring, returns it each fall), are three good hotels, though not pretentious, the *Freeman*, the *Belmar* and *La Siesta*. The Freeman is owned and run by an architect-builder named Guillermo Freeman, who is 50 per cent American by birth. It is a 12-story structure, said to be the tallest building on Mexico's western coast. All the front rooms have private balconies and, from any one of them above the third floor, one feels as though perched in the crow's nest of a liner well out to sea. They're truly marvelous, these balconies, especially up until about two o'clock in the afternoon, at which time the sun begins to hit them too strongly. Up aloft there's the Sky Room restaurant, with music and dancing nightly. The view from all sides is thrilling, for Mazatlán is a veritable "little Rio." Dramatic hills such as Cerro del Vigía and Creston Island, with its lofty lighthouse, shoot up from the heart of the city and from its nearby waters, and most of the hillsides seem "dotted with fires," from the brilliant red-flowering tabachín trees. The Hotel Freeman sometimes closes its restaurant in the slack summer season, but a good restaurant called *La Copa de Leche* (The Cup of Milk) is only a block away. This is under the same management as the like-named place in Guadalajara.

The Mazatlán of tourism is springing up *fast* along the beach, lined all the way by a shore boulevard, the Avenida del Mar, despite the fact that the more distant parts of this area, adjacent to marshes, are still battling the mosquito problem.

Newest hotel (as of this writing) is the large *Hotel Playa Mazatlán*, on Playa Las Gaviotas (Sea Gull Beach). On North Beach, the newer accommodations include the *Hotel de Cima*, most expensive of the tourist hotels, a real palace of pleasure with every expected amenity and luxury, boasting refrigerated air-conditioning, a private beach, a swimming pool and so on. Other inns are *El Dorado*, *Las Arenas* (The Sands), and the *Agua Marina*.

More hotels and motels are fairly jumping all along the beach, two more of which I will name. The *San Luis* is a bungalow hotel, American-owned and managed, which advertises "children welcome." The water is purified and the milk pasteurized. The *Motel Playa del Rey*, on El Camaron beach, comprises 20 suites, air-conditioned, with swimming pool and a special pool for children.

Sand and surf are far from being Mazatlán's only attractions. Its fishing fame (marlin and sailfish) has long lured those addicted to this sport. Many companies rent fishing boats or take out fishing parties, and the five-story *Balboa Fishing Club* is called by the city's boosters the largest such club in the world.

The name, Mazatlán, means place of the deer. It is a town of rare gentility. Any morning finds Mazatlán in a leisurely mood. Its 72,000 inhabitants are mostly involved in catching and exporting shrimp or in catering to tourists. Huts of thatched palm, like witches' hats, dot the immaculate sands, pounded by waves from the rock-edged Olas Altas Bay. Open-air bistros provide native mariachi bands and vendors of mangoes, bananas, papayas and coconuts rattle their little carts along Olas Atlas Street. For a few pesos you can ride in an *arana*, a two-wheeled horse-drawn surrey. On the hills, pastel Spanish-Moorish houses and villas look down upon the crowded streets, where burros and carts zip in and out between automobiles, and boys on rickety bicycles dart out of hidden corners. I like this lazy town and would not wish to pass through or over it without at least a night or two in one of its oceanside hotels, lulled by soporific surf.

A new travel facility of interest is the motor ferry, *La Paz*, sailing nightly from Mazatlán to La Paz, the capital of the long Mexican peninsula called Baja California. You leave at five P.M., arriving in La Paz at nine A.M., and have your choice of a reclining chair or a private cabin. There's a cafeteria and dining room aboard, and, all in all, the sea voyage across the Gulf of California can be a genuine delight.

CHAPTER 16

ALLURING TOWNS OF INDEPENDENCE

Freedom's Cast of Characters

THE state of Michoacán, with its capital Morelia, is the Morelos country of Mexican patriotism, but the abutting states of Querétaro and Guanajuato to the north are the actual *cradles of liberty*, where the first cries were heard. Morelos did not enter the nursery of rebellion until things were already very lively. Dolores Hidalgo, where the first leader uttered the first *grito*, is not of interest except for its historical associations, but three towns that fought for liberty have such special allure that I would place them unhesitatingly among the most interesting and charming towns of all Mexico, yet no one of them has yet been very much favored by tourists. They are Querétaro, San Miguel de Allende and Guanajuato. The first and last are capitals of their like-named states. San Miguel is in Guanajuato State, not far from the capital town.

Certain characters of the first ill-starred phase of the struggle —and most of these heroes were martyred within ten months— come into the story again and again, and the towns of their fame are not to be fully enjoyed without keeping their names and their deeds ever clearly in mind. They have all been discussed in Chapter 5, but by way of recapitulation here is the cast of characters.

La Corregidora, the mayor's lady of Querétaro, was the rugged patriot who sounded the alarm that saved the rebellion from being stillborn. Her Christian name was Josefa Ortiz de Domínguez.

Ignacio Pérez was the city jailer of Querétaro to whom La Corregidora signaled instructions. He carried the warning that the revolutionary plans had been discovered.

Aldama and *Jiménez* were officers who came into the rebellion with their friend Allende. To Aldama the warning message was given by Pérez when he could not at first find Allende.

Ignacio Allende, a dashing young officer stationed in his native town of San Miguel, was a leading spirit in the independence movement. He brought his regiment over to the rebel side.

Miguel Hidalgo y Costilla, a devoted but often bewildered village priest, was the heart and soul of the independence struggle, a man of noble character whose motives were far loftier than those of the military men on whom he leaned. They thought of the whole thing as a military rebellion to win Mexican independence from Spain. He thought of it as a social revolution as well, designed to bring not only independence but justice for the oppressed. He fought for a democracy that should exist in Mexico, under the nominal sovereignty of the king of Spain. He faced a firing squad on July 30, 1811, and died with the conviction that his cause had utterly failed. But it has been "gradually succeeding" ever since.

Querétaro, Birthplace of the Plan

The *City of Querétaro* is among the richest in interest in the Mexican republic and to it, I'm glad to report, a good highway from Mexico City has been built, supplementing the main railway line from the capital, which line passes through Querétaro, connecting it with the chief centers north and west, including Guadalajara, El Paso, Monterrey and Laredo.

The actual birthplace of the plan of Mexican independence is the area in and immediately around Querétaro's Plaza Independencia. This is not, however, the center of the modern city's life, so it is well to get one's bearings before starting out in search of the past. The plaza that centers modern Querétaro eschews the customary names and calls itself Plaza Zenea in honor of a local celebrity. Here one finds the veteran *Gran Hotel* (a newer one, but less favorably located, is *Hotel del Marqués*), the best shops and almost everything that is lively. It is an appealing garden-plaza, with the usual palms and splendid laurel trees, the usual benches and shine boys, the usual flirtation walk at band-concert time, and, in short, the usual "restful animation" that obtains in all central plazas in Mexico.

The best hotel, though, at least for atmosphere, is probably the *Motor Hotel La Mansión*, just outside town at Km 180, between Querétaro and San Juan del Río. It is a remodeled 16th-century hacienda, with exceptionally large rooms, heated swimming pool, putting green and horseback riding.

A good, up-to-date city map, bought at a local *librería*, will be of special value in Querétaro, for there is much to find and many of the old street names have been altered. The Square of Independence, in name and fact, lies two blocks east of Plaza Zenea. Near the southeast corner of it, Number 14 on the street now called Calle Pasteur Sur (South) is the actual incubator of the independence plan. Here met the dreaming patriots who so cooly called themselves an "art study club." The building is now a museum.

On the north side of the square is the *Palacio Municipal*, being the very building where the Corregidor and his Corregidora dwelt. Both were earnest art students—in the strictly patriotic sense of plotting to throw off the hard yoke of Spain. The business affairs of the city are conducted here now, as they were in 1810, and I found it a bit difficult to view the actual quarters where La Corregidora lived; but persistence was rewarded and finally a city official relaxed to the point of calling his daughter and instructing her to show me the historic rooms. Only one phrase properly describes this girl. She was a cute number; and she wore a cute gray jacket with bright-red pockets and red-bound buttonholes, a style then affected by young Queretareñas. I hope you will find her father (in an office at the southeast corner, ground floor) and then find her, though she'll be a "big girl now." She or someone else will, I hope, show you the exact spot on the floor where Doña Josefa tapped her signal to Jailer Pérez, the determined tap that touched off the fuse of rebellion.

This was by no means the only occasion on which Querétaro trod the stage of history. Here, in a building that is now used by an undertaker (Cosio, at Calle Hidalgo 29), the Treaty of Guadalupe Hidalgo was ratified, for Querétaro was briefly the nominal capital of Mexico. Here, too, Emperor Maximilian made his last stand and was finally done to death in scenes so dramatic that they rival in interest the most vivid scenes of the birth of independence.

It was at the insistence of Benito Juárez that the emperor paid the last penalty for "bearing arms against the government," and the penalty was exacted chiefly to teach Europe that it must not interfere. The man who had *been* the government and who was the symbol, to liberty-loving Mexicans, of foreign exploitation, was executed on the *Cerro de las Campanas* (Hill of the Bells), just outside the city, on June 19, 1867. He was a personally gentle and kindly man, and his last words were by no means the pious hypocritical screed they seem in a cold reading of them. "I forgive all," he said solemnly, "and I pray that all may forgive me. And I pray that my blood, about to be shed, will flow for the good of Mexico. Viva México! Viva Independencia!"

There is scarcely a more pathetic figure in all history than Maximilian of Austria, who became Maximilian of Mexico. He was tricked by conscienceless Mexican reactionaries and by a conscienceless general of the French army of occupation into believing that the Mexican people had overwhelmingly voted for him as their ruler. Perceiving the trick too late, he was not strongminded enough to leave Mexico in indignation, so he carried on, trying to regenerate and liberalize the country of his adoption and trying also, though this scandalized his fellow monarchs in Europe, to introduce real democracy into his "empire." He honestly believed he was advancing that independence that he hailed in his last spoken word.

Carlota tried, in her own high-spirited way, to aid her husband in his ambitions. Both of them exercised astonishing tolerance and good sportsmanship, finding everything practically perfect in Mexico and bringing in the frequent phrase "we Mexicans," which must have had an extraordinarily hollow ring to all who heard it. The empress broke her health on the impossible task of trying to secure aid in Europe for her husband and she went down into madness as he went down before the firing squad.

The *Provincial Museum* of Querétaro, located in a fine building adjoining the San Francisco Church on the Plaza Zenea, contains stirring souvenirs both of the independence struggle and of the Maximilian interlude. One sees the very lock through whose spacious keyhole La Corregidora whispered final instructions to Ignacio Pérez and risked her life by so doing. And of Maximilian and Carlota one sees many tragic memorials. There is the Capuchin Church clock, for instance, whose hands long pointed to six o'clock, the exact hour of the morning when the emperor was executed. The clock was stopped in tribute to him by sympathetic clerics, but has since been set going again. There are the original rude crosses that were first erected on the hill where the emperor and his two chief generals were shot. (Maximilian was given the chance to escape but refused unless they also could escape.) The crosses are simply lettered M. A.; M. M.; T. M. The last two are for General Miguel Miamón and General Tomás Mejía, but the first is wrongly lettered, at least as regards the wishes of the man whose place of execution it marked. M. A. stands for Maximilian of Austria but he passionately desired, even in death, to be considered Maximilian of MEXICO. Even had Mexicans desired this—and they certainly did not—the Hapsburg imperial line could hardly have countenanced it. Austria erected, in 1901, a showy $10,000 chapel on the Hill of the Bells to mark the spot where a Hapsburg fell, but the body of the unfortunate emperor rests with those of his family line in the gloomy imperial vault of the Capuchin Church in Vienna.

QUERÉTARO, BIRTHPLACE OF THE PLAN

The artistic appeal of Querétaro is quite as great as the historical and those who enjoy searching out superb old buildings of the colonial period will be repaid for a week spent in this city. Francisco Eduardo de Tresguerras ("Three Wars") was the architectural genius of Querétaro, as he was of Celaya, his birthplace, and many another town in the independence region. He has been called the most gifted architect ever produced by a Latin-American country, and one of his Querétaro churches, that of *Santa Rosa de Viterbo*, is a magnificent architectural achievement. It may be emphasized here, for the benefit of those travelers who "do not bother with churches while on holiday," that if only two churches in the whole republic outside of the capital are to be taken seriously as sightseeing specials, the two are inevitably Querétaro's Santa Rosa and Oaxaca's Santo Domingo.

Santa Rosa, on the narrow calle of the same name in the southwestern quarter of the city, is constructed so that it flanks the street, sending flying buttresses almost to the very sidewalk. The roof balustrade and the dome and tower are most interesting, but from the Calle Santa Rosa they cannot be seen, so the church should be approached from the north where several streets give something of a view, though not an unimpeded one. A close-up examination does, however, enable one to see comfortably a much more unusual feature, namely two large faces, like theatrical masks, that look out from the outer curves of two inverted arches, these in turn being purely decorative ornaments attached to the flying buttresses. These faces are of Saracens, and they are Mexico's only examples of that rather unchristian feature of various churches in southeastern Spain. They are a public and permanent vaunting of Christianity's military triumph over the Moors. But you will gaze at them with admiration just the same, for they are bold and original, like the mind of the great man who designed them. Tresguerras is supposed to have had virtually unlimited money for the decoration of this church, money derived from government confiscation of rich caches of smuggled goods, and you can well believe the story when you see the interior. Its churrigueresque lavishness surpasses anything else of the kind and the gold leaf is prodigally thick, but fortunately an artistic genius of the first rank controlled the outlay of wealth, and the result is worth all that it cost—the smugglers. And do not neglect to see also the sacristy, where a beautiful painting of a convent-garden close, by the same Tresguerras, is the chief masterpiece. It is universally considered the greatest mural done in Mexico in colonial times. It is as opposite as possible to the art of Mexico's modern muralists, but you will think its naïve pieties no less interesting in their field.

Tresguerras proved himself as able in secular architecture as in religious, as you may judge for yourself by entering the patio of the *Government Palace* (not the Municipal Palace). You will immediately see the very scene that is pictured on the back of 20-peso notes and you will not wonder that Mexico has selected this beautiful courtyard as a decoration for its money.

A final Querétaro note will especially interest Californians. In the extreme eastern portion of the city, on the highest point of ground, is the *Plazuela de la Cruz*, dominated by the *Templo* and *Convento de la Cruz*. This was an early Franciscan stronghold and from it the earnest Franciscan friars set out southward to Nicaragua and northward to California to establish their chain of missions and to convert and civilize the Indians. Father Junípero Serra, the beloved pioneer who made his way to California and now rests in his own Mission Church in Carmel—the only Spanish colonial to be honored by a statue as a "great American" in our National Hall of Fame in the Capitol rotunda in Washington—was one of these Querétaro friars. The rude cell where he prayed for the success of his venture is pointed out to visitors.

As there are several mines in the vicinity, visitors should look for the legitimate opals and amethysts sold in the shops. But *be sure* they're authentic. There is quite a racket going on of glassy imitations being sold to Indians who turn around and resell them as "stolen from the mines," to tourists along the highway.

As another note of holiday interest to motorists I might mention here that a new and little-known spa called Tequisquiapan, with 60 spring-fed swimming pools, is being developed near Querétaro. It used to be of such pleasant unsophistication that its posadas asked only three or four dollars a day for lodging and meals. Today, the tariff is more like $10 minimum single, $18 minimum double! The *Rio Hotel Spa* is one of these hostelries. Sixty rooms, all with private terrace, pool surrounded by gardens, thermal springs, bar, restaurant and coffee shop. Others are *Balneario Del Relox*, *Hotel Las Delicias*, *La Granja* and *Tequisquiapan*, while smaller hotels include the *Casa Michauz*, *Posada del Virrey* and the *San Francisco*.

Tequisquiapan is 43 miles east of Querétaro, by Route 45 to San Juan del Río and a short branch road from that point.

San Miguel, a Patriot's Hearth

A good road connects Querétaro and San Miguel and an all-weather road, via Dolores Hidalgo, goes on to Guanajuato, a stretch of some 70 miles. Querétaro and San Miguel both lie also on the direct rail line, mentioned above, that leads west and north from Mexico City, the distance between them being but 50 miles.

San Miguel, which tacked on the name Allende in honor of its native patriot, is one of the picture towns of Mexico. It is now, as I've mentioned, officially called a "National Monument," in the same sense that Taxco is so called, and consequently much care is taken to prevent its appearance from being spoiled. This means that no new construction and no structural alterations to existing buildings or homes may be undertaken without due authority. Architectural harmony is to be maintained, even at the sacrifice of commercial gain or personal convenience.

San Miguel is a jewel of unspoiled Spanish-colonial aristocracy, for it was the home of many pedigreed families who had extracted wealth from the Guanajuato mines. A steep road leads up from the railway station to the central plaza of the town, and if you have elected to come by the National Railways' train service you may be delayed in securing a taxi for the climb, but when you finally reach the main plaza you will quickly forget the delay, for the sight is a picture of romance.

One of the most comfortable inns is actually an art school, the *Instituto Allende*, part of the Allende Institute for the study of arts and crafts, writing and the Spanish language. It has a garden setting and much "atmosphere."

The home of Ignacio Allende is at the corner of the above-mentioned main plaza, with an appropriate tablet to identify it. The old street that runs past this building is called Calleja de la Cuna de Allende (Lane of the Cradle of Allende). Aldama's house is also on the main plaza, one corner away from Allende's.

The central hotel, *Posada de San Francisco*, strikes just the right note, being a pleasant structure in the colonial style with two patios, fountained and flowered in exquisite taste. Its rooms are modern, with private baths, its table fare is good, and its location, directly on the plaza, is decidedly convenient in so up-and-down a town.

Across the plaza from this posada is an astonishing church inevitably named San Miguel. Sylvester Baxter called it "Gothesque" and perhaps that manufactured word is as good as any. It was the grandiose effort of a local architect who had more ambition than artistic knowledge, yet it by no means spoils the town. Its oddity, with a wide straddling tower cutting sharp lines against the sky, is a positive enhancement rather than a defect, and as the rays of an early sun stream upon and through it, illumining its pink stone, the effect is glorious. Ceferino Gutiérrez, who did this, did many other things for his own town and averaged very well indeed. Two other good hotels are the *Posada de las Monjas* and *El Atascadero*. If you enjoy spas you may wish to headquarter yourself at the near-to-town, *Spa Fuentas de Taboada*, where swimming in mineral waters is the big attraction.

Walking in this steep town at an altitude of 6000 feet may tax your "bellows," but it will tax your supply of adjectives, too, for every vista is lovelier than the last. Little rivers flow through most streets from the abundant springs on the hillside above called Cerro del Chorro (Hill of Springs), and they lend a freshness to the whole atmosphere, as well as a brisk obbligato to the normal sounds of small-town life. One walk—and it is only one of many—I would stress for its great rewards. Go uphill from the plaza, by Calle de Correo (Post Office Street), and you will see straight ahead of you a *campanario* with four bells, in a horizontal row, silhouetted against the sky. Turn right at the bells and go for half a block until you find a rough boulder-strewn street ascending the cerro steeply. Climb this (slowly) and you will find yourself at the top of the world, with the whole of San Miguel spread out below you. From this superb natural belvedere, look down and pick out whatever you wish to find, for the town is like a map on a great table. There is, for instance, in the right middle-distance, the enormous *Basílica San Felipe Neri*, with fine old cypresses accentuating its venerable charm. And there is the lively town market, close by Neri; and the bullring in quite another quarter; and in the distance the arty vignette of the village of Atotonilco.

But the map is yours and you will make your own selections without much help from anyone. This is a town where you cannot make a mistake, for whatever you do or fail to do will work out just right. With the whole of San Miguel a lovely monument to the past, it matters little what details compose it.

Guanajuato Silver

Guanajuato is considered by many to be a true rival in picturesqueness of that other old town of silver, Taxco. I would not go quite so far, but it is at least a good second in setting and in romantic appearance, and it has the advantage over Taxco—so far—of being relatively undiscovered by tourists. But this will change, as it is being heavily promoted by the Mexican-tourist industry. The name is Tarascan for "Frog Hill," but it actually occupies a deep cleft between two hills and ambitiously climbs their very steep sides. Formerly, this cleft contained a river and the river occasionally went wild with floods, wrecking the town and drowning scores of inhabitants, but it was finally tamed and more or less obliterated by means of an expensive tunnel to divert the waters.

The central plaza is Mexico in miniature, with a special heritage of Andalusia (whence came some of the early settlers) and with a somewhat incongruous touch of classicism in the imposing modern Juárez Theater, with its columned portico. The congested square is called Plaza Mayor but it should rather be called Plaza Menor, for it must certainly be the smallest central square (actually, a curious triangle) of any town in the republic. Space is at a great premium in the narrow valley and this is all that could be eked out. But life goes on marvelously here and the flirtation walk at dusk, with a moon peering over the hillcrest and a band playing popular airs, is like something out of an operetta. So small is the space for walking that the señoritas are often quite inadvertently bumped by the young caballeros, but this gives a chance for a handsome apology and a charming acceptance of it, all done with the proper proportions of admiration and confusion.

The *Posada de Santa Fe*, on a curve of this plaza, focuses much of the local life, but a newer and better hotel, the *Orozco*, not on this center of centers, offers the traveler more creature comforts; *Hotel Castillo de Santa Cecilia*, an extraordinary inn in a baronial castle converted to this public use, is perhaps the most desirable of all. *Posada de la Presa* is also attractive.

Guanajuato was a conspicuous center of activity in the Wars of Independence, and its grim old granary, Alhóndiga de Granaditas, has been mentioned as a scene of heroism and tragedy. In this huge pile of masonry the royalist troops took refuge in September, 1810, only a few days after Hidalgo had uttered his Cry. The rebels stormed the place but could not force their way in. On September 28, a young Indio named José Barajas and nicknamed Pípila undertook to make a solo attack against the great main door, under a murderous hail of assorted missiles. He was successful and smashed it in. A terrible slaughter of the royalists ensued and a few days later this was capped by a mass lynching in which the town mob killed about 250 royalist prisoners who were being held, unarmed, in the massive structure. In a counterthrust the royalists recaptured Guanajuato and murdered all the citizens—men, women and children—whom they captured in the attack. And a few months later, piling brutality upon brutality, the royalists—as we have noted earlier—brought the severed heads of the four slain leaders, including that of Hidalgo, and callously fixed them upon hooks on the four corners of the Alhóndiga, where they remained for a gruesome decade.

Pípila is the town's personal hero of the independence movement. A statue of him, with a decidedly silly mustache of real hair superimposed, stands in the hallway of the Alhóndiga; another statue, of huge proportions, showing the Indio in the act of charging the granary, has been erected on the crest of one of the hills, immediately overhanging the Plaza Mayor.

Guanajuato strolling, unguided by any cicerone, is of unending delight. You will surely find the pretty *Jardín de la Unión* and you will probably find, around the corner and up from the plaza, the *Compañía Church* (for "Company" of Jesus; hence, Jesuit, as everywhere in Spain and Spanish America). It is identifiable by the four tall cypresses that rise from an elevated parapet fronting a tiny plazuela and seem fairly to pierce the sky with their thin green shafts. You may find *Callejón del Beso* (Kiss Alley), so named because of its narrowness, fancifully enabling the houses, not to mention their residents, to kiss across it. And if you wander to the hilltops you may even find the *Catacombs*, with their horribly realistic mummies lined up *in a standing position* against the walls. The rich men of this rich town have nice graves, kept inviolate for all time, but the poor have only *leases* and their bodies have to be exhumed when the leases expire, some of them, as I've said, being stood up in the Catacombs. The exceedingly dry air of the heights has a sufficient embalming quality to preserve their bodies in ghastly "naturalness."

Three miles from the center, if your wanderings take you that far, you may find the extremely rich Valenciana silver mine and its *Church of San Cayetano*, built by the Conde de Rul. According to a splendid legend, suitable to the town's traditions, the supporting mortar was made of powdered silver moistened with fine Spanish wines. If this is a bit fantastic, it is at least a fact of history that the count built the lavish edifices with peon labor, which was almost slave labor, since the wages were six centavos a day, with no payment for religious holidays, though full work was expected. And it is a fact that he demanded from each miner a weekly *piedra de mano* (fist-sized chunk of silver ore) as religious tribute for the upkeep of the church's pompous ritual. There was something a good deal less than noble in Rul's attitude, and the story of this Valenciana church, one of the great curiosities of Mexico, is worth keeping in mind for purposes of comparison when you see the church of that other silver plutocrat, Borda of Taxco.

Guanajuato silver has made this amazing town what it is and isolation has kept it what it is. But there are good roads to it now from several directions, and some day, not far distant, it will be a Mecca for tourist thousands. Already, travel agencies are offering three-day packaged tours, combining Querétaro, San Miguel de Allende and Guanajuato, for less than $75, hotels, meals, transportation and guide all included. Soon Guanajuato may be almost another Taxco, at least in terms of popularity.

CHAPTER 17

THE SIRENS OF THE SOUTH

The Call of Cuernavaca

CUERNAVACA–TEQUESQUITENGO–TAXCO–ACAPULCO are generally seen in a chain of ecstatic travel by those who drive a car of their own or who elect to hire one in Mexico City. But it is a five-hour drive clear to Acapulco (264 miles), even by the excellent new toll road, and many travelers make an overnight round trip as far as Taxco only (109 miles), with a halt one or both ways at Cuernavaca, and then fly by Aeronaves from the capital's airport to Acapulco. Cuernavaca is only about 50 miles from the capital, and for those who wish to save the expense of hiring a car, an impressive saving indeed; there is a quarter-hourly limousine service from six A.M. to nine P.M., the address of the Mexico City terminal being—easy does it—Calle Netzahualcoyotl 163. To pursue this topic a bit further, two bus lines serve Taxco, a fast line of six-passenger microbusses called *Los Galgos* (The Greyhounds), starting from—you'll find this address easy—Calle Fray Servando Teresa de Mier 148, and a so-called Pullman service by a company called *Estrella de Oro* (Gold Star), with large but slower busses. For the long pull to Acapulco the Gold Star uses double-deck deluxe busses not unlike the Scenicruisers of our American Greyhound lines.

The whole subject of Mexican busses is nowadays an item of travel news, for the improvement has been truly spectacular, yet tariffs are so low as to defy belief. The 264-mile ride by deluxe bus to Acapulco costs less than $5, and the one-way fare to Taxco, a 100-mile journey, is only around a dollar.

Cuernavaca is a much-loved residential town whose history is as romantic as its present appearance. Being almost 3000 feet lower in altitude than the capital, its climate is semitropical and its floral luxuriance beyond description. There are glorious twin plazas in the center of the town, named for Morelos and Juárez. All of Cuernavaca's better hotels have outdoor swimming pools and various trappings of sport, and all are brilliantly bowered in flowers. Hibiscus, vast masses of purple and rose bougainvillea, and scarlet and even yellow poinsettias dominate the show; you may have the good fortune to see some fine magenta-and-white passion flowers. These are named for the Lord's Passion and the origin of the name is interesting. The corolla forms a perfect crown (of "thorns") and from it emerge three stamens ("nails"), which pious folk consider represent the spikes that nailed Christ to the cross.

The best hotel of a resort type is the *Posada Jacarandas*. For honeymooners, there's a "Love Nest" on top of a tree. Other features include a Japanese suite, a swimming pool, a golf course, and deck tennis. *Las Mañanitas* is also pleasant and luxurious in a quiet, unshowy way. The *Casino de la Selva*, despite its name, is a garden hotel whose rooms have private terraces. The *Casa de Piedra* is also recommendable, as is the *Papagayo*, the latter of special interest if you have children with you, since this hotel has two swimming pools, one specifically for youngsters.

An excellent restaurant, located on a pleasant knoll that can be seen as one enters the city from the north, is the *Terrazas Majestic*. Its conversation piece consists of glass-topped dining-room tables, beneath which is a small pool. If you toss a coin into the water a jet of spray hits the bottom of the table and gay lights illuminate the miniature fountain. Each day the coins are collected for the benefit of local charity. Las Mañanitas has also a fine restaurant, with atmosphere provided by peacocks that strut about the lawn.

Cuernavaca is the capital of Morelos State. Its name means "Cow's Horn," but this was merely the conquistadores' lazy way

THE CALL OF CUERNAVACA

of saying Cuauhnahuac, the Indians' word for "Beside the Woods." A more luxuriant setting for a town can hardly be found or imagined anywhere than this of Cuernavaca. No wonder Cortés loved it and built here his palace in the country. No wonder Borda loved it and spent his millions building here his own Versailles—but definitely without showiness. No wonder ambassadors have loved it, including Dwight Morrow, and have made it their Mexico home. No wonder Mexico City's privileged thousands and you and I and all other travelers love it.

The Cortés Palace, now used for the state legislative offices, is the center of the city. Its lofty loggia, with the Rivera frescoes, the gift that Dwight Morrow presented to the people of Cuernavaca, is the center of the palace, so far as visitors are concerned. This great mural is in the process of being restored from the ravages of dampness and fungus. It is typical of the artist, including his ruddy bias and his savagery toward privilege and toward the Church. Typical of his social sentiments is that portion of the picture which portrays Indians being branded with red-hot irons to indicate whose property they were; and typical of his sentiments toward the Church are the ghastly representations of human sacrifice as practiced by the Aztecs, shown at one end of the loggia, and the similar "human sacrifice," practiced by the Holy Inquisition, shown at the other end. Both are made to seem equally horrible and perhaps they were, though certainly the scale of the Aztec slaughters was a thousandfold greater.

Interesting anecdotes of the Conquest are shown, including Cortés' dismantling (not burning) of the boats at Veracruz; and interesting persons include Bartolomé de las Casas and, of course, La Malinche. From conspicuous points on either side of the loggia Morelos and Zapata gaze earnestly at us, and Morelos' eyes follow us strangely wherever we go.

A technical effect is invoked by Rivera to dramatize his fiery preaching. At the north end of the mural, where the historical narrative commences and where capitalistic and ecclesiastical greed are at their worst, the colors are very somber indeed. The effect softens gradually as the picture moves along until finally the bright Social Revolution bursts through triumphantly. Zapata is the key figure of this wondrous change, since his operations were chiefly in the Cuernavaca region and farther south. He is clad in dazzling white and he rides a white horse. The skies over him are as blue as Cuernavaca's own.

This town, if we may exploit the Spanish reflexive so commonly encountered, "sees itself" and "enjoys itself." You will hardly have difficulty in finding the things that need seeing and enjoying, but it will be a practical aid if you find, perhaps in the lobby of your hotel, some illustrated and mapped brochure of Cuernavaca, presumably put out by Pemex or the Mexican Tourist Association. These publications are always coming and, alas, going.

Your strolls will inevitably include the dreamy *Borda Gardens* with their mirror pools; the *cathedral* and its adjoining *Third Order Church*, both of Franciscan origin; the Morrow home, *Casa Mañana*, where the ambassador lived with his family and where Charles Lindbergh courted Anne. This is on Calle Dwight Morrow and at the extreme end of it rises the *Tepetate Chapel*, framed by two cypress sentinels. The Tepetate Chapel, always associated with Mrs. Morrow because of her affection for it, is one of the loveliest "artist's bits" in Mexico.

On a warm afternoon I found a seat in the humble *Salón Ofelia*, on the Plaza Morelos, chiefly because it is far more shady at that time of day than the Marik's porch, but partly in tribute to a book about Mexico. I refer to Gertrude Diamant's *The Days of Ofelia*, which has not been surpassed for charm nor for its sympathetic view of Mexico's "lower brackets." As I watched the life of the plaza I saw many a potential Ofelia and many an Eduardo, but the touch that seemed to me most agreeably typical of Indian Mexico, though not mentioned in the book, was the row of evangelistas. In this city they have made their "office" on the plaza's pavement. I watched the Cuernavaca scribes as I had watched others in other cities, as they sat patiently behind their typewriters, waiting for business, and finally one of them landed a client.

He was a diffident cocoa-skinned youth and evidently found it most difficult to start dictating his letter. Finally he plucked up courage and the words came. Of course I was for him all the way, hoping hard that he was not as nervous as he looked and that he would not forget to put in lots of *abrazos* and *besos*. It would be perfectly safe to do so. The wooden-faced scribe would not be beguiled into any show of mockery, for he was in much the same position as a father confessor in his confessional box; and furthermore, a client is a client.

Tangents to Tepoztlán and the Caves of Cacahuamilpa

A half-hour's drive northeast of Cuernavaca is an attractive, sleepy little village named Tepoztlán, dotted with trees and surrounded by cliffs. The people here still prefer to speak Aztec rather than Spanish, and cling to many of their old traditions. Every September 8 there's a brilliant fiesta in honor of the town's patron god, Tepoztecatl, with Indian dancing and theatrics. An interesting shrine in his honor stands on a pinnacle high above the valley and the village. If you're not troubled by claustrophobia you may enter it. Inside an inner shrine are carved, bold-relief hieroglyphics. A pleasant village inn, where you can get a good meal, is the *Posada del Tepozteco*, with a swimming pool, and a magnificent view of the village from its hilltop.

If caverns intrigue you, you may wish to seek out the Caves of *Cacahuamilpa*. The largest yet discovered in Central Mexico, they are rather similar to the Carlsbad Caverns. Although discovered in 1835, they haven't yet been completely explored. They are illuminated, and regular conducted tours are made several times a day. The caves are southwest of Cuernavaca, on the border between the states of Morelos and Guerrero.

Lake Tequesquitengo, Five Syllables of Water Fun

Lake Tay-case-key-ten-go, to phoneticize these syllables, is a holiday lake 22 miles southeast of Cuernavaca. In August of 1958 the lake received most of the blow from a severe flood that wrought havoc in many parts of Mexico, but it has bounced back to life and is now not only floodproof but a very popular resort. Unfortunately, the road leading to it is still in very poor condition, but the lake is worth the effort all the same. *Hotel Tequesquitengo* is the chief place on the lake. All rooms face the water.

Your meals may be had, if you wish, on your own balcony and you may toss breadcrumbs or other tidbits straight down into the water at the hotel's base, where a horde of hungry fishes will make short work of your discarded delicacies. Lunching and dining on the terrace, just at the water's edge, shaded by big umbrellas, is a relaxing delight, and on Sundays the hotel puts on a help-yourself buffet lunch that is so lavish and excellent that it has reminded me, in a rather more tropical way, of the buffet luncheons offered by the shorefront hotels on the beach at Waikiki. A frequently offered specialty of this lake-edge buffet is a Mexican-slanted shish-kebab, which is nothing short of marvelous when accompanied by a bottle or two of Carta Blanca.

Water sports, especially swimming (in the lake or large pool, illuminated at night), are the chief diversions, eagerly practiced and eagerly watched, too, for there are special water-ski shows given on the lake for the entertainment of the hotel guests. Wonderful stunting is done by a group of Mexican youths who have become exceedingly expert. They can ski-jump, of course, from an inclined raft, and they can water-ski in patterns and crisscross "skeins," in complete 360-degree turns and standing on their heads on a round disk and even—hardest of all—*on their bare feet*, with no skis, no ski shoes, no disk—nothing.

Of the two other tourist inns in the Tequesquitengo region, only one is also on the lake, a smaller place called the *Oasis Hotel*, owned by the owners of the Hotel Monte Cassino in Mexico City. The other, at some distance from the lake, is the *Hacienda Vista Hermosa*, with a charming pool and view. The hotel has an interesting history having started out, in 1529, as a ranch; and been, successively, a monastery, a sugar mill, a ranch again, and finally a hotel.

The name Tequesquitengo is said to mean "Saltpeter Market" and in the name we find an interesting fact of history, for Hernán Cortés, who had his hacienda here, built a church and village in a volcanic crater that had valuable deposits of saltpeter but was destined to fill up over a period of some two centuries to become the present Lake Tequesquitengo. There is still a strong saltpeter content in the water and this has one property that should recommend it to all visitors, for *mosquitoes can't endure saltpeter.* The very suspicion of it drives them away, so lake-shore dwellers and holiday-seekers need give no thought at all to this pest. I have sat on the terrace of the Hotel Tequesquitengo for all the hours of a long dinner and much postprandial chat, without being bothered by the incursion of a single mosquito, and this despite the fact that there were bright lights all over the terrace. And as for the church that Cortés built, it's still there, a hundred feet or more under the surface, and divers have more than once explored its remains. The surface of the lake is rather large for southern Mexico, being oval in shape and some five or six miles in width at its widest point. It lies about 3000 feet above sea level and the water temperature in winter averages 79 degrees, the air being a trifle warmer at 82 degrees.

Taxco the Incomparable

Whatever places you miss in central Mexico, including the capital itself, do not miss *Taxco!* Its romance is true, its beauty *total*. In an article called *Taxco Done in Silver*, written on the spot when I first visited the town some years ago, I burst into such an enthusiastic panegyric that I was almost ashamed to send the piece to any editor, lest it seem overexcited—but it was printed without setting the pages afire. I called this town the absolute equal of any hill town in France or Italy, and that statement I have never desired to take back. Knowing all the chief European hill towns, I am in a position to do my personal comparing and I still feel that this treasure of Mexico is as good as the very best in the Old World.

Taxco (correctly pronounced Tasco) is, to repeat this bit of information once again, a "National Monument," protected by the federal government, and it is zealously supervised, in this respect, by federal architects. Every home and every business building in the town has—and must have—a red-tiled roof and this law alone adds measureless beauty to the place. Survey in certain other potentially pretty towns the hit-or-miss roofs, some of tile, some of concrete, some even of rusty metal, and then feast your eyes on Taxco.

Cortés was the founder of this town, but Borda, originally Joseph le Borde, born of Spanish parents in the French city of Toulon, was the man who really built it. His horse is supposed to have sunk a hoof in soft ore that proved to be an outcropping of a vein of silver. This became the fabulous San Carlos vein and on the exact spot where the horse was so richly trapped, the cathedral ultimately rose. "God gives to Borda and Borda gives to God" is the much-worn saying. The 18th-century millionaire did at any rate suit the action to the aphorism by building in 20 years the sumptuous cathedral that dominates the whole region. It is supposed to have cost ten million pesos and these were Borda's pesos, though doubtless they were sweated from humble laborers in the manner of the times. The material of the church, which gives forth a wonderful warm glow, is a pink rock called *cantera* and the chiseling of it, especially in the façade and the tall slender towers, is as delicate as though the whole church were a *châsse* intended to house the relics of a saint.

The inside is of very handsome churrigueresque adornment, with much gold leaf and with the Quetzalcoatl-Christian symbol of the shell constantly recurring. It will be noted that the images of Christ in agony always show plenty of *blood*. This was for the simplest of reasons. The Indians have always understood blood and what it means to shed it. They could and still can read these images like open books. The paintings, as against the decorations, were all done by the great Miguel Cabrera, whose blues and reds some Mexican critics consider unique in the field of art.

Silver made Taxco and silver still forms the dominant motif of business, but in these days relatively little ore is mined—except from the pockets of tourists. Numerous shops—two of the best known being *Talleres Borda*, which was Borda's own home, and *Los Castillo*—sell pins and brooches and silver ornaments of every kind, wrought by the hands of local artisans. Many of the items are exquisite and temptation demolishes the last vestige of sales resistance. Taxco urchins, all of whom speak tourist American of the most fluent if limited sort ("What's cookin', sir?" and "That's the real McCoy, lady."), appoint themselves as cicerones and drag the unresisting shoppers here and there. My self-appointed guide on one occasion was a most charming and lively youngster supporting the name of Jesus German, which loses its comic aspect if one dresses it up with accents and pronounces it in Spanish.

To watch the artisans, as one may do in either of the above establishments, is a sheer fascination, and old-time visitors think with deep nostalgia of William Spratling.

Some 300 persons were employed here by Mr. Spratling and most of them worked on silver, though some devoted themselves to woodworking and cabinetry and some to ornamental objects in tin. Mexican silver, the chief material of that or any *taller* (which word will be recognized as the Spanish cousin of *atelier*) was, and still is, seen in great bars and it is of such purity that it is far too soft for direct use. An alloy to the extent of 2 per cent must be used to harden it. The Spratling artisans started learning their craft when they were mere boys, but in time they became finished craftsmen and then teachers.

One should not assume that Bill Spratling has disappeared from the silver scene merely because he no longer lives and works in Taxco. Far from retiring, he is quite as active as ever, though he has now taken up his headquarters down in the valley, near Iguala, where he has instituted a taller for the making of his celebrated articles in silver. The remarkable work of this founder of

Taxco's silver industry, for such "Bill" Spratling is, can be bought in an exclusive Spratling Shop of the Talleres Borda, conspicuous on the north side of the Zócalo. Bill himself, still spry, dashes about all over Mexico in his private plane, which he hops aboard with the nonchalance of a cyclist mounting his bike. Sometimes he flies to Mexico City and back three times in a day. Once he made a famous flight, alone, to Alaska and arranged to have 24 Eskimos sent to Taxco (or Iguala) to work on silver, but the venture was not a success. The Eskimos proved better adapted for fishing and sealing than for making fine silver articles. Spratling's charming book *Little Mexico*, has long been a classic.

Above the cathedral the town climbs hundreds of feet—you may take a hair-raising ride, *by jeep only*, to lofty viewpoints named *Guadalupe* and *La Vista*—and below the cathedral the town falls away other hundreds, but the house that Borda built for God (in return for the mining concession) is the center of everything. The plaza from which it rises is even the center of unchurchly revelry—of a most innocuous sort, for here is *Paco's* very humble veranda bar, with a straight-on view of the cathedral towers that surely few other bars in the world can match for romance; and here, too, is the original *Bertha's* tiny café-bar. Bertha won the distinction of being written up in such sophisticated publications as *Esquire*. She made substantial money to match her international fame, but some years ago, advancing years caused her to retire and leave her business to a nephew. The Bertha "nightclub" was, and still is, so humble that fastidious tourists sometimes hesitate to enter it, but it is the life of the Taxco evening, the rendezvous of spontaneous Latin songs, the trumpet of the Silver Symphony.

I have saved to the last my mention of Taxco's hotels, for they are a distinguished company. They are "sights" in themselves and each one has a view that you will swear surpasses all the others. In the upper town are two.

The *Rancho Taxco-Victoria* is a recent merger between the old Rancho Telva and the Victoria hotels. It is owned by Hoteles

TAXCO THE INCOMPARABLE

Mexicanos Dubin, Señor Dubin being the indefatigable Jimmie Dubin of Mexico Travel Advisors. The hotels were always next door to each other, which makes the merger a sensible arrangement. The Rancho is the more attractive property, with a string of terrace gardens virtually roofed over by brilliant bougainvilleas, and a swimming pool, but the Victoria is noted for its food. Guests, incidentally, may interchange meals at either hotel and also at the de La Borda, another Dubin property, in the lower town.

Santa Prisca is the other hotel in the upper town. It is a bit lower in location than the Rancho Taxco-Victoria, and considerably lower in tariff, with a homely atmosphere and a broad open roof that sits just under the stars.

Los Arcos, graced by a lovely patio where one may dine in the open, is below the Zócalo, above the lovely Casa Humboldt, where the great German naturalist-explorer lived—and you will envy him.

Loma Linda is a well-run motel magnificently situated on a ledge beside the road to Acapulco.

Hotel de La Borda, a swanky hostelry on a separate knoll at the base of the town, is the favorite of Mexico City society and one readily sees why. It has grown smarter with the years and now has a splendid glassed-in belvedere, with a fireplace in the middle for cool evenings, and a very flossy swimming pool. As mentioned above, it is owned by Hoteles Mexicanos Dubin, and guests have reciprocal privileges at the Rancho Taxco-Victoria.

Posada de la Misión (Mission Inn) is, to my mind, the most flawless in picturesque charm. This whole "Mission Inn," in general and in particular, is a work of art, and, in the words of the old hymn, "every prospect pleases." To the west, Taxco climbs its hill before the very eyes of the Posada's guests and the sight is one of the tourist world's most utterly unforgettable, whether by dawn's early light, by full daylight, by gloaming light or after dark. The night view has been recently enhanced by a very skillful floodlighting of the cathedral by a sort of pastel illumination that brings out the gentle pinkish glow of its cantera-rock material.

On a wide and high retaining wall, back of its kidney-shaped pool—I've saved the best for last—is a huge mosaic mural by Mexico's most celebrated living muralist, Juan O'Gorman. The whole vast picture, which tells the story of the hero-emperor, Cuauhtémoc, last of the Aztecs, the man who "wouldn't talk," even when Cortés has his bound feet placed over a fire, is made from natural stones garnered from Taxco's own State of Guerrero and mostly from near Taxco itself. Their range of colors—red, mauve, rust, yellow, black, white and that's not all—is as astonishing as the scope and artistry of the picture. A leaflet explaining all the details of the scene is available at the Posada, and in the inn's presidential suite, where several Mexican presidents have stayed, there is a vivid oil painting of Cuauhtémoc's trial by fire. Señora Razó de T. Amézaga, who owned and managed the Posada, was criticized by other hotel people for her "folly" in engaging O'Gorman to do the swimming-pool mural. Said one, "You could have built 20 new rooms and baths for what that mural cost you." This she admitted, but she had no regrets, nor will you when you see the stirring work. Juan O'Gorman is a devotee of Taxco and of this Posada.

I have to report that a few years ago the Balsa chain took over the management of La Misión, bringing to nine (and soon it will be ten) the links, in Mexico, of the Balsa chain, but the quality, and personality, of this lovely hotel seem not to have been at all disintegrated by becoming one-tenth of a group instead of a loved hotel enjoying its individual fame.

For convenience in making short strolls from Taxco's Zócalo-cathedral center, the upper hotels are recommendable, but those who drive their own cars generally prefer the lower ones because they are on the main highway. From considerations of view I am inclined to vote for the lower ones, specifically the La Borda or the Misión, for two reasons. First, the whole town hangs before the eyes like an incredible tapestry, red of hue by day from the innumerable tiled roofs, a banner of scintillant lights by night. And second, there is the thrilling outlook from the tiny shrine in the rear of the inn. You naturally assume that you are on very low ground at the Mission Inn, with Taxco high above; but no—you are still a mile above sea level. As you sit on the parapet behind this shrine you feel that you are on the edge of the "bottomless world." You look straight down at the twisting ribbon of the road that leads down to Iguala and on to Acapulco. And you look down far below that to a hamlet in a deep ravine where life goes on, even as it does at your level and in the loftier levels of the town. The activities of that hamlet are on the same scale in your eyes as are your activities in the eyes of the plane pilot who cuts a path in the cobalt sky a thousand feet above you. Taxco is like that—a vertical town where every view of it rivals every other. It is romance itself, done in stone and tile and dazzling plaster and bougainvillea and birds. As Shakespeare might have put it: The soul that hath no Taxco in himself—but you and I *have*.

Another Taxco attraction is its Sunday market. The mercado is downhill and just south of the plaza. You'll find its displays of fruits, vegetables, handicrafts and whatnot unfailingly colorful.

Three miles south of Taxco, then two miles more, over a spectacular road, brings you to a charming resort hotel called the *San Francisco Guadra*. A hacienda dating from 1540, it is a miniature village in itself, with cobbled streets, tiny church and rustic walks. There is a swimming pool, and guests are provided with transportation to and from Taxco.

Acapulco in Her Bathing Suit

Acapulco looks wonderfully well in her bathing suit. She is as beautiful as any of her most favored rivals in the Old World or the New and if she is a "warm number" she is certainly neither torrid nor sultry. Her temperament, moreover, is amazingly even and you need look for no storms nor tantrums nor even many clouds to shadow her lovely serenity.

To retreat from this risky metaphor and find a place to stay in Mexico's most popular resort is a practical necessity, and a poser, too, for during many months of the winter, when Acapulco's magnetism is at its strongest, all the hotels are full, and this despite the enormous recent increase, a phenomenon of the first travel magnitude, in accommodations of every type.

You can fly here direct (and probably before you read these words, nonstop) from California, and nonstop flights to Acapulco from the U.S. East Coast are also just around the corner of the sky. Aeronaves de México shuttles jets all day long between Mexico City and Acapulco. In addition to this influx, the resort receives hundreds of private cars daily and numerous good busses and tourist limousines. The double-decker busses of Estrello de Oro are air-conditioned and serve luncheon aboard.

To meet and sustain such waxing popularity, Acapulco now has over 150 hotels (more, in the official listing for tourists, than the capital itself) and several of them are large and of luxury status. The reeking dust of the town's Zócalo and radiating streets is no more. Every street has been paved—in one burst of energy, it is said, within a period of 45 days. And the bumpy little pasture that formerly served as airfield has been long since replaced by a fine modern airport.

To keep the following report under any sort of control I'll have to condense and abridge the story of Acapulco's hotels most stringently; so here goes, naming the most deluxe places first.

The *Pierre Marqués*, on exclusive Revolcadero Beach, five or six miles from the center, is in the very front rank of expensive luxury and elegance and it operates, contrary to the usual Acapulco custom, on the European Plan. It was built and is owned by the owners of the Hotel Pierre in New York, which is to say the billionaire oil man, J. Paul Getty, who is generally considered to be the richest man in civil life in the world. Perhaps I need not say more.

Las Brisas Hilton (The Breezes) is absolutely unique in my experience. It is an extremely sumptuous cottage colony, rising steeply on a hillside. Every cottage has a view of the magic scene of Acapulco Bay and very much more. There are 200 (at this writing) rooms, and 100 swimming pools, and 150 pink-and-white jeeps, at a modest charge per day, for your jaunts to town or elsewhere.

Las Brisas' private double beach, La Concha (The Shell), where bathing-suit luncheons are a daily feature, is actually several salt-water lagoons, one or two of them deep for adults, others shallow, with a little beach, for the children. There's a separate, supervised luncheon place for the kiddies, too, so their parents can be mercifully "shet of them" while they enjoy their swim, lunch and siesta.

The *El Presidente*, a Balsa (Sheraton) hotel, is the last possible word in skyscraping luxury and also in setting, for it rises straight up in part from a glorious beach, dramatized here and there by huge round boulders, and in part from a sort of tropical park. It is *the* place for well-to-do guests who wish to be within close range of Acapulco, yet not in the bustling center of it. It is located rather far out on the "afternoon beach" called Los Hornos (The Ovens—but it is cool there), yet within an easy ten minutes of downtown by taxi.

The *Acapulco Hilton* is a 13-story holiday palace whose most distinctive feature is a restaurant called *La Isla* (The Island), completely surrounded by a 900-foot circular swimming pool. Three bridges link the restaurant to the hotel grounds. The hotel has a nightclub called *Kon Tiki* that is rated one of the resort's best.

Las Hamacas features 25 acres of coconut groves, a private beach and fishing pier, a lavish pool, and music piped in all over the grounds.

Among the many other newish hotels and motels are:

The *Elcano*, a Balsa (Sheraton hotel) of deluxe status, still farther out on the afternoon beach. Every room has a sea-facing balcony and there is a delightful seaside pool. Near this hotel is Acapulco's 9-hole golf course.

The *Noc Noa* is another of the Balsa group.

The *Boca Chica*, at Caletilla Beach, is ultramodern and it strikes a fresh note by including a fine breakfast in the published prices of its rooms.

El Pozo del Rey (The King's Well), small and delightful, is in a luxuriant tropical garden.

The *Monaco* is a good motel on the afternoon beach.

Probably the most deluxe of the motels is the *Hotel Miami & Courts*, featuring Swiss cuisine and a Swiss chalet-style wing—with Florentine-mosaic tiling!

Three other excellent motels are the *Tampa*, the *Ritz* and the *Acapulco*.

New hotels, as in Mexico City, seem to spring up every year in Acapulco. *Hotel Maris*, on Los Hornos Beach, rises like El Presidente, straight up from the sea's edge. *Hotel Pan Americano*, on the Acapulco peninsula opposite the Hotel Majestic, is another of good quality, though not luxurious.

Among the old standbys in Acapulco are: the just-mentioned *Majestic*, rising on a steep slope with several terraces, and a glass-enclosed outside elevator; the *El Mirador*, located on a clifftop (this is where the famous divers perform), with a funicular that takes guests down to its pools, one halfway down the cliff, the other cleverly built into an inlet of the ocean. Western Hotels International manages this hotel, a longtime favorite; the *Hotel Prado Americas*, another in the Balsa chain, is on a hill cliff, 280 feet above the bay. The bay-section bungalows are the coolest, and their bay view, by day and night, is thrilling. The hotel has a two-level pool on the cliff.

Hotel Club de Pesca (meaning Fishing Club, but this is *only* a name, selected at random) is on the edge of the bay, with a wonderful cross-breeze to keep it cool throughout, though it is air-conditioned, too. Its pool, its restaurant, its *Tropicana Nightclub* and its Turquoise Bar, with gay music every night till three A.M., are all of top quality and it boasts its own private sea beach—and wharf.

Hotel Caleta, on the high bank above the like-named "morning beach," has advanced to the front rank of the centrally located hotels. It is a large and cheerful hostelry, under the management of Western Hotels International, as is El Mirador.

Other pleasant places are *Hotel Bahía*, on the peninsula not far from the Yacht Club, finely located and inexpensive; *Los Flamingos*, on a high ridge; the *Costero*, secluded, select and expensive; *Palacio Tropical*, with a pool in a hillside garden and a dinner-dance restaurant, up aloft, called the Starlight Roof; and *Hotel del Monte*, with a palm-fringed pool, a tropical bar and a terrace dining room that fairly hangs in the sky.

Virtually all of Acapulco's hotels operate on the American Plan, meaning with meals, but if, in spite of this, you wish to try some separate restaurants, you'll find the *Belair*, near Hotel El Presidente, very good, as a sort of society restaurant, and for Italian food you'll like the new *Dino's*, on the afternoon beach; also *Armando's* and the *Sao Paulo*.

Nightclubs are of considerable variety and some of the chief ones cleverly *stagger* their floor shows—no pun intended by the italicized word—so that customers can see several successively in a single evening. Outstanding are the *Jacaranda Room* at El Presidente, the *Kontiki* at the Acapulco Hilton, *La Perla* at the El Mirador, *Cocoteras* near Las Hamacas, the *Flamingo*, the *Tropicana* at the Club de Pesca, the *Starlight Roof*, in the Palacio Tropical, the *Cantarana*, on a spectacular sea cliff near Las Brisas Hilton, the *Varadero*, on the coastal road approaching town, and the smart *Club de Esquies* (Water Ski Club), on the harbor, offering an exciting water-ski show every night of the year. Most of these places operate the year around, but some of the hotel nightclubs close down in summer.

Of all the night shows the most thrilling—don't watch it unless your heart is in good repair—is that of *La Perla* at La Quebrada, seen from open-air terraces of Hotel El Mirador. For its climax, a diving boy, spotlighted all the way, descends the cliff by a long flight of steps to a platform on one side of a narrow indentation of the sea and dives some 40 feet into the churning waters. He swims across and climbs the almost perpendicular cliff on the other side of the indentation, clinging on by a toe here, an eyelash there, to a flat rock at a height of 40 meters, which is 132 feet! He poises on the brink and then the spotlight is turned off, for its glare would blind him. On a ledge across the inlet, far below him but well above the water, newspapers are set afire to give him enough light to see where he's diving and to enable the watchers to witness the plunge. Then he gets set and makes the perilous 132-foot dive. It has to be perfectly done every evening, for this is a really narrow "sea ravine," with jagged rocks on both sides.

Among Acapulco's sights, other than its pervasive, Naples-like beauty, the cheerful, rebuilt Zócalo and the long quay are conspicuous. From the latter you may go water-skiing, or rent a launch and go out to the open sea in search of big sea game, notably the prized sailfish, or if you're in less ambitious mood you may take your choice of a number of excursion boats. The *Fiesta I* makes a popular five-hour cruise, putting into Puerto Marqués for a treasure hunt, lunch and a swim. *Fiesta II* makes a three-hour afternoon cruise, and also a three-hour moonlight cruise, where the bar is on the house and there is entertainment and dancing. The *Sea Cloud* is another fine cruise yacht, making a three-hour "cocktail" cruise, with dance orchestra and free unlimited drinks, and also evening sailings glamorously named *lunadas*.

Acapulco has three local beaches in addition to the less central *Pie de la Cuesta* (Foot of the Hill) and the more distant strand called *Revolcadero* ("Wallow"). *La Caleta* (The Cove), its perfect crescent split and dominated by an island castle originally built by Avila Camacho's brother, is the lovely morning beach, always crowded until one or two but comparatively deserted thereafter. *La Roqueta* is an island beach reached by motorboat (three pesos round trip) from La Caleta. It is much more secluded than the other, and from it one may climb to the lighthouse on the high ridge above it. *Los Hornos,* the afternoon beach, is a far longer, more rugged stretch of sand than either of the other local ones and with much bigger, though not dangerous, surf.

One afternoon I encountered on Los Hornos Beach a giggling group of young Mexican girls. They saw me from afar and spotted me as a gringo. As I drew near, one of them rushed up to me and said prettily, "Excuse me, sir. Do you know where we can buy a whale?"

I didn't. But I thought the incident charming.

The Call of Zihuatanejo

Long known to Mexican vacationists and just beginning to catch on with the American beachcomber seeking new beaches to conquer is Zihuatanejo. A tiny hideaway resort, it is 147 miles northwest of Acapulco. You can drive or bus there from Acapulco, a fairly rugged drive but not too difficult. You can also fly there direct from Mexico City in an hour and 25 minutes by Aeronaves DC-3. The beaches are far superior to Acapulco's, as is reflected in such charming names as *La Solitaria*. Although the number of hotels is limited, their quality is good. There is *Brisas de Zihuatanejo*, with private beach, restaurant, bar, and a reservations office in Mexico City. There is also *Hotel Catalina*, on a hillside overlooking the bay, with funicular service to the beach (and complementary jeep transportation back and forth to town). Others are the *Hotel Belmar*, a pleasantly rustic place in the village, and the *Zafari*, of bungalow type, with an excellent dining room and swimming pool, the latter being a great favorite with fishermen and other sportsmen. Until very recent years this part of the Mexican coast, known as the Costa Brava, has been practically unknown to tourism, being hidden behind the massive natural barriers of the Sierra Madre del Sur. But now that the road is in and there is regularly scheduled air service, this charming resort is bound to come into its own.

CHAPTER 18

TO PUEBLA AND THE FORT OF FLOWERS

Cholula and Its Calendar of Churches

NATIONAL highway Number 190 leads over the lofty pass on the flank of snow-crowned "Ixtaci" and so through Cholula (76 miles) and Puebla (84 miles) to a fork that carries on by two alternative routes to Veracruz. The southern route, which chiefly concerns pleasure travelers, passes through Tehuacán (160 miles; with the pleasant spa called *Peñfiel*), Orizaba, Fortín (210 miles), and ancient Córdoba, and so, continuing by a paved road the entire distance, the remaining few miles to the gulf port. A rather good bus service of the so-called Pullman category runs between Mexico City and Veracruz. As on other lines of acceptable quality, only reserved seats are sold, so there should never be mad scrambles and never massed standees. (We may interpolate an important travel thought here, reminding ourselves that in coming from the capital we have been on the Pan American Highway, which, however, strikes off south—from our present route—at Puebla and continues to Oaxaca and Guatemala.)

By air, the travel time between Mexico City and Veracruz is a mere 70 minutes.

Cholula is a sort of ganglion of villages with 160 churches whose polychrome tiled domes illumine the countryside for miles around. It will be recalled that Cortés vowed to replace each of the 400 heathen teocallis hereabouts with a Christian church (see Chapter 5), but he and his descendants have done well to miss the mark by only 60 per cent. The most conspicuous of the churches, and one of the least beautiful, rises from the large pre-Aztec pyramid on the edge of the chief village. This pyramid was erected to honor Quetzalcoatl and the basic reason for the choice of its site is of prime interest. The gentle god, who was born of a virgin in a far eastern land (!), had incurred the wrath of some more potent god on the Mexican plateau and had been forced to "leave the premises." In doing so, he halted for a matter of 20 years in Cholula, teaching the arts of civilized living to the people of the region. Then he continued to the coast and set sail in a magic boat of serpents' skins for his mythical eastern home, vowing to return one day and liberate his people. When he finally did return he had transformed himself, as we have seen, into the doughty warrior, Hernán Cortés. Mexico has dramatized this transformation by naming the handsome mountain that looms above Cholula and Puebla for Cortés' handsome mistress, La Malinche.

Convoyed by a guide with a lantern, one may wander through seemingly endless labyrinthine passages in Quetzalcoatl's pyramid, far beneath the church upon its crest, and wonder, as always in the presence of such monstrous works of antiquity, at the endless, patient labor that must have gone into the building of it. To the humble folk who performed such immense toil, this god of the evening star, mysterious offspring of a mysterious virgin, must have been as real as any god or saint has been to any people.

The Weathered Wealth of Puebla

Puebla de los Angeles, fourth city of Mexico, is the most Spanish and most Catholic city of the republic. They call it the Rome of Mexico. Aside from the capital it is probably the wealthiest and most learned city. Its traditional manufactures are majolica in many colors, chiefly cheerful yellows and blues, and onyxware; and both of these pleasant materials are lavishly used in its churches, public buildings and plazas. The city is practically awash in venerable charm and you will feel repaid for spending several days here, instead of the usual three hours of the agency trips. *Hotel Lastra*, an Azteca hotel located about five minutes by car from the center of the city, is the best hotel, with the *Palace*, the *Royalty* and the *Imperial* as downtown possibilities.

The sights of the great and various Puebla of the Angels are so delightful and unusual that they cry to be seen, but some of them are elusive if you don't have a guide. A good city map is needed and one is found in the brochure called simply Tourism Department's *Puebla*. Take time to study it. It is simple to understand, though the wording is somewhat awkward.

The main streets of the city, intersecting the central plaza, have traditional names, but virtually all the others have numbers. The east-west thoroughfare is Avenida *Reforma* (in its more important portion); the north-south thoroughfare is Avenida *Cinco de Mayo*, north of the plaza, Avenida *16 de Septiembre*, south of the plaza. The plaza itself is the dividing point for the numbered streets. North (*Norte*) and South (*Sur*) streets have odd numbers west of the plaza, even numbers east of it; East (*Oriente*) and West (*Poniente*) streets have odd numbers south of the plaza, even numbers north of it. The text hereinafter will Anglicize addresses, but the sights are so numerous that even the chief ones can only be catalogued.

1. The *Cathedral*, second in size and importance to that of Mexico City, is a massive and somewhat gloomy affair whose interior is relieved by much Puebla onyx, including a great gray altar by Manuel Tolsa.

2. The *Biblioteca Palafoxiana* (entered from a courtyard at 5 Calle 5 Poniente, which is to say 5 West 5th Street, just back of the cathedral) is one of the most wonderful old libraries of incunabula in the world. Its three-tiered shelves of carved cedar, its worn brick floor, its gold-leaf "altar," its onyx-and-inlay tables, combine with its remarkable literary treasures to make it a venerably glamorous masterpiece. I have never seen its equal, save in some of the famous colonial libraries of Portugal and in the Benedictine Abbey library of Admont in Styria, which is lavish

and exuberant, in rococo style, whereas this of Puebla is mellow, reserved and cedar brown. Among its more valuable old tomes, seen under glass, you will find a beautifully illuminated Bible, which may test your Latin nicely. These are its opening words: *In Principio Creavit Deus Celum Et Terra. Terra Autem Erat Inanis Et Vacua.* Bishop Juan de Palafox y Mendoza gave this library and many other benefactions to 17th-century Puebla.

3. The *Santo Domingo Church* and its *Rosary Chapel* (on Avenida Cinco de Mayo, three blocks north of the main plaza) is an amazing ensemble of glittering and almost pagan ornament. Nothing else quite so artistically voluptuous exists in Mexico.

4. The *Hidden Convent of Santa Mónica* (far north on Avenida Cinco de Mayo, corner of West 18th Street) is the most curious in Latin America. When all of Mexico's conventual establishments were closed by the Reform Laws of Juárez, this one secretly defied the edict and kept functioning continuously for *over 70 years*, and that despite the fact that a municipal police station was located directly across the street. The façade of Santa Mónica is that of an ordinary dwelling house but its character is now openly revealed, for it is a religious museum open to the public. Visitors are conducted through its trap doors and camouflaged corridors so that they may see exactly how the convent's 60 nuns escaped when finally the federal police discovered the place in May, 1934. It is assumed that the local Puebla police, sympathetic to the sisters, simply refused to be aware of their religious neighbor-across-the-way.

Another odd note about the establishment is the origin of its name, for Santa Mónica was not a virgin! She was the mother of Saint Augustine. It seems that when the convent was founded the names of all the chief feminine saints were written on separate slips of paper and placed in an urn, from which receptacle one name was to be drawn at random so that Heaven might decide the weighty matter. To the consternation of all, the name of the married and motherly Mónica was first drawn by the officiating prelate. This might be a mistake of some kind, they thought, so he tried it again, and again Mónica's name emerged. A third time the same thing occurred, so the prelate and the pious sisters were compelled to conclude that through some inscrutable whim the Virgin Mother desired this particular "matron saint" to be the convent's sponsor.

5. The *Santa Rosa Convent Kitchen* (on North 3rd Street, between 12th and 14th, a block north of where it is wrongly shown on the above-mentioned brochure map) is a majolica miracle of olden times, and its shiny copper pots will make you want to steal them for your own so-different kitchen.

6. *La Casa del Alfeñique* (meaning Sugar Paste House), located at the corner of East 4th and North 6th Streets, is Mexico's most famous example of secular churrigueresque. It is so strangely, impudently gay as to be beyond belief. Wait until you see this strawberry shortcake covered with whipped cream and then say if you believe it is real. Perhaps, though, entering the place will bring conviction, for it is now the State Museum. Its collection of aboriginal and Spanish-colonial treasures is full of interest, but the simple bed and the worn slippers of the original China Poblana will easily win first place in your attention. The "Puebla China-girl" was a Chinese princess who has become partly legendary and who is much beloved throughout Mexico. She is supposed to have been captured by slavers, brought to the port of Acapulco, sold to a wealthy but pious man and brought finally to Puebla, where she was converted to Christianity and took the name Catalina de San Juan, devoting the rest of her life to works of charity. Accepting the new and austere religion, she discarded her Oriental modes of dress and wore a rough red skirt and white blouse, which have been touched up and glorified to become the present national costume. It now appears as a red skirt with a green border, embroidered with flowers, a white blouse of fine material with elaborate embroideries in many colors, much costume jewelry according to taste and a delicate shawl (*rebozo*) draped in gay fashion. There is nothing in the least austere about modern adaptations of the China-girl's coarse garments.

7. Nearby the Sugar Paste House, on North 8th Street, is the *Barrio del Artista*, a group of some 20 shops remodeled into artists' studios. Visitors are welcome.

8. *La Compañia*, or Jesuit Church (on South 4th Street, a block east of the plaza), is a huge and bizzare affair with as strange a majolica dome as you will ever see, and with a great deal of Puebla onyx in the interior. The church is interesting chiefly as containing the marked burial place of the China Poblana, under her very Christian and very Spanish name, of course.

9. *Agua Azul* (Blue Water) is a large and palatial *balneario* (watering place), four or five miles south of the city. If you have your car and like warm sulphur pools and holiday crowds, the resort warrants the short trip. There is a pleasant, modern hotel here, heavily named *Hotel Spa Reforma Agua Azul*.

The old glories of Puebla are eclipsed, in the thought of many tourists, by the city's unusual offerings to zealous shoppers. China Poblana costumes have, of course, a special appeal here, but *talavera ware* and tiles arouse equal or greater excitement, and the workshops of such conspicuous firms as *Iriarte* and *Guevara Brothers* can be readily located with help from the hotel porter. The name of this form of majolica pottery originated in Spain, where its chief place of manufacture was Talavera de la Reina, near Toledo, but it was early introduced into Mexico and notably to the city of Puebla. It has remained a chief product of this city and is so identified with it that one cannot see good majolica anywhere in Mexico without instinctively calling it Puebla ware. Onyx is the other specialty and this greenish-white chalcedony, with its darker parallel stripes, lends itself to the finest working by expert craftsmen. However, its lavish use in Puebla churches (even the floor is of onyx in the Rosary Chapel of Santo Domingo) has cheapened it somewhat and the positive prostitution of it by arcade shops of the central plaza has done much to rob an attractive stone of artistic merit. Paperweights, inkwells, ornaments, buttons and doodads of every sort are on sale by the thousands, and many of them have crossed Mexican and American flags painted on them, together with such ringing mottos as "My Country, My Honey" and "My Country, My Harry" (or Joe or Ben or Lois or Dorothy). If you can shut your eyes to these horrors you will find, especially in the onyx shops just off the plaza rather than on it, some very alluring souvenirs.

Fortín, a Floral Millionaire

The *Fortín de las Flores* ("Fortress" of the Flowers), once a wayside stronghold of the conquistadores while on their toilsome way up the sierra from Veracruz to the high plateau, has become the horticultural show of Mexico, far surpassing in floral magnificence Xochimilco and all other competitors of longer standing. There is, in fact, nothing quite like Fortín anywhere else in Latin America. To speak of the flowers in paltry millions is to understate the case; and, furthermore, they are not the commoner garden flowers such as petunias or marigolds, but are the kind that we buy in shops and greenhouses by the bloom or by the half dozen. Gladioli and lilies are seen in Fortín fields by the millions, but gardenias are seen surely in the tens of millions.

The *Hotel Ruiz Galindo* is the center and almost the sum of life in Fortín, though there is also a pleasant halting place for motorists called *Posada Loma Motel*, on the highway just east of the resort. Each table in the dining room of the Ruiz Galindo is brightened at every meal by a huge vase of gardenias. And the open-air swimming pool is made to look like the dream of a spendthrift film producer, by having a few thousand fresh gardenias tossed into it each morning, after those of the day before have been raked to the edge and thrown away. Swimming amid myriads of flowers, one feels like Marie Antoinette disporting in the pools of her luxuriant *hameau paysan*.

The Ruiz Galindo is the official permanent headquarters of the Inter-American Hotel Association and one can very well understand why the sophisticated *hoteleros* of 21 Americas should agree on this as their common gathering place, but you and I have come without waiting for a convention or a directors' meet-

FORTÍN, A FLORAL MILLIONAIRE

ing. If we have made the trip from the capital or Puebla by motor, we have passed Peñafiel (at Tehuacán) and then plunged over the plateau's edge to descend by a score of hairpin turns to Orizaba, Fortín, Córdoba, all valley towns at a modest 3000-foot level but dominated by Mexico's loftiest mountain, the superb peak of Orizaba, which mounts to the height of 18,225 feet. Those who have come by the night train of the *Ferrocarril Mexicano* from the capital's Buenavista Station have been delighted to find that their sleeping car was sidetracked at nearby Orizaba and left there, permitting them to finish out their sleep until eight o'clock.

Fortín is more than a resort. It is an experience. It is more than luxury-at-ease in the international style. It is a story to tell when you get home.

Veracruz, if you push on another 85 miles to reach it, or if you have arrived at that port by steamer or plane, will hardly warrant any prolonged visit, despite its historic interest as the landing place of Cortés. It does have an excellent hotel, the big and air-conditioned *Veracruz*, on the Plaza Constitución, offering three restaurants, three bars, a cafeteria, a roof garden and a heated pool. The *Diligencias*, under the same management, and *El Nacional* are two other recommendable downtown hotels. A pleasant beach hotel is the *Mocambo*, six miles south of town, and the *Emporio* has an attractive waterfront location. For an excellent seafood meal, try the restaurant at the old *Prendes* hotel. From Veracruz, National Highway Route 180 leads all the way to Mérida, a distance of 700 miles, with the Island of Carmen crossed en route. Time is obviously a necessary ingredient for this road-and-ferry trip. In these hurried days, of course, almost everybody flies.

CHAPTER 19

WONDERS OF OAXACA

Plaza Life at Its Best

Oaxaca (pronounced Wah-háh-cah) is the "farthest south" for most visitors to Mexico, though with the great strides in highway improvements, more and more motorists are continuing to *Tuxtla Gutiérrez*, 340 miles beyond, the colorful capital of the border state of Chiapas, and even to *San Cristóbal las Casas*. The best hotel in T.G. is the *Bonampak*, named for a Mayan town of antiquity discovered in 1947 by an expedition sponsored by the United Fruit Company and the Carnegie Institute of Washington. The hotels *Esponda* and *Serrano* are also recommendable.

In San Cristóbal las Casas, the *Hotel Español* is the focus of visitor life. In this town, in a home that is something of a museum, lives a most interesting couple named Mr. and Mrs. Frans Blom, who run Chiapas Tours. Beyond San Cristóbal, almost at the Guatemalan frontier, is the town of *Comitán* and beyond that are the *Montebello* lakes, a lovely scenic region whose shores abound in orchids and in tropical birds, but so far there is no place there where visitors may stay. Chiapas, hitherto virtually undiscovered, is undoubtedly destined to attain its place in the tourist sun.

For those who cannot venture to Mexico's far south, Oaxaca makes a fitting climax to any tour, for its background is immense, its present glows with soft allure and its future, tied to that of the Pan American Highway, is full of practical promise. One of the best-equipped service garages in Mexico is near the city's northern entrance and it seems that half of the ambitious young Mexicans one meets talk of opening up a shop in Oaxaca, or perhaps a motor camp or a *lonchería* (steakery). No doubt tourist inundations will rob the city of its pristine character as capital both of Zapotec and Mixtec civilizations, past and present, but much of its special charm will be indestructible.

The history of the Valley of Oaxaca is a pageant in itself. The Zapotecs probably built the great structures on the acropolis of *Monte Alban*, above the city, and also those of *Mitla*, 25 miles to the southeast, but Mixtec incursions confused these regions. The Aztecs later surged into the valley and then came the Spanish conquistadores. The whole region was granted by the Spanish crown to Hernán Cortés and thence came his sounding but inappropriate title (for he preferred Cuernavaca), Marqués del Valle de Oaxaca. Three centuries after the arrival of the conquerors came the Great Reformer. Benito Juárez was a pure Zapotec Indian native of the city. He became a schoolteacher here and then a professor of law. One of his students was another young Indian named Porfirio Díaz, who was destined to be the very opposite of a social reformer.

A city with so vast a background could not fail to be interesting, but Oaxaca is much more than a museum of past wonders. I think its plaza life is the most appealing in all Mexico, not even excepting that of Guadalajara. These pleasures can be reached and experienced with such ease that one rather wonders at the tardiness of tourism in taking full advantage of them. CMA has long served Oaxaca, making the trip from Mexico City in a little over an hour, and Aerolíneas Vegas serves this city directly from Acapulco and Puebla. Nacionales de México has a good train service from the capital on a highly scenic route.

The plaza life is a double life, for there are two large plazas lying corner to corner, the Zócalo or Plaza Mayor, and the Alameda. The Zócalo is, of course, the chief one and it is very large. On three sides it is flanked by spacious portales, with the usual shops, the usual evangelistas and very *un*usual cafés. There are astonishingly few attractive outdoor cafés in the Mexican republic, considering how the climate encourages such relaxation. One would expect to find thousands of them in the manner of France or Austria but, barring hotel terraces, there are scarcely a score of good ones in the whole country. Two or three of them are under the arcades of Oaxaca's Zócalo, which is in itself one of the pleasantest of siesta parks.

I have mentioned that three sides of this central square are flanked by arcades. The fourth is graced by the cathedral and a good hotel bearing the name *Marqués del Valle* in honor of the first marquis of the valley. The best hotel, however, is the *Victoria*, with swimming pool and purified drinking water, located on high ground on the Pan American Highway, a mile and a half north of the city. An excellent motel is the *Oaxaca Courts*, on the highway at the northern edge of town. This is a genuine bit of America-in-Mexico, its owners are an ingratiating couple from Texas. Among other good tourist hotels in Oaxaca are *Las Margaritas, Monte Alban, Señorial* and *La Mansión Imperial*. An excellent travel agency for this entire section of Mexico is *Centroamericana de Viajes, S.A.*, at 50-A Avenida Hidalgo, in Oaxaca.

Two Double Stars for Strolling

Of two dozen interesting sights of Oaxaca two stand out so brilliantly that they dim the others. These are, as you have guessed, a church and a museum, but *this* church and *this* museum are wonders of Mexico.

The *Church of Santo Domingo* is the one mentioned in Chapter 16 as the only one in the country capable of rivaling in baroque splendor the smaller church of Santa Rosa de Viterbo in Querétaro. Together with its adjoining monastery it forms a huge medieval fortress with immensely thick walls built to resist the frequent earthquakes of the region, but once inside the church one forgets the fortress aspect, for this is altogether as gay and giddy a spectacle, for a Christian house of worship as the mind can possibly cope with. There are, for instance, two "genealogical trees," one on the ceiling of the organ loft, the other over the main entrance. The branches spread out like the spreading chestnut tree and its leaves are of glistening gold. Amid this mass of aureate foliage are the busts of numerous saints, diminishing in size at the top until the uppermost ones are mere faces peeping out coyly or slyly from the tangled leaves. The Virgin is, of course, the central figure in both of these quaint trees.

The sight is enough to dazzle the eyes, yet the Santo Domingo ensemble is considerably less rich than once it was. This is supposed to have cost 13 million pesos, but unhappily it was desecrated on two or three occasions by being used as a military stable, and vandalism reached a shocking peak when some of the French troops who had imposed Emperor Maximilian on Mexico used it as a barracks. They smashed off part of the reredos for firewood, removed valuable religious paintings for use as sacking and chipped off large amounts of the thick gold leaf just for fun. This sort of thing has been the traditional sport of occupation troops in many countries in many periods of history. Europe's churches offer scores of examples, as, for instance, Santa Maria delle Grazie of Milan, where Leonardo da Vinci's *Last Supper* was defaced by Napoleon's cavalry to while away some boresome hours.

The *Museo Regional de Arqueologia* of Oaxaca State is every whit as interesting, in its smaller way, as the Anthropological Museum in the capital and it is far more intimate. It contains as its chief feature numerous plaques, religious decorations, urns and household and personal articles exhumed by archeologists from the ancient Zapotec and Mixtec tombs of Monte Alban, and no such thrilling collection of small wonders is to be seen either in the Aztec areas of Mexico or in the Maya areas of Yucatán and Guatemala. Even Peru, with all the gold wealth of the Incas as background, can muster no such miracles of craftsmanship. The articles are chiefly of pure gold, but there are others of green and gray jade, of amber, of obsidian, which is volcanic glass, of rock crystal and quartz, and there is even a case of real pearls that once adorned the great ladies of aboriginal Oaxaca. One of the pearls, a beautiful oval of enormous size, bulks about as large as a macadamia nut in its shell.

By far the richest cache of treasures on Monte Alban was found in 1932 by the Mexican archeologist, Professor Alonso Caso. This was the world-celebrated Tomb 7, which yielded no less than 500 separate items, many of them of very great intrinsic as well as artistic worth. It is said that when Professor Caso found it, quite by accident in connection with the building of a new road to the summit of the hill, he was literally struck dumb, for this was the event that happens once in the lifetime of one archeologist in a thousand. His wife and two Indian helpers were with him and they spent 24 consecutive hours, without sleep, delving into this almost unparalleled treasure house. Tomb 7 is thought to have been built originally by the Zapotecs and to have been appropriated by the Mixtecs and used as a special royal tomb. The bones of nine celebrities, presumably kings and high priests, were found here. The relics of this special tomb, lodged for a time in Mexico City, are now in a special room in this Oaxaca Museum and one may spend absorbed hours examining them. For once, museum attendants are neither over-officious nor tip-hungry. You may browse at will, asking them questions only if you wish to do so. The gold masks of the various Mixtec gods, and especially that of Xipetotec, the god of jewelers, will perhaps capture your first and greatest interest. This last, once covered with human skin to transfer the god's blessing of craftsmanship to human artificers, is a work of magnificent intricacy. The visitor feels like offering a libation to the jewelers' gold. He was by no means a handsome fellow but his inspiration was certainly effective.

Monte Alban and Mitla

The two great archeological sites of the Oaxaca Valley are easy to visit and are of supreme interest, quite aside from the treasures that they contained before looters and then authorized archeologists removed so many of them. Monte Alban was probably founded as a dwelling place by archaic peoples, developed as a religious center by the Zapotecs and captured by the Mixtecs only a few decades before the arrival of the Spanish conquerors. Mitla is a legacy of dubious origin stoutly ascribed to the Zapotecs—by present Zapotecs.

Monte Alban, reached by an easy paved road, would be worth visiting for its superlative view, even if it had no structures of early America. One may wander about among the temples and public buildings on the meadowlike summit, picking wild verbena but avoiding the poisonous weed called *mala mujer* (bad woman). The blossoms of the *casahuate* trees fleck the hill's sides with patches of white and this effect did, as a matter of fact, suggest to the conquerors the name White Hill, which is Monte Alban. Its original name was Oseotepec, meaning Tiger Hill Town. The word *tepec*, recurring frequently in place names of southern Mexico (not to mention Chapultepec in the capital), means Hill Town and one of the buildings on Monte Alban illustrates this rather neatly. The hieroglyphics of the astronomical observatory record various captured towns of the region and in most cases the symbol for hill is part of the name. Four such towns seen in these sculptured records and still more or less prominent on the map of modern Mexico are Ixtepec (Flint Knife Hill); Tolstepec (Rabbit Hill); Caltepec (House Hill); Chiltepec (Pepper Hill).

Among the undeciphered carvings exhaustively studied by Professor Caso, the numerous stories representing human deformities constitute the most mysterious. Unlike the depicting of conquered kings upside down, which was a common way of humiliating a defeated monarch, these strange deformities are beyond the present grasp of scholarship. Cripples of every sort are in conspicuous evidence. Bodies are bent or contorted, heads are squashed down between the shoulders, arms are knotted, legs bowed and feet twisted. They are on the oldest parts of the wall constructions and are considered to be even pre-Zapotec. Were the men who persistently sculptured these cripples indulging in mockery of beaten foes? Or were they, as Professor Caso seriously suggests, perhaps publicizing miraculous healing powers of the gods of Tiger Hill? The subject is a fascinating one and no doubt the primitive glyphs accompanying these carvings tell the story. We may hope that some day they will be read as easily as Spanish or English inscriptions.

Mitla yielded no jewels of importance (the Spanish colonials are thought to have looted the tombs), but the architecture equals in interest anything found in Mexico or in all Latin America. It was the City of Repose, of Death, as its name literally says, yet the Indians of Mexico have always thought rather pleasantly of death and this civic sarcophagus suggests nothing gloomy. Mitla's palaces of the departed are hard-stone structures of very great stability laid out with enourmous corridors whose chief glory is a type of stone-mosaic walls seen nowhere else. The individual stones are very small, but not minuscule. Most of them are a few inches in length, one inch or less in thickness, but they are cut in curious geometrical fashion and are fitted together without mortar to form a fretted pattern or frieze as perfect as the massive walls of Inca masonry in Cuzco. This seems far to surpass Cuzco in "mass craftsmanship" because the individual blocks at Mitla are numbered in the tens of thousands, yet each one had to be chiseled with as much care as if it had been a two-ton block. And the whole work displays such consummate skill that one would think it had all been done by an individual master craftsman.

The Mitla trip has much more than mighty ruins to recommend it. On the outward or homeward trip you will presumably stop at *Tlacolula* to see the quaint church of the farmers' saint (San Isidro) and to see the reeking market of the village. I think the adjective is moderate but let it not deter you from seeing Tlacolula's market, for this is one of the most colorful in Mexico. You can pick up almost anything here, including a live armadillo "dillowing in his armor." And you will *see* almost everything, including a wandering mendicant who carries a tiny statue of the Virgin from stall to stall, permitting the market women to kiss it (to stimulate trade) and to give him a centavito in recompense. You will halt, perhaps on the homeward trip, to see the giant *ahuehuetl* tree (cousin to the patriarchs in Chapultepec Park), at *Santa María del Tule*. It is supposed to have been 1600 years old when Cortés was Marquis of the Valley. Now it is nearly four and a half centuries older than that, and the circumference of its trunk—but you cannot believe this until you see it—is over 150 feet. It requires 25 men, each with a good "wingspread," to form a circle around it, finger tips touching. The height, according to the inscription, is 140 feet and the weight of its trunk 600 tons. If your mind rejects figures as big as that, just leave it to the testimony of your senses and roll along homeward.

Perhaps you will learn that a fiesta is in progress in some nearby village such as Zimatlán or Ocotlán, for Oaxaca State, as we have seen, is the most fiesta-minded region of Mexico, and if so, a side trip to see the rich rural pageantry of Zapotecs and Mixtecs (compare Chapter 5) will recompense you a hundredfold. These gorgeous drama-dances are presented with no thought of tourists and we find ourselves utterly ignored as we stand in the crowd watching. This is as it should be, and rarely is, in the more picturesque parts of foreign lands.

If fiestas fail you, there is always the free show of the arcade cafés on the city's Zócalo. Oaxaca is the home and habitat of mezcal, but you will need no fiery beverage to paint the scene in dreamy colors. A glass of mild sangría will do the trick or even that popular pop pronounced *oranhay kroosh* (orange crush). The pleasant plaza life of this most languorous of towns will build its own engaging dreams of times far past and of travel lures ahead. Occasionally, the mind may even harbor a passing thought of this quite perfect present.

CHAPTER 20

YUCATÁN, HEARTLAND OF THE MAYAS

Routes to Mérida

YUCATÁN-OF-THE-MAYAS is as different from the central tableland of Mexico as, for instance, Louisiana is different from New England. It ties in more closely, both geographically and historically, with Guatemala. Yet Mérida, its capital, should definitely be considered by anyone planning a Mexico tour. It is only an hour and a half by Mexicana jet from Mexico City, and it takes but two and one-half hours to fly there direct from New Orleans. Not only that, but if you're flying to Mexico City from the East, you can come, via Yucatán, for no extra fare, while, if you're starting your Mexico trip from the Midwest or West you would do well to make it a round trip to Yucatán, for this will permit you to stop over in Mexico City for no extra fare!

The Island of Carmen on the Way

Mexicana also serves a little island with the charming name of *Carmen* that lies in the Gulf of Campeche along the coast midway between Veracruz and Mérida. Serving as an extra bonus for the Yucatán tangent, this is another escapist isle, with simple inns bearing such names as *Motel Lino*, *Hotel Las Campanas*, *Hotel Zacarias*, and even, rather intrusively, *Hotel Jet!* A few short years ago the top hotel rate here was a mere $2.25, but those days are gone forever. Tarpon and snook fishermen may be interested in the deluxe fishing camp *La Cabaña* ($35 a day), reached by taxi across the island through a coconut plantation and then a boat trip across a two and-one-half-mile channel.

Mérida, the Modern Hub of Mayaland

The "Story of the Mayas" is set forth in detail in the author's *All the Best in Central America*, but the essentials of today's Yucatecan Mayaland, which is at least equal in importance to the Guatemaltecan Mayaland, will be given here, some passages being repeated from the Central American volume, though this report is based on fresh and recent travels.

The qualifying adjectives Yucatecan and Guatemaltecan call for a bit of explanation, for in Yucatán we are viewing the "New Empire" of the Mayas, which began to take form in the latter half of the sixth century and was brought to an abrupt end, over 900 years later, by the Spanish conquistadores. The "Old Empire" took form in Guatemala in the first century A.D., but some five centuries later it transferred to Yucatán in a most remarkable hegira. In that period the Old Empire picked itself up by its bootstraps (anachronism conceded) and moved north bodily to Yucatán, where the New Empire slowly took form. Dr. Thomas Gann, F.R.G.S., who has headed the British Museum's scientific expeditions to Central America, called this "one of the most remarkable events ever recorded in the history of any nation." The book he wrote in collaboration with J. Eric Thompson, leader of the Marshall Field Expedition to Central America, is the reverse of lurid. It is entitled simply *The History of the Maya* and presents the story in straightforward language, with a tendency toward cautious understatement rather than impressionistic fireworks. I have found it a good and satisfying book. Dr. Gann stresses the enormous effort involved in this mass migration and confesses that there are half-a-dozen explanations, each as farfetched and unconvincing as all the others. Temples, palaces, stelae, homes, vast fields of maize, good forests, abundant water supply—all these things were deserted forever in favor of a new site, the present Yucatán, where the soil was poor and the water supply very dubious. "It was," says Dr. Gann further, "as if the entire population of the towns in the English southern counties were suddenly, for no apparent reason, to migrate to the north of Scotland."

Since no one knows the reason for this strange performance (which was not done in panic but deliberately over a period of decades), we need not waste our time in speculation. The fact itself, however, is of immense importance to us as travelers. Had this transplanting of a nation not occurred, Yucatán would be merely an outlying province of Mexico. Because it did occur Yucatán is a second and greater Mayaland, the stimulating, challenging Mayaland of the New Empire.

The first capital of the New Empire—and it is the capital of today's tourist interest as well—was *Chichén-Itzá*, lying a few miles east of the present Mérida. This "City of the Sacred Well," as folders call it, was also the city of the Itzás. That word was the family name of the rulers of the region and it also means "sacred," so two tributes were offered in a single word. Chichén means literally well mouth and there were three large wells or *cenotes* in this immediate area. They were caused by cave-ins of the earth's crust above subterranean lakes and they furnish the obvious clue to the early selection of this site as capital. The sacred well that was the home of the water gods still exists and has a diameter of about 150 feet. It lies 60 feet below the ground surface and is another 60 to 80 feet in depth. The thought of it, as drinking water, is not enhanced by the knowledge that the gods who dwelt in this cenote demanded and received human sacrifices from time to time.

The first beginnings of this city seem to have been made by aboriginal cousins of the Old Empire Mayas just before the Great Migration, but the influx of new energies from the south was the real cause of its growth. About the year 650 a period of confusion developed in which two great families, the Itzás and the Xius, alternately dominated the region. They were the Montagues and Capulets of their day and age and sometimes even broke the peace and pushed each other around Yucatán, a thing quite contrary to the peaceful practice of Old Empire Mayas. The Itzás, despite many wanderings and vicissitudes of fortune, placed their family stamp upon this city and it is to them that we owe the real glory of the place, achieved during its Great Period or "Elizabethan Age," as Mr. Thompson called it. This period extended roughly from 1100 to 1300. The Xius built *Uxmal*, a few miles due south of Mérida and second only to Chichén-Itzá in present-day interest to travelers. Uxmal of the Xius, like Chichén of the Itzás, is a name to plant in your itinerary of anticipation. You will see there the finest and best preserved building (the House of the Governor) existing in any part of Mayaland, Old Empire or New.

One other city of the New Empire needs definite stress and a firm place in one's "advance memory." This is *Mayapan*, lying very near Mérida to the southeast and founded about the year 1250. (Unfortunately the word "about" must be introduced with almost all dates connected with the New Empire, for the Old Empire custom of erecting dated stelae had largely gone out.) Mayapan became the civil capital of the entire New Empire in Yucatán while Chichén-Itzá remained the religious and cultural capital. For two centuries after the advent of Kukulcan, the hero-god whom we have already "met," a central government was efficiently maintained in Mayapan. All the local chiefs were required to take up residence there and a sort of imperial court was established. Mercenaries were brought in to maintain order. The League of Mayapan was highly successful. Peace reigned. Art and architecture flourished mightily. But—force induced restlessness. Restlessness induced rebellion and even war to mar the wonderful record of Mayan tranquillity. In 1451, one of the few definitely established dates of the New Empire, civil war brought about the complete destruction of Mayapan. There is little to see of it today and its site is rarely visited except by explorers. With that catastrophe began the rapid disintegration of the New Empire, which had endured for nine centuries and had been great for the last two.

Mérida, capital of Mayaland and of the Mexican state of Yucatán, is a charming city, not only for its historic buildings and churches and its delightful animated plazas, but for its attractive, pint-sized Maya inhabitants, who are certainly the *cleanest* of all aboriginal folk in the Western Hemisphere. The best hotel is the *Panamericana*, air-conditioned throughout and with an inviting pool and an equally inviting nightclub. The older *Hotel Mérida*, of the Balsa chain, is of a pleasant colonial type, with a tropical patio, pool, and a "skyscraping" (ten-story) wing, with many air-conditioned guest rooms. Two excellent hotel-motels are the *Tropical Maya* and the *Gran Motel Yukalpetén*.

Hotel Colón, a smaller hotel of very moderate rates, boasts a Turkish bath that is one of the sights of the city. There are several well-equipped steam rooms and two gaily tiled and much-mirrored "suites" within the bath, where one descends to a pool whose water can be changed in 90 seconds for each guest—or group of guests.

Fernando Barbachano has been called the tourist king of Yucatán. He has a travel office in the lobby of the Panamericana, which he operates, and his simple mail address is Box 90, Mérida. He also owns the fabulous *Hotel Mayaland* and the *Hotel Hacienda Chichén*, at Chichén-Itzá (more coming up on this), a comparable glamour inn called *Hacienda Uxmal*, at Uxmal, and the new *Cozumel-Caribe*, on the island of Cozumel. He is also the Hertz agent in Mérida. This tribute to a dynamic promoter of tourism should not obscure the fact that other important men and agencies are in the field in Yucatán, the most effective competitors being the agency called *Yucatán Trails*, built up and headed by an able and energetic fellow countryman named Felipe Escalante, in the Mérida office at 482 60th Street and Mexico City office at Reforma 36-5.

It is easy to merge oneself with the life and tempo of modern Mérida. Taxis for cruising are to be had for about a dollar an hour within the city limits but these seem a bit highfalutin, since Mérida is one of the world's few remaining strongholds of the horse-drawn vehicle. You see the cabs and cabbies everywhere in little groups and constellations. You enter and mount your old-fashioned throne, in a sort of *caléche*, and proceed to roll along at a five-mile-an-hour shamble. For any given ride within the city, three pesos is sufficient and seven pesos is ample by the hour. I think you will love the clatter of your horse's hoofs and the soft rumble of the rubber-tired wheels. You are back in the horse-and-buggy era—of blessed memory.

Streets in Mérida are numbered. The even-numbered streets run north and south, the odd-numbered streets east and west, and the great shaded plaza lies in the center of the diagram. It is easy to find your bearings, and a couple of key addresses may help you to a good start. The *Hotel Mérida* is on 60th Street at the corner of 57th. The Pan Am and Mexicana offices are on 58th Street, at the corner of 61st. The chief streets of shops are 63rd and 65th Streets. Of the three leading movie houses one is on the central plaza and two are on 60th Street, near the Hotel Mérida. *Cinema Cantarell* is attractive and more or less air-conditioned. The *Peon Contreras* is huge and palatial but less modern. A theater offering revues and other light fare is the *Fantasio*, and there is a pleasant nightclub garden at the edge of the city (on 42nd Street) called *Los Tulipanes*, meaning The Hibiscuses. It provides dancing, and the gourmet specialty of the house is chicken barbecued in banana leaves, a typical Yucatecan dish, as are *pibal* and *venado*.

Before leaving the subject of shops too far behind I should mention that Yucatán's sisal is woven into very appealing articles for tourists. Mats, doilies, handbags and even sport shoes are beautifully fashioned by patient craftsmen and craftswomen.

Mérida is easy to explore. You stroll and drive through a lovely world that has been forgotten by the Restless Age. Its heart, the central plaza, is peculiarly appealing since it is not yet in any sense dominated by tourism. Under the shade trees one sees not only the usual park benches but many *confidentes*, which are flirtation seats scattered about at points where lights will not be inconveniently bright in the evening. They are S-shaped doubletons as confidential as their name. (Other parks of Mérida also go in for confidentes in a big way. It's an old Yucatecan custom.) Surrounding the main plaza are arched arcades, government buildings, the large but simple *cathedral* and the *Casa de Montejo*, the first Spanish house built in the city.

The extensive *market*, seen best in the early morning, reaches its peak of activity on 65th Street, at the corner of 56th. Its chief charms are its abundant flowers, filling several blocks with fragrance, and the amazing cleanliness of the Mayan vendors, which is not a matter of propaganda but a fact that any traveler will attest with delight. The costume of Mayan women is the tuniclike *huipil*, often enhanced with wide borders of intricate embroidery, and the garment is not draggled and soiled but scrupulously clean in almost all cases, as are the hands and face of its wearer. A special feature of this market, as of all others through Mexico and Central America, is the *tortilla*, which you may see being made on many a curb. Its base is corn paste, the Mayan staff of life, which is spread into thin sheets and then filled with meat or, quite literally, with "what have you."

Two beverage facts of local interest may find a place here. An excellent light beer called *Carta Clara*, quite as good, I think, as its more famous cousin Carta Blanca of Monterrey, is made in Yucatán. Good coffee is brewed in the numberless cafés of Mérida, and when served in a demitasse it has a special local name. It is called a *greca*.

The *chewing-gum tree*, or more properly the *chico-zapote*, will be first encountered by many tourists in the heart of Mérida itself—perhaps in front of the penitentiary, where there is a little park of them. The fruit of the tree is the zapote and its sap is—chicle. Eastern Yucatán Peninsula (the state of Quintana Roo) and northern Guatemala (the Petén region) provide the world's chompers with practically all of their chomping material, and here in Mérida—in front of prison bars—you may see the tree that made Chicago famous.

A sight that is quite as interesting and a great deal more beautiful is the *Campo Deportivo* or Sports Stadium. This vast structure was designed by an architect who had a bright idea, though not strictly original in Yucatán. The wall that shuts off the view from neck-craners without the price of an admission ticket is pierced by more than a hundred half circles cut down into the cement from the top of the wall. Into each of these is fastened an intricately wrought iron grille about the size and shape of a good cartwheel. The upper half of the wheel protrudes above the wall. Behind the cartwheels have been planted bougainvilleas of purple, pink and red persuasions. Bougainvillea, as every traveler in the tropics knows, is the rankest, most riotous, most violent of all nature's floral products. It grows like an undesired weed and at the annual peak of its flowering (November in Mérida) it spreads its brilliance in the unruly profusion of blossoms-by-the-billion. You cannot see through bougainvillea, once it has a bit of a start, so the grilled cartwheels, when fully in bloom, offer no peepholes. But the effect is truly magnificent, checked and subdued as it is by the handsome ironwork. I know of few buildings where architectural ingenuity has so cleverly and effectively harnessed nature as in Mérida's Campo Deportivo.

Three civic developments have brought pride to Mérida: an extremely impressive *Monument to the Country* (at the end of Paseo Montejo), with a full, pictured story, in relief, of Cortés' conquest of Mexico; a vast, ultramodern *Centro Educacional* (named for Felipe Carrillo Puerto, a champion of the modern Mayas); and a Good Neighbor park named *El Parque de las Américas*. This last is a genuinely hemispheric achievement, for it honors each of the Americas with a stela, or pillar, containing the name of the given country and a map of it. The entire, extensive development is, however, in the appropriate Mayan style of architecture, from the open-air theater, library and exposition hall to the *Fuente* (Fountain) *Monumental*, whose half-dozen serpents spit noble jets of water in honor of the god-man, Kukulcan.

Rolling back to the center of town, perhaps through Avenida de Colón, whose broad way is lined by fine estates with emerald lawns of *frescura* and with majestic royal palms, you will rest a bit and then be ready for—more rest, since that is the keynote of Mérida. Find a seat in the central plaza, but kindly not one of the confidentes, unless you have someone with whom you wish to be confidential, and when soft evening falls just listen to the music of the band and watch the flirtation parade, or more strictly the parade of the oglers and the ogled. The oglers are the young men about Mérida. The ogled are the timid maidens burning with amorous curiosity but wrapped in layers of modesty, real or assumed, for the occasion. The masculine strollers, as always in Latin-American cities, walk in one direction, the feminine in the other, and glances bold and shy weave through the air like shuttles of desire. This old Spanish custom, transplanted to the New World, must be a fascinating one for the participants. It is certainly fascinating to watch, since it rouses the matchmaker's instinct to the fever point. Try your heart at it in Mérida's pleasant plaza.

Entering Antiquity

One should enter Mayan antiquity in Mérida itself in the Yucatecan Museum, being careful, incidentally, to accent the word Yucatecan on its penultimate syllable. This fine collection, introductory to the wonders you will see in Chichén-Itzá and Uxmal, is housed in a large mansion on Paseo Montejo.

The contents of the *Museo Yucateco* are exceedingly interesting and I say this with due sympathy for museum dodgers whose attitude, when on vacation, I can readily understand. You will see models of the pyramids and temples of Chichén-Itzá; a Chac-Mool, which is a curious reclining human figure so typical of

Chichén-Itzá and of all Mayaland that it is frequently pictured on travel folders and hotel stationery; heads of feathered serpents honoring the god Kukulcan. You will certainly notice, too, some elongated skulls flattened in the infancy of their ancient possessors by Mayan "beauticians" and you will see innumerable ornaments, amulets and implements of jade, obsidian and flint. Turtles and frogs will predominate in the field of pure ornament, reminding us that the Mayas greatly venerated the rain god, patron of their maize crops, and hence any and every zoomorphic symbol that suggested water.

Some things you might miss if you go without an alert guide are the following:

A bas-relief of a Mayan astronomer amid a circle of planets explaining to his monarch the mysterious meanings of the universe.

Curious and artistic Mayan murals from the Temple of the Warriors at Chichén-Itzá.

Figures of heads with depressions in the crania for copal (incense), a prime essential of old Mayan worship.

A lintel depicting a brave and pious Maya who passes a rope through a hole bored in his tongue. He is shown performing this heroic act in front of a god to demonstrate his courage.

Gross phallic symbols, hermaphroditic monoliths, copulating jaguars and other items that you will pronounce "disgusting" if your sensibilities are easily bruised and if you forget that the worship of fertility-deities was of deep religious meaning to the Mayas.

Sacrificial knives of tan-colored flint with which the *Nacons*, or priests of sacrifice, cut out the hearts of their victims.

A curious fact is that every article that was sacrificed to the gods was first made "dead." The implements for this use are always found to be broken in some way. The bowls are mutilated. The plates have holes punched in them. Even the bells of gold that were tossed to the rain god in the sacred cenote of Chichén-Itzá will be seen to have had their clappers removed so that their voice should be stilled.

From the city of Mérida modern highways of good quality carry you into the very presence of antiquity. One leads east to Chichén-Itzá, some 80 miles distant, the other south to Uxmal, 50 miles distant. We may turn our attention first to the east.

Hotel Mayaland, Comfort Amid History

The *Mayaland Hotel* is a dreamer's dream of tropical luxury and beauty. In the main building the rooms and baths, screened against possible marauding insects (though these are rarely noticed in the open), are the last word in comfort, as are the individual cabins, all with Mayan names and decor, scattered about the ample, parklike grounds. The swimming pool, with a poolside bar, is a popular feature, and for sheer loveliness you will see no landscaping in the tropics to surpass that of the Mayaland's setting. The whole ensemble is brilliant with coconut palms, flowering shrubs and tropical fruit trees such as mangoes, papayas and aguacates (avocados), and one of its well-loved features is a pool filled with aristocratic purple water lilies. For evening entertainment of the guests, Yucatecan peasant dances are often given by the hotel staff and these are quite as lively as any folk dances you will see in other parts of Mexico. One is performed by a woman dancer with a glassful of *xtabentun*, a local liqueur, balanced on her head and she never spills a drop, despite her intricate gyrations.

Meals are surprisingly ample, considering the hotel's remoteness from any town. Perhaps you expect to find for breakfast merely the Continental coffee and rolls, but you will actually be served griddle cakes and syrup, eggs and ham or bacon, coffee, buttered toast and jam. For lunch or dinner venison is a common delicacy, being easier to secure in Chichén-Itzá than in New York.

I stress, perhaps unduly, my personal delight in this lodge-in-the-wilderness, which rests in its Edenlike jungle almost in the lee of the pyramids. To see great ruins and pay for their educational value in the form of hardship and discomfort, before and after,

CHICHÉN-ITZÁ, PRIDE OF THE NEW EMPIRE

may have its disciplinary value, but to see them comfortably, while living in luxury's own lap—well, confidentially, I prefer it. Two other hostelries, recommendable if you can't get into the Mayaland, are the *Cunanchén Hotel* and the *Hacienda Chichén*.

Chichén-Itzá, Pride of the New Empire

Three great families dominated three sections of Yucatán's Mayaland, the Xius in Uxmal, the Cocoms in Mayapan, the Itzás in Chichén-Itzá. The sacred city of the Itzás has preserved the most interesting relics for posterity. Uxmal pushes it fairly hard, but Mayapan is only a name in books and a few rough mounds in the jungle.

Chichén-Itzá is compelling and wonderful in its lure, not quite equaled, I think, even by Copán, a stronghold of the Old Empire. The sacred city of the New Empire was to other Mayan cities as Athens was to lesser cities of Hellas, or so it seems to the modern beholder. Your guide, and you will be provided with an intelligent one who knows and loves what he is showing, will spend a day with you, or two days, merely indicating the high spots. If you can afford a whole week to look again and again it will still be too short a time. The human guide may be supplemented by a printed guide purchasable on the spot. I refer to that of José A. Erosa Peniche called *Guide to the Ruins of Chichén-Itzá*. Its text makes simple reading and its charts and illustrations are a big help.

You will probably see first the *Cenote de Sacrificios* (Well of Sacrifice), since it lies in a forest beyond the ruins and furnishes a dramatic opener to your great day. The circular cenote, typical of many lesser ones found in Yucatán, lies 60 feet below its rim at forest level, and the water is about 80 feet deep. Its sacrificial victims were often young girls—delectable tidbits for the importunate rain god—and before being hurled from the brink they were taken to the top of the great pyramid for a religious ceremony of consecration. They were then led to the cenote, anesthetized, and in the presence of hundreds of eager spectators were hurled down into the well. The spectators simultaneously tossed in all sorts of implements and jewelry—every such sacrifice being broken first to make sure it was "dead." Occasionally the shock of the victim hitting the water broke the spell of the anesthetic and she would swim about battling for life. Rarely she won the battle, was fished out at noon and became a sort of saint venerated by all her fellow citizens.

The newest discovery in the area is the *Cave of Balancanché*, a subterranean shrine of the Toltec rain god, Tlaloc. It was discovered by a Barbachano guide named José Humberto Gómez in September, 1959, after it had lain untouched for a thousand years where it was secretly sealed by the Toltec priests. The cost of exploring and opening up the cave was borne by the National Institute of Anthropology, the National Geographic Society and Tulane University, with help also from Mr. Barbachano, and the cave was inaugurated by the wife of President López Mateos. It lies ten minutes by car from Mayaland Hotel and takes three hours to see in satisfying leisure. The cave is superbly lighted and is a National Monument of Mexico, with all its finds left intact right there.

The finds include mass offerings of urns averaging about three feet in height, mostly carved in the likeness of the rain god, brilliantly painted in blue, green, red and yellow and unlike anything previously found in Yucatán. The paintings all look as though the artists had done their work only yesterday. Accompanying the urns are bowls, jars and vases of pottery, carved clay spindle whorls, tiny ceremonial corn grinders, miniature plates like a child's tea set—all of which is only the beginning.

The spectacular ruins of Chichén-Itzá, a city which once covered six square miles, need not be enumerated here, as their very number would make a tiresome listing. Perhaps I may concentrate on the two most conspicuous items.

The *great pyramid*, which is somewhat over 100 feet high, with two of its sides carefully restored, is really a Toltec pyramid capping an earlier Mayan pyramid in token of military conquest.

One may enter it to see certain priceless relics. Students have found in this important structure a great deal of symbolism, including that of the Maya-Toltec calendar. The 52-year cycle is seen in 52 panels found on each side; and the 365-day year is seen in the 91 steps multiplied by four (364), plus the square base of the pyramid common to all four sides. One may enter the castillo and climb to a double chamber, dim and spooky, whose prized possessions are a Chac-Mool and a monolith in the form of a ferocious jaguar. Both are wonderfully preserved, since they have not been exposed to the open air. The Chac-Mool has eyes, teeth and nails of shell resembling mother-of-pearl. The jaguar (*tigre* in Spanish) is painted red and is of remarkable artistic merit. The eyes are hemispheres of jade and the spots, 74 in number, are little disks of jade. On the tail, which seems to be switching angrily, are jade markings. The fangs are of flint and the teeth are painted white. Most curious of all, the *tigre rojo* carries on his back a sort of plate like a card tray and when the beast was first discovered this tray contained a coral necklace and a piece of jade the size of a crab apple fashioned into the likeness of a human head. These bibelots have long since been removed.

The *ball court* of Chichén-Itzá is, to my thinking, the most exciting ruin left anywhere by either empire of the Mayas. It is, in fact, so wonderfully preserved and restored that it seems hardly a ruin at all. It is a playing court for one of the fastest games ever invented, the Mayan game of pelota, which I have mentioned as father, or perhaps I should say "co-father," of jai-alai. Fashioned marvelously of clean blocks of masonry, the immensely thick walls are surmounted by several temples. With tribunes at either end of the court for high priest and king respectively, the whole rectangle is of noble dimensions, the width being about 120 feet and the length, from tribune to tribune, about 490 feet.

High in the wall of either side was a stone ring through which the players had to strike the ball—if they could—and one of the rings, intricately carved with twisted serpents, is almost perfectly preserved. The umpires stood on the parapet just above either ring to see and announce if a goal was scored. In the elaborate frieze of the west wall of the court we may see something of the ferocious quality and hazards of sport in Mayan times. We see that there were seven men to each team, clad in the "armor" of the game and wearing tall and fancy headgear. The captain of the winning team shouts his paean of triumph and a stone cartoon shows the words emerging from his mouth exactly as in modern cartoons. Then we see action. He celebrates his victory by cutting off the head of the losing captain and holding up his trophy. But the sculptor was, after all, a bit squeamish, for he shows the blood dripping from the severed head not in drops but in the form of serpents. It was a small thing to any brave Mayan sportsman to suffer death, since the king and the high priest and thousands of spectators were looking on. It was like being sacrificed on a public altar. Only hereditary nobles of high degree played pelota in the big matches and the temples on the parapets prove the religious nature of the game.

An amazing echo exists in this vast ball court. Stand on the grass beneath the west wall and shout the command "Play!" The order will be repeated to your ears nine times by count, and if your hearing is especially acute it may mount to 12 or 15 times. From the high priest's tribune at the north end, shout the greeting (to the king) at the far south end "How do you do?" and the king will respond clearly and in full "How do you do?" You may even try it in the longer Spanish "*Como está usted?*" and he will courteously reply in that tongue.

The wealth of interesting things in Chichén-Itzá discourages all who would write of them in anything less lengthy than a full-sized tome, but I may set down a few notes that will at least guide your eyes a bit. Watch for Kukulcan, the feathered serpent, in the sculpture of many a temple. Watch also for the rain god, always identifiable by a colossal nose, somewhat like an elephant's trunk but turning up at the end. Watch for symbols of water—snails, fishes, turtles—repeated in the sculptures everywhere, for water was all in all to Mayan religion and economy. In *El*

Templo de los Tigres (The Temple of the Jaguars) surmounting the east wall of the ball court, look for the most interesting of all Chichén-Itzá's sculptures, the Story of Creation. You will note that the rain god created man by either of two evolutionary processes. His tears made him in this sequence: ocean, duck, fish, serpent, man; or in this: river, fish, serpent, man. He made woman not by taking a rib of the man but by the very same sequences as listed above, ending the job by draping her in a Mayan huipil, to prove that she really was a woman. In both sequences of evolution, be it noted, not a monkey but a *snake* was the immediate progenitor of man. In Mayan theological science that was thought of as a definite compliment to man, since the serpent was venerated as a symbol of divinity.

Returning to a cool drink on the porch of the hotel you will hear, if it is dusk and if the season is right (late autumn), an occasional musical note—long, piercing, mysterious. It is the "swan song" of a dying locust. He "goes out singing."

Uxmal and Its Thousand-Year Palace

Uxmal (pronounced Ooshmal) may be easily visited in a day trip, or even a half-day trip from Mérida, since it is only 50 miles distant by a paved highway, but there's a fine inn for stayers-over. The ruins, though less extensive, are almost as interesting as those of Chichén-Itzá. You'll need a guide and the tour company will provide a good one for you. For a printed, mapped and illustrated guide, you may purchase at the ruins (as in the case of Chichén-Itzá) the workable and simple volume by José A. Erosa Peniche, *The Ruins of Uxmal*. My own brief text, unable to discuss the pyramid called *El Adivino* (The Fortune-Teller), the Quadrangle of the Nuns, the House of the Turtles, the House of the Doves and other piles of masonry, feels inclined to stress and underline merely the *Casa del Gobernador* (House of the Governor), possibly the most admirable structure left by the Mayas anywhere. It attracts me personally rather less than does the ball court of Chichén but the two structures are so different that they cannot sensibly be compared.

The Casa del Gobernador was the pride of the great family of Tutul Xiu, which reached its zenith of power in the tenth century, but the building's name is slightly misleading since this derives not from the structure's former use so much as from a sculpture of a presumed "governor" seated on a throne above the main doorway. Probably priests, nobles, bigwigs of every sort actually dwelt here. It rises in its rectangular bulk from a great triple terrace built by human labor. Erosa, in his prideful preamble, rates this structure among "the most important archeological constructions of the world," and he cannot be far wrong for it is truly imposing and the intricacies of its sculpture warrant the highest admiration. The length of this "house" is about 325 feet and its width but 40 feet. The main façade is almost entirely covered with bas-reliefs in which geometrical designs are entangled with serpents, animals and human faces.

The name Uxmal, originally Ox-Mal, means "Thrice Built" and students, though arguing amiably with each other, more or less agree that the first building probably occurred in the seventh century. In its present state its architecture seems rather more Mayan (and less Toltec) than does even Chichén-Itzá. You will note the feathered serpent constantly recurring in the decorations, and, of course, the big-nosed rain god. A famous "false arch," looking like an isosceles triangle, is seen conspicuously in the Nuns' House and a similar one is in the Governor's House.

As for your own house of repose and refreshment, you will find the *Hacienda Uxmal* delightful. The building is constructed like a big U, enclosing a tropical patio and swimming pool, and each bedroom, cooled by cross ventilation, has its tiled bathroom with tub and shower. The property of 740 acres includes many tropical plants and flowering trees, one of the interesting plants, a shiny purple one, being called Moses-in-the-bulrushes because its pods are like cradles, with Moses reclining inside. The property contains also an orchard of 1000 fruit trees, oranges, lemons, limes, bananas, mameys, mangoes and avocados, and this is being constantly tended and improved. In one part of the orchard you'll find pavilions where two Mayan weavers and three potters are industriously making articles for sale in the hotel's gift shop. There's a relaxing atmosphere about this select hacienda that is rare even in Mexico.

Returning from anywhere to Mérida is a sheer delight. You begin to have the sensation of getting home whenever you see once more its sleepy streets, its cool plazas and its lovely patios glimpsed through open doorways. (A good example of a private patio is the one seen at Number 443 on 60th Street.)

Windmills are the very banners of Mérida. There are 25,000 of them in the region and they rise singly, in twos and threes, in serried ranks. From my hotel balcony I once counted 34 of them though much of the skyline was cut off from my vision. They race in the wind or whirl lazily in the zephyrs and often they stop completely for a long siesta. Lush tropical vegetation attacks them at their bases and unless this is counterattacked it will clamber clear to the top and choke them. I noticed three which were thus choked by impudent vines that had fastened their tentacles even around the wheels, preventing their movement. The effect was so utterly beautiful, green against the sky, that perhaps their owners could not bear to disengage those clinging tendrils. But between you and me, I think the owners have been likewise choked by the lush laziness of the tropics. I am sure that they intend to do something about those vines—sometime.

The Island of Cozumel, an Escapist's Dream Come True

Just off the coast of Quintana Roo, a state of Mexico occupying the eastern half of the Peninsula of Yucatán, in the Caribbean, between this peninsula and the western tip of Cuba, lies a tropical island of the never-never sort called *Cozumel*, where flowers and palm trees fringe fine beaches of whitest sand and in whose adjacent waters one can see *and* catch tropical fish, clad in all the colors of the rainbow and some, like creamy white and rich chocolate, that elude the rainbow. On this island Fernando

Barbachano has erected a luxurious resort hotel called the *Cozumel-Caribe*. Some of its rooms have private balconies, and a few have private gardens as well. It is located in a grove of coconut palms on a beach of fine white sand. There are two patios, one with a fountain, the other with a children's wading pool. The adults' pool has a recreation area for games and is connected by a separate wing to the dining room and the bar.

Two other good hotels are the *Caribe-Isleño* (Islander), also a Barbachano property, located downtown in the port of San Miguel, and the *Playa Azul* (Blue Beach), an Azteca hotel, on San Juan Beach two miles out of town. Here all rooms and terraces face the sea, there is music nightly and the dining room specializes in regional island dishes. Older hotels are *La Playa*, *Las Cabañas del Caribe* and the *Mayaluum*. The latter has excellent food, and something of a nightclub.

Slowly taking shape is what will eventually be the island's largest hotel, the *El Presidente*, of the Balsa chain. There is one very good restaurant, *Casa de Denis*, run by the island's former health inspector.

Cozumel is an ideal goal for the escapist. Skin diving in the limpid waters, which the eye can penetrate, it is claimed, to 200 feet, is a popular sport, as is fishing, as is, of course, sheer sun loafing, with an occasional swim. The island's name means "Land of Swallows" in the Mayan language. The place is a masterwork of nature, serene and beautiful. Let's hope that the incursion of many tourists, ourselves, will not serve to dim its pristine luster. You can reach Cozumel easily by Mexicana Airlines, which flies in by jet from Mexico City, stopping at Mérida en route.

Mexico has another Caribbean island about 50 miles north of Cozumel and six miles off the coast, namely, *Isla Mujeres* (Island of Women), and to get there you must either charter a plane or ride four or five hours by car from Mérida to Puerto Juárez (200 miles) and then take a 40-minute ferry ride. Actually, this island is nothing but a long sand spit, with one small village and

ISLAND OF COZUMEL, ESCAPIST'S DREAM COME TRUE 271

three or four hotels, the *Zazil-Ha* (Luminous Waters) and the *Pasado del Mar*, this an Azteca unit, and the best. It is my understanding that the Zazil-Ha has a six-passenger twin Beechcraft that may be chartered for flights from Mérida, but this should be checked, at the time of your coming, through one of the agencies in Mérida. I have not visited the Island of Women but have been told that its beaches are as good as those of Cozumel, which is high praise. The island's main attraction, aside from its superescapism and its beaches, is its name, which derives from nothing more exciting than the terra-cotta figurines of fertility goddesses, found back in 1517 in the island's temples, by the Spanish conquistadores. However, the pirates who came afterward must have found living women, for many of today's native islanders are light-haired and have French or Italian names. Both Cozumel and Isla Mujeres are relative newcomers to the tourist scene and both are destined, beyond a doubt, to win more and more popularity.

INDEX

Aborigines, 43-50
See also Aztecs; Incas; Mayas
Academia de las Bellas Artes, 126-127
Acapulco, 229-235
  air service to, 9, 10, 180, 230
  car rentals, 34
  city plan of, 13
  climate, 6
  distance from Mexico City, 217
  highways to, 12, 180
  hotels, 230-233
  nightclubs, 233
  rail service to, 23
  restaurants, 233
  ship service to, 22, 23
Aerolineas Vegas, 10, 181, 245
Aeronaves de México, 9, 10, 230, 235
Agriculture, 194
Aguamiel, 157
Aguascalientes, 21
  rail service to, 24
Aguilar, Jerónimo de, 52
Agustín the First, Emperor, 60
Air France, 9
Airlines, 8-10
  tourist cards issued by, 36
  within Mexico, 9, 10, 181, 230, 235, 245
  See also names of airlines
Aldama, 205
Alemán, Miguel, 68
Alitalia Airlines, 9
All the Best in Central America, 253
All Saints' Day, 98
All Souls' Day, 98
Allende, Ignacio, 59-60, 205, 212
Allende Institute, 212
Altitude, 37-38

Alvarado, Pedro de, 55
American Airlines, 8
American Athletic Association, 167
American Automobile Association, 11, 13, 35
  tourist cards issued by, 36
American Bookstore, 35
American Express, 39
Amigos (magazine), 4
Anthropology, National Museum of, 105-107
Antigua Morelos, 17
Architecture, 56-57, 209, 224, 259-260
  Mexico City, 101-110
Art, 57, 68, 104, 126-139, 195-196, 212, 264-265
  classic, 126-127
  courses in, 35
  Mexican School, 127-132
  modern, 138-139
  murals, 132-138
    Mayan, 261
  mosaic, 136-138, 228
August Fair, 98
Auto Rent, 34
Automobiles
  rentals, 34
  See also Highways
Avis Rent-a-Car, 34
Aztecs, 43-50, 53-56, 102, 105, 219, 247
  calendar stone of, 28
  dances of, 159

Ballet, 92, 158
Barajas, José, 214-215
Bargain shopping, 120-122, 175-178
Bargaining, 176-177
Barra de Navidad, 200-202
Bars, 157, 226

273

INDEX

Baseball, 167-168
Beauty-parlors, 26
Beer, 27, 91, 258
Birds, 35, 244
Birds of Mexico, 35
Blake, Emmett Reid, 35
Books, 34-35, 94
Borde, Joseph le, 224
Border barriers, 35-37
Braniff International Airways, 8
Brenner, Anita, 44-45
Bullfighting, 163-165
Busses, 12, 88, 109, 199, 230, 236
    prices, 26, 217

Cabrera, Miguel, 224-225
Cacahuamilpa, caves of, 221
Calendars, 125
Camacho, Manuel Avila, 67, 68
Camarena, Jorge González, 138
Campeche, 11
    air service, 10
Canada, Mexican tourist offices in, 33
Canadian Pacific Air Lines, 9
Canadian Pacific Steamship Company, 8, 22
Cantinflas, 137-138
Cárdenas, Lázaro, 49, 68
Carmen, Island of, 10-12, 243, 252-253
Casa del Conde de Santiago de Calimaya, 113
Caso, Alonso, 248
Castillo, Bernal Díaz del, 44
Castles, 107-109
Caves, 221, 264
Chalma Festival, 96-97
Chapultepec, castle of, 107-109
Charles I, 52
Charles V, 52
Charlot, Jean, 135
Charro Festival, 97
Chewing-gum trees, 258
Chichén-Itzá, 11, 254, 260, 263-267
    highways to, 262
    hotels, 262-263

Chihuahua, 11, 21-22
    climate, 5-6
    rail service to, 23, 24
Chihuahueno (dogs), 21
Cholula, 53, 236-237
    churches in, 57
Christmas festivals, 98, 158-159
Churches, 56-57, 113-116
    Chihuahua, 21
    Cholula, 57
    Guadalajara, 57
    Guanajuato, 57, 215-216
    Mexico City, 57, 101-102, 113-116
    Oaxaca, 246-247
    Puebla de los Angeles, 238-239
    Querétaro, 209
    San Luis Potosi, 20
    Taxco, 224
Churriguera, José, 57
Churrigueresque architecture, 56-57
Cigarettes, 91-92
Cinema, 158
Ciudad del Carmen, 10
Ciudad Jiménez, 11
Ciudad Juárez, 11
    rail service to, 24
    visiting without a permit, 36
Ciudad Mante, 11
    hotels, 17
Ciudad Obregón, 22
Ciudad Valles, 17
Ciudad Victoria, 11
    hotels, 17
Climate, 5-6
Colorful aspect of Mexico, 3-7
Columbus Day, 98
Communism, 127-132, 135
Concerts, 92
Conquest of Mexico, The, 43, 44
Conquest of Peru, The, 43
Conservatism, 49-50
Constitution of 1857, 62
Copper, coins of, 29-30
Copperware, 96, 188
Córdoba, 236
Corn, 46

INDEX

Corpus Christi celebrations, 97
Corregidora, La, 204, 206, 208
Cortes, Hernan, 43, 44, 45, 47, 48, 50-56, 99, 116, 219, 224, 236-237, 245
Costumes, 16, 94, 125, 159, 258
Courtesy, 49
Covarrubias, Miguel, 35
Cozumel Island, 181, 269-270
   air service to, 10, 270
   hotels, 270
Crafts, 94-96, 175-178, 212, 257
   prices, 26
Creoles, 58
Crow, John A., 35
Cuauhtemoc, 55-56
Cuautla, 97
Cuba, 51, 52
Cuernavaca, 68, 217-221
   altitude, 38, 218
   city plan of, 13
   distance from Mexico City, 217
   festivals, 96-97
   flowers, 218
   highways to, 12, 38, 180
   hotels, 218
   museums, 107
   rail service to, 23
   restaurants, 218
   shopping, 94
   tours from, 221
Curios, 94
Currency, see Money
Customs, 35-36
   liquor, 92
   tobacco, 91-92

Daily Bulletin, 90
Daily News, 90
De la Cruz, Sor Juana Inés, 57-58
Díaz, Porfirio, 45, 49, 63-66, 104, 130, 131, 245
Díaz Ordaz, Licenciado Gustavo, 68
Diego, Juan, 170, 172
Dollars, exchange rate, 27
Dolores (town), 59-60

Domínquez, Josefa Ortiz de, 204
Don Pasco, Bishop, 186
Drinks, 27, 91, 155-156, 258
Durango, 11, 21
Duties, see Customs

Easter season, 97
Eastern Air Lines, 8
Ecuador, 48
Education, 117-120, 212
   Communism in, 128
   summer courses, 35
English-language publications, 90
Esta Semana, 90-91
Ethnic groups, 43-50
Europe
   air travel from, 9
   ocean travel from, 22-23

Ferrocarril del Pacífico, 24
Ferrocarriles Nacionales de México (FNM), 24
Festivals, 50-51, 64, 96-98, 172-173, 251
   Christmas, 98, 158-159
   Easter, 97
Fiesta Lands, 35
Fishing, 194, 252-253
Flower Fair, 97
Flowers, 92-93, 124, 218, 242, 244, 249, 269
   floating gardens of Xochimilco, 173-174
   wild, 183, 184
Fonda Del Sol, La (NYC restaurant), 143
Food, 92, 142-147
   health aspect, 91
   Indian-Mexican, 143-146
   See also Restaurants
Football, 166-167
Ford, Norman D., 34-35
Forests, 108
Fortín de las Flores, 97, 236, 242-243
   altitude, 38
   climate, 6
   highways to, 180-181

INDEX

Francisco I, 64-65
Fuente del Salto de Agua, 117
Furniture, 94

Gachupines, 58
Gann, Thomas, 253, 254
García, Genaro, 44
Garci-Crespo table water, 91
Gazer, The, 91
Glassware, 94, 95, 96
Gold coins, 30
Gómez, José Humberto, 264
Green Fleet, 10-11
Grito de Dolores, 60
Guadalajara, 193-203
  air service to, 9, 10
  altitude, 38
  car rentals, 34
  churches in, 57
  city plan of, 13
  entertainment, 195
  guides in, 194
  highways to, 179-180
  hotels, 194-195
  museum, 195-196
  orphanage in, 197
  population, 193
  pottery-makers' suburb of, 197-198
  rail service to, 24
  restaurants, 195
  shopping, 94, 96
    bargain, 121
  sightseeing, 195-197
  tour from, 198-199
Guadalupe Hidalgo, 170-173
Guanajuato, 29, 60, 180, 213-216
  altitude, 38
  churches in, 57, 215-216
  hotels, 214
  packaged tours to, 216
  shopping, 96
Guatemala, 44, 46, 47, 236
Guaymas, 11, 21-22
  rail service to, 24
Guide to all Mexico, 34
Guide to Mexico, 34

Guide to Mexico City, 34
Guide to the Ruins of Chichén-Itzá, 263
Guidebooks, 34-35
Guides, 38-40
Gunther, John, 48-49

Haircuts, 26
Health, 91
Hermosillo, 21
Herring, Hubert, 44, 61
Hertz de México, 34
Hidalgo y Costilla, Miguel, 59-60, 103, 170, 205
Highways, 10-22
  en route, 15-22
  See also under names of cities and towns
Historia Verdadera de la Conquesta de la Nueva España, 44
History of the Maya, The, 253
History of Mexico, A, 43
Hoban, Bernard A., 166
Holland-America Line, 22-23
Holy Week, 97
Horse racing, 168-169
Hospital de Jesús Nazareno, 116
Hotels
  bars in, 157
  prices, 26-27
  at spas, 178, 183
  stamps sold by, 89
  tipping, 31
  travel agencies in, 39-40
  See also under names of cities and towns
Huitzilopochtli (god), 48
Human sacrifices, 49, 219

I Columbus (musical comedy), 138
Iberia Air Lines, 9
Iguala, 61
Incas, 43, 44, 46, 247, 250
Indian-Mexican food, 143-146

INDEX

Indians, 43-50, 185, 245, 247-248
  festivals, 96-97
  social status of, 59
  See also Aztecs; Incas; Mayans
Instituto Allende, 35
Interpretative Guides (pamphlet), 132-133
Isla Mujeres, 270-271
Iturbide, Agustín de, 60-61
Ixaccíhuatl (volcano), 53
Ixtapán de la Sal, 12

Jai-alai, 165-166
Jalapa, 11
James, Neil, 199
Janitzio, Island of, 187-188
  festivals, 98
Japan Air Lines, 9
Jewelry, 121, 122, 176, 225
Jiménez, 205
Juárez, Benito Pablo, 49, 62-63, 207, 245
Juárez (town), 4
Juarista victory, 63
Judas (effigy), 97

Kany, Charles E., 87
KLM Royal Dutch Airlines, 9
Kubler, George, 136
Kukulcan, 46

Lacquerware, 94, 96, 189
LACSA (airline), 10
Lake Chapala, 198-199
Lake of Pátzcuaro, 185
Lake Tequesquitengo, 221-223
Lake Texcoco, 48
Language, 40, 47, 185
Las Casas, Bartolomé de, 56
Leather, 94, 95
Leighton, George B., 45
León, 11
Leonard, Irving A., 44
Letters, 89-90
Libraries, 93-94, 137, 260

Lindbergh, Charles and Anne, 220
Liquor, 36, 92
Literature, 35, 57-58

Machete, El (newspaper), 127
Made in Mexico, 35
Madero, Francisco Indalecio, 64-66
Maize, 46
Malinche, La, 50, 52, 53, 237
Many Mexicos, 35
Manzanilla, 22
Maps, 11, 13, 15
  city plans, 13
Markets, 123-125
Martin, Lawrence and Sylvia, 34
Matamoros, 12
Matehuala, 18
Mateos, Adolfo López, 68, 264
Maudslay, A. P., 44
Maximilian, Emperor, 63, 108, 207-208, 247
Maya-Toltec calendar, 265
Mayan language, 52
Mayapan, 255
Mayas, 46-47, 253-256, 260-268
Mazatlán, 11, 201-203
  air service, 9, 10, 180
  highways to, 12, 179-180
  hotels, 22
  rail service to, 24
  ship service to, 22
Means, Philip Ainsworth, 44
Mejía, Tomás, 208
Mérida, Carlos, 35
Mérida, 11, 243, 253-260
  air service, 10, 252
  car rentals, 34
  highways to, 10
  hotels, 256, 257
  market, 258
  museum, 260-261
  shopping, 257, 258
  windmills, 269
Mestizos, 58-59
Mexicana Airlines, 9, 10, 181, 270
Mexico, 34

INDEX

Mexico City, 73-169
  acquiring tourist cards in, 36
  addresses needed in, 93-94
  air service, 8-10
  altitude of, 37-38
  American Bookstore, 35
  car rentals, 34
  castle of Chapultepec, 107-109
  churches in, 57, 101-102, 113-116
  climate, 5, 37
  early name for, 45
  entertainment, 157-162
  festivals in, 96-97
  folklore, 159
  guidebooks, 34
  guides in, 39-40
  health in, 91
  highways to, 11, 12
  hotels, 73-86
    bars in, 157
  luxury section of, 109-110
  markets, 123-125
  murals of, 132-138
  museums, 28, 95, 103, 105-109, 126-139
  nightclubs, 159-160
  palaces, 103-105, 111-113
  population of, 73
  postage rates, 89-90
  practicalities in, 86-93
  prices, 26-27
  rail service to, 23
  red-light district, 161-162
  restaurants, 146-155, 165
    in hotels, 73-86
  Sanborn's, 140-142
  shopping, 94-96
    bargain, 120-122
    Sanborn's, 140-142
  sightseeing, 99-110
  sports, 163-169
  student sector of, 117-120
  telegrams, 89-90
  telephones, 89-90
  tourist offices in, 33-34
  tours from, 170-178
  transportation in, 87-89
  unguided strolling in, 111-125
Mexico City Times, 90
Mexico, the Making of a Nation, 44
Mexico by Motor, 13, 35
Mexico? Si, Señor, 39
Mexico South, 35
Mexico, Three-Storeyed Land, 34
Mexico Today, 35
Mexico Travel Advisers, 39-40
Mexican Folklore Center, 159
Mexican food, 143-146
Mexican Government Today, The, 35
Mexican Government Tourist Department, 10-12, 13
Mexican Government Tourism Department
  calendar of festivals from, 96
  locations of offices of, 33
  tourist cards issued by, 36
Mexican National Tourist Council, 33
Mexican War of Independence, 59-61
Mexitl (god), 48
Mezcal, 156
Miamón, Miguel, 208
Minatitlán, 10
Mitla, 245, 250
Mixtecs, 50, 247, 251
Moctezuma, 52, 54, 55
Modern art, 138-139
Money, 25-32
  border controls, 36
  exchange rate, 27
  informative value of, 27-30
Monte Alban, 248-250
Monterrey, 11, 15-18
  air service to, 9, 10, 15-16
  city plan of, 13
  climate, 5-6, 16, 19
  highways to, 15-18
  hotels, 13-14
  motor trips from, 17
  population, 15
  rail service to, 24

INDEX

restaurants, 14, 16
Sanborn's in, 16
scenery, 16-17
shopping, 16
Morelia, 11, 60, 183-185
  altitude, 38
  churches in, 57
  highways to, 183
  hotels, 184
  shopping, 96
Morelos, José María, 60, 184
Morrow, Dwight, 68, 219, 220
Mosaic murals, 136-138, 228
Movies, 158
Murals, 132-138, 186
  Mayan, 261
  mosaic, 136-138, 228
Museo de Antropologia, 105-107
Museo de Tepoztlán, 107
Museum of Modern Art, 107
Museum of National History, 108
Museums
  Cuernavaca, 107
  Guadalajara, 195-196
  Juárez, 4
  Mérida, 260-261
  Mexico City, 28, 95, 103, 105-109, 126-139
  Oaxaca, 247-248
Music, 157-158, 195

Nacional Monte de Piedad, 112, 120-122
Nacionales de México, 245
Nahua migrants, 47
National Museum, 28
National Museum of Anthropology, 105-107
National Palace, the, 103-104
National University of Mexico, 35
Newspapers, 90
Nogales, 11
  rail service to, 24
  visiting without a permit, 36
Norman, James, 34
Nuestra Señora de Loreto, 114

Oaxaca, 28, 50, 62, 63, 156, 236, 244-251
  air service to, 10, 181, 245
  altitude, 38
  churches, 57, 246-247
  city plan of, 13
  festivals, 98, 251
  highways to, 10, 180-181, 244-245
  hotels, 244
  museum, 247-248
  outdoor cafés, 245-246
  railroad service to, 245
  shopping, 96
Ocean travel, see Ships
Ocotlán, 251
O'Gorman, Juan, 137, 186, 228
Opera, 195
Orbis Turismo de México, 39
Ordaz, Diego de, 53
Orizaba, 236
Orozco, José Clements, 104, 107, 128, 135-136, 196
Our Lady of Guadalupe, 170-173

P & O-Orient Lines, 22-23
Padilla, Ezequiel, 68
Palace of Fine Arts, 104, 157-158
Palaces, 103-105, 111-113, 219, 253
Palacio de Iturbide, 112-113
Pan American Airways, 8, 10
Pan American Union, 34
Paricutín (volcano), 59, 188-192
Parkes, Henry Bamford, 43, 45
Partida Autentico de la Revolucion Mexicana (PARM), 68
Partido de Acción Nacional (PAN), 68
Partido Popular (PP), 68
Partido Revolucionario Institucional (PRI), 68
Pátzcuaro, 180, 185-188
  mural, 186
  shopping, 96
Pemex Travel Club, 12-13, 33-34, 93
Peñafiel, 91
Peniche, José A. Erosa, 263, 267

INDEX

Pennsylvania Museum (Philadelphia), 58
Pérez, Ignacio, 205, 207, 208
Perfume, 36
Perro pelón (bald dog), 21
Peru, 43, 44, 48, 247
Peso taxis, 88
Peso, exchange rate of, 27
Petróleos Mexicanos, 12-13
Pillow, Gideon, 107
Piñatas, 96, 159
Pípila, 214-215
Pizarro, Francisco, 43, 53
Plan of Iguala, 61
Poetry, 57-58
Political parties, 68
Popocatépetl (volcano), 53
Porters, tipping, 31-32
Posada (Mexican custom), 158-159
Postage rates, 89-90
Pottery, 94, 95, 96, 176, 197-198
Pre-Churriguera, 57
Prescott, William H., 43, 44, 51
Prostitutes, 161-162
Provincial Museum, 208
Publications
  English-language, 90
  See also names of publications
Puebla de los Angeles, 53, 63, 236-242
  air service to, 181
  altitude, 38
  churches in, 57, 238-239
  city plan of, 13
  highways to, 38, 180-181
  hotels, 238
  shopping, 94
    bargain, 121
Puerto Juárez, 11
Puerto Vallarta, 199-200
  air service, 9, 10, 180
  highways to, 179-180
  hotels, 199-200
  ship service to, 22
Puertocarrero, Alonso Hernández, 51
Pulque, 156-157

Pyramids, 174-175, 260, 264-265, 267

Quantas Airways, 9
Querétaro, 11, 29, 59, 180, 205-211
  altitude, 38
  churches in, 57, 209
  hotels, 19, 206
  museum, 208
  packaged tours to, 216
  spa near, 210-211
Quetzalcoatl, 46, 47, 51-53, 54, 175, 237

Radio Patrulles de Auxilio Turistico, 10-11
Railroads, 23-24
  prices, 26
  service on, 23
Rebozos, 19, 95, 176
Relics, 95
Religion, 56-57
  in revolutions, 61, 62, 67
Restaurants
  prices, 26-27
  tipping, 30-31
  See also under names of cities and towns
Revolutions
  1810–21, 59-61
  1858–61, 59, 61-63
  1910–11, 59, 63-68
  religion in, 61, 62, 67
Rivera, Diego, 68, 77, 104, 107, 127-132, 135-137, 219-220
Rockefeller, John D., Jr., 131-132
Ross, Patricia Font, 35
Ruiz, Guillermo, 187

Sabena Belgian World Airlines, 9
Sacrifices, human, 49, 219
Saltillo, 18-19
  climate, 5-6, 19
  festivals, 98
  hotels, 18-19
  parks, 19
  restaurants, 18

INDEX

scenery, 19
shopping, 19
San Antonio, 96
San José de Purúa, 11, 179-180
   hotel, 183
   spa at, 182-183
San Luis Potosí, 11, 20-21
   climate, 20
   hotels, 18-20
   rail service to, 24
   restaurants, 20
San Miguel de Allende, 11, 177, 180, 211-213
   altitude, 212
   architecture of, 211
   churches in, 57
   highway to, 211
   hotels, 212
   inns, 212
   packaged tours to, 216
   spa near, 212
   summer courses, 35
San Pedro Tlaquepaque, 197-198
Sanborn's, 16, 140-142
   eating at, 143, 147
Santa Ana, General, 62
Santa María del Tule, 251
Santísima Trinidad, La (church), 114
Santo Domingo (church), 114-115
Sarapes, 16, 95, 176
   quality of, 19
Señor Pico (San Francisco restaurant), 143
Serra, Father Junípero, 210
Servants, 26
Shaw-Saville Company, 23
Ships, 8, 22-23
   tourist cards issued by, 36
Shopping
   bargains, 120-122, 175-178
   customs allowances, 36
   prices, 26
   Sanborn's, 140-142
   See also under names of cities and towns
Shrines, 170-173

Silks, 125
Silver, 16, 94-95, 213-216, 225-226
   coins of, 27, 29
Simpson, Lesley Bird, 35
Siqueiros, David, 107
South America, air travel from, 9-10
South American Handbook, The, 33, 37
Spain, 50-58
   conquest of, 43, 50-56
Spanish Line, 23
Spas, 178, 179-180, 182-183, 211, 212, 236
Spoken Spanish, 87
Sports, 163-169
   baseball, 167-168
   bullfighting, 163-165
   fishing, 194, 252-253
   football, 166-167
   horse racing, 168-169
   Jai-alai, 165-166
   swimming, 199-202, 222, 234-235, 269-271
Spratling, William, 225-226
Stamps, 89-90
Standard Guide to Mexico, 34
Sucesión Presidencial, La, 65
Swimming, 199-202, 222, 234-235, 269-271

TACA International Airlines, 10
Tamayo, Rufino, 107
Tamazunchale, 17
Tampico, 11
Tapachula, 10
Tardiness, 6, 49
Taxco, 177, 223-229
   altitude, 38
   architecture of, 224
   bars, 226
   churches, 57, 224
   distance from Mexico City, 217
   festivals, 97
   founding of, 224
   highways to, 12, 38, 180
   hotels, 226-228

INDEX

Taxco *(continued)*
  rail service to, 23
  shopping, 94, 95
  silver of, 225-226
  Sunday market in, 229
Taxco Done in Silver (article), 223
Taxis, 87-88
  peso, 88
Tehuacán, 236
Tehuantepec, 28
Telegrams, 89-90
Telephones, 89-90
Temples, 186, 253, 260, 266-267
Tenochititlán, 45, 47-48, 49, 54, 81
Teosinte, 46
Teotihuacán, 47
  pyramid at, 174
Tepic, 11
  hotels, 22
Tepoztlán, 221
  churches, 57
  festivals, 98
Tepozteco, El, 98
Tequila, 155-156
Terry's Guide to Mexico, 34
Tezontle, 111-113
Theaters, 92, 137-138, 158, 195, 257, 260
This Week, 90-91, 93
"Thomas and Charlie," 17
Thompson, J. Eric, 253, 255
Tijuana
  cleanup in, 4
  visiting without a permit, 36
Tipping, 30-32
  taxis, 87
Tlacolula, 250-251
Tlaquepague, 96
Tobacco, 91-92
Toltecs, 46-47, 264-265
Toluca, 11, 175-177
  altitude, 38
  highways to, 12, 177
  shopping, 175-177
Tony Perez (travel agency), 39
Toor, Frances, 34, 132
Torreón, 24

Tortillas, 49, 258
Tourism Department's Information Bureau, 93
Tourist-assistance patrol cars (Green Fleet), 10-11
Tourist cards, 35-36
Toys, 176
Trains, *see* Railroads
Transportation, *see* Airlines; Busses; Highways; Railroads; Ships
Travel agencies, 38-40
Treasury of Mexican Folkways, A, 34
Treaty of Guadalupe Hidalgo, 207
Treguerras, Francisco Eduardo de, 209-211
Trolleys, 26
T'Serstevens, A., 34
Tucker, William P., 35
Tuxtla Gutiérrez, 10
Tzintzuntzan, 97, 185, 186
  fair, 97

Uiski, 156
United States of America
  border barriers, 35-37
  duty allowance, 94
  importing gold coins to, 30
  Mexican tourist offices in, 33
  returning to, 36-37
Uruapan, 180, 188-192
  hotels, 189
  shopping, 96
Uxmal, 255, 267-269
  highways to, 262, 267
  hotels, 268-269

Valladolid, 60
Valle de Bravo, 177
Varig Airlines, 9
Velásquez de León, Diego, 51
Veracruz, 11, 63, 236, 243
  air service, 10, 236
  climate, 6
  founding of, 52
  highways to, 10, 236
  ship service to, 23

INDEX

VIASA (airline), 10
Villa, Pancho, 67
Villa Gustavo Madero, 170-173
Villahermosa, 11
   air service, 10
Virgin of Guadalupe, 61, 64, 170-173
Virgin of los Remedios, 61, 64, 98
Vizcaínas, Las, 117
Volcanoes, 53, 59, 180

Wagons-Lits-Cook, 39
War of the Reform, 59, 61-63
Watches, 122
Water, 91
Wells Fargo, 39
Western Airlines, 8
Wild flowers, 183, 184
Wilhelm, John, 34
Windmills, 269
Wines, 27
Wind That Swept Mexico, The, 44-45

Women, Island of, 270-271
Wood carvings, 96

Xochimilco, floating gardens of, 173-174

Yácatas, 186
Yucatán Peninsula, 252-271
   air service to, 252
   Chichén-Itzá, 254, 260, 263-267
   highways to, 10, 262
   hotels, 262-263
   Island of Cozumel, 269-270
   Mayan antiquity, 253-256, 260-268
   Mérida, 253-260
   Uxmal, 255, 267-269
   windmills, 269

Zapata, Emiliano, 67-68, 97
Zapotecs, 50, 247-249, 251
Zihuatanejo, 235
Zimapan, 17
Zimatlán, 50-51, 251
Zumáraga, Bishop, 172

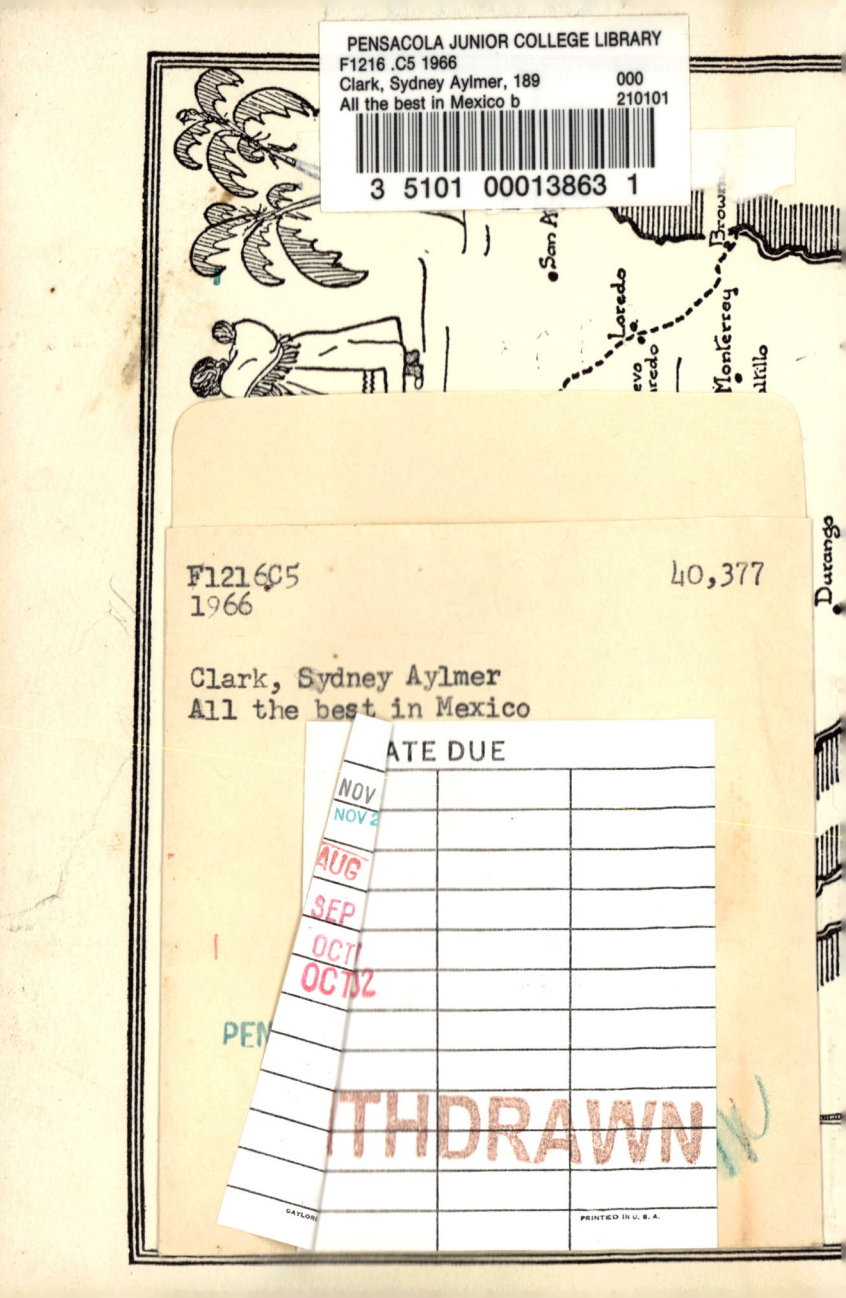

PENSACOLA JUNIOR COLLEGE LIBRARY
F1216 .C5 1966
Clark, Sydney Aylmer, 189   000
All the best in Mexico b   210101

3 5101 00013863 1

F1216C5
1966

40,377

Clark, Sydney Aylmer
All the best in Mexico

DATE DUE